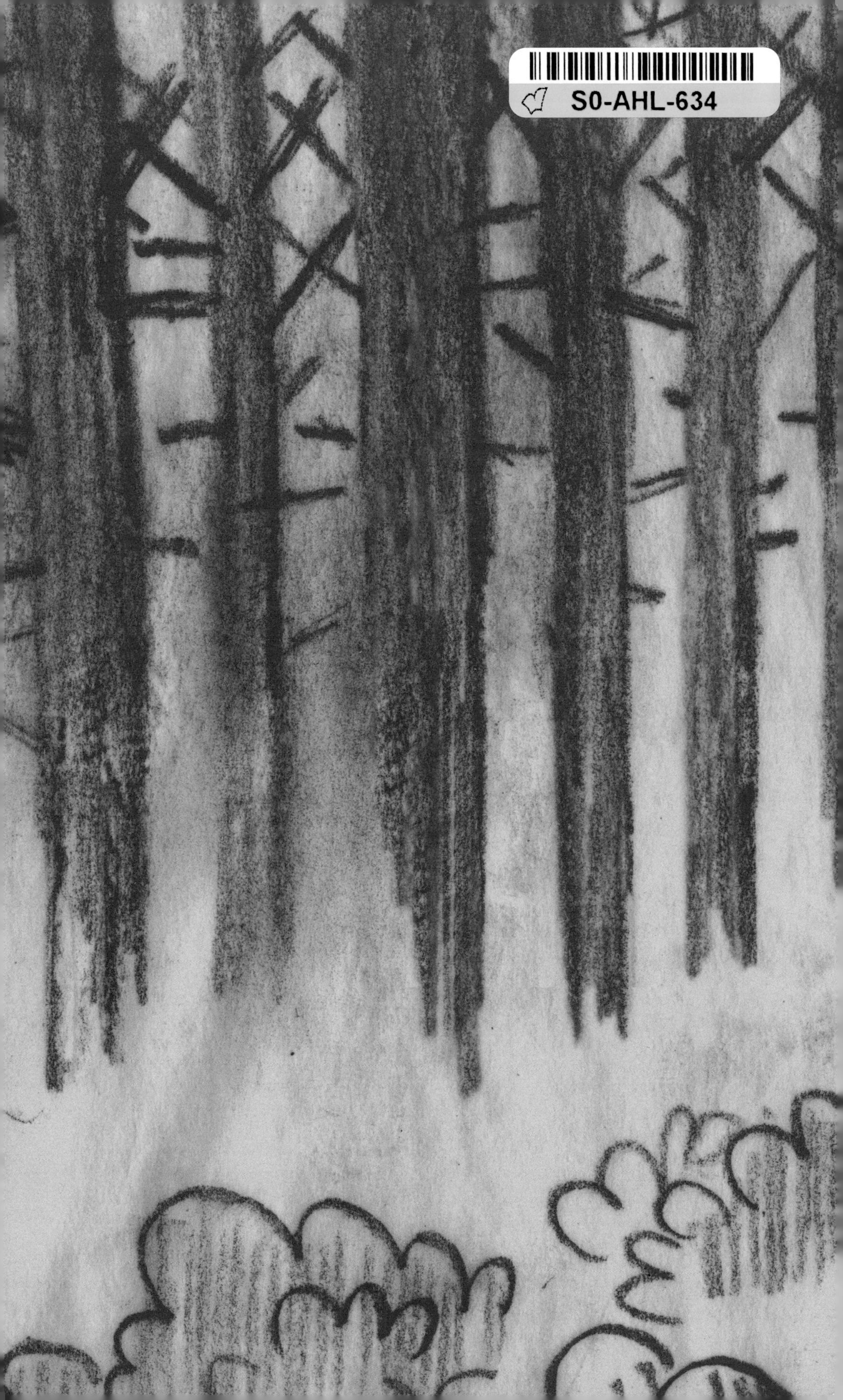

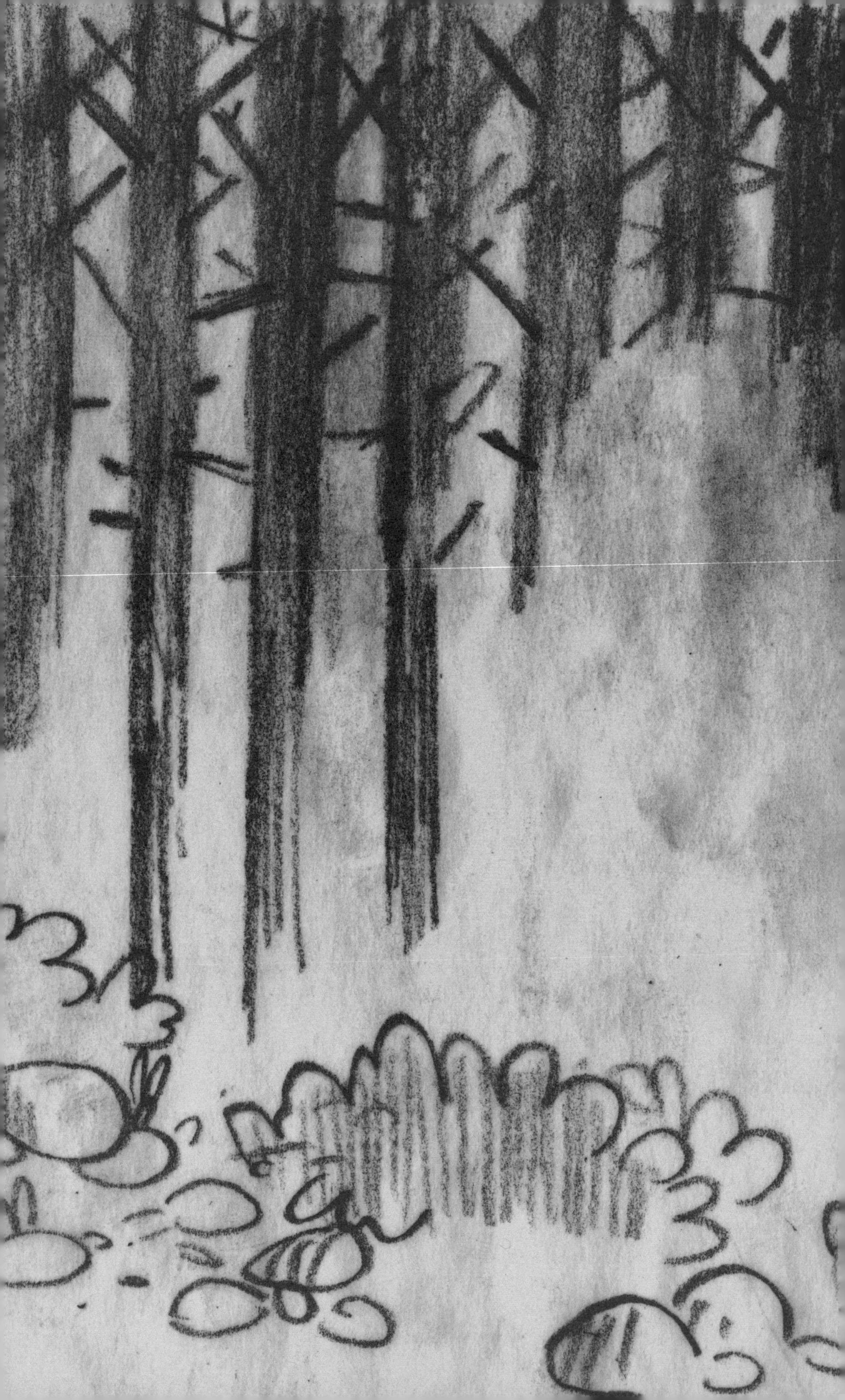

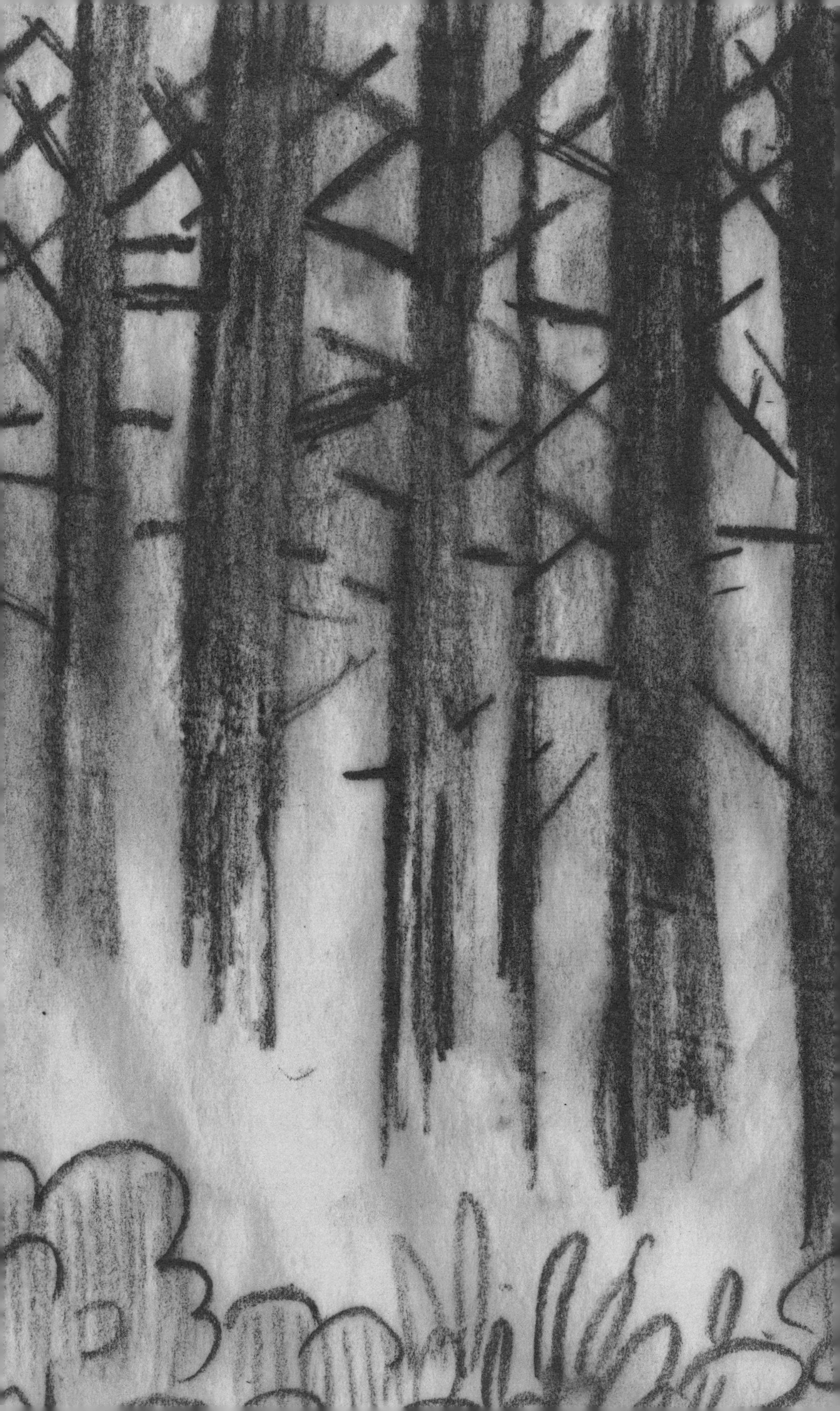

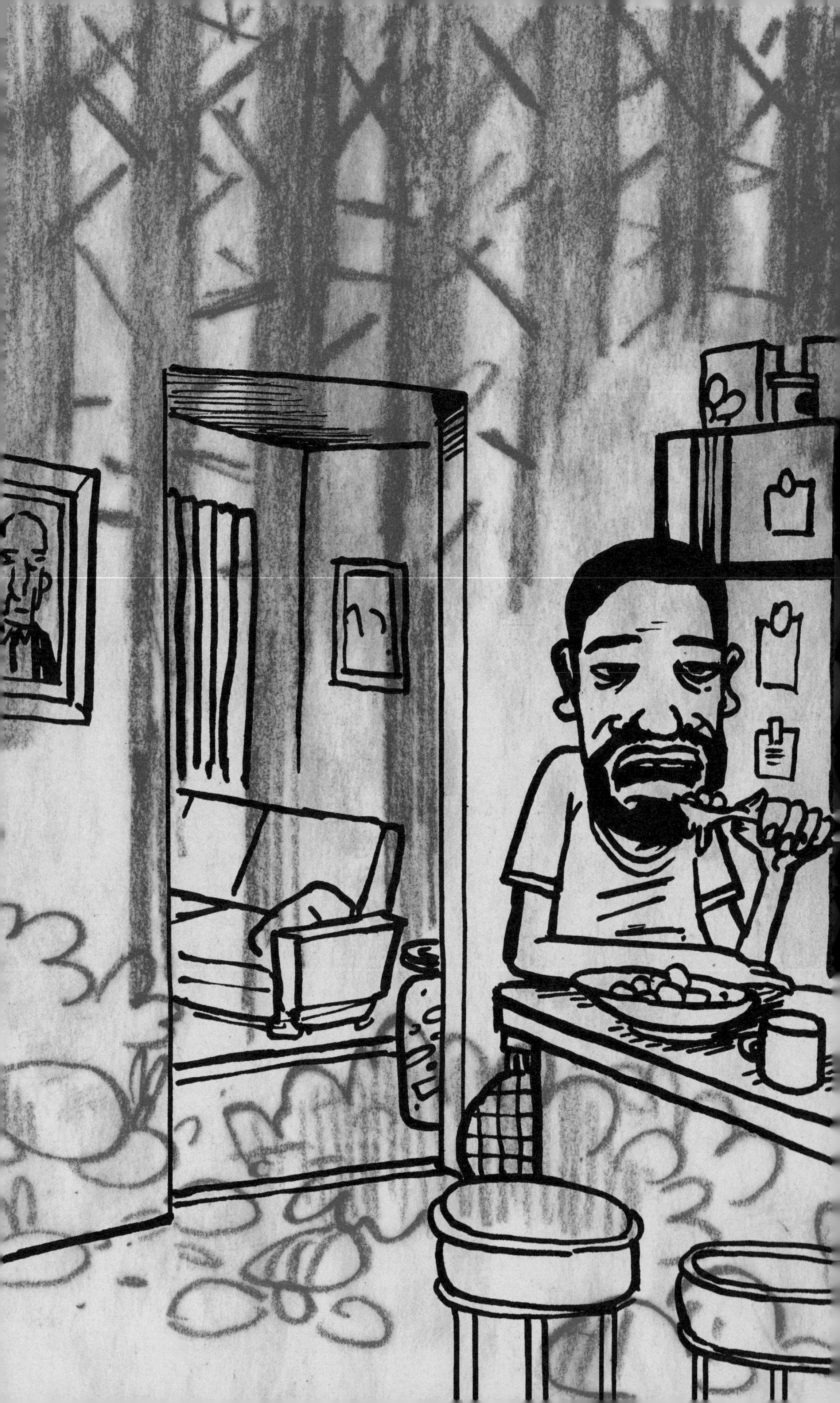

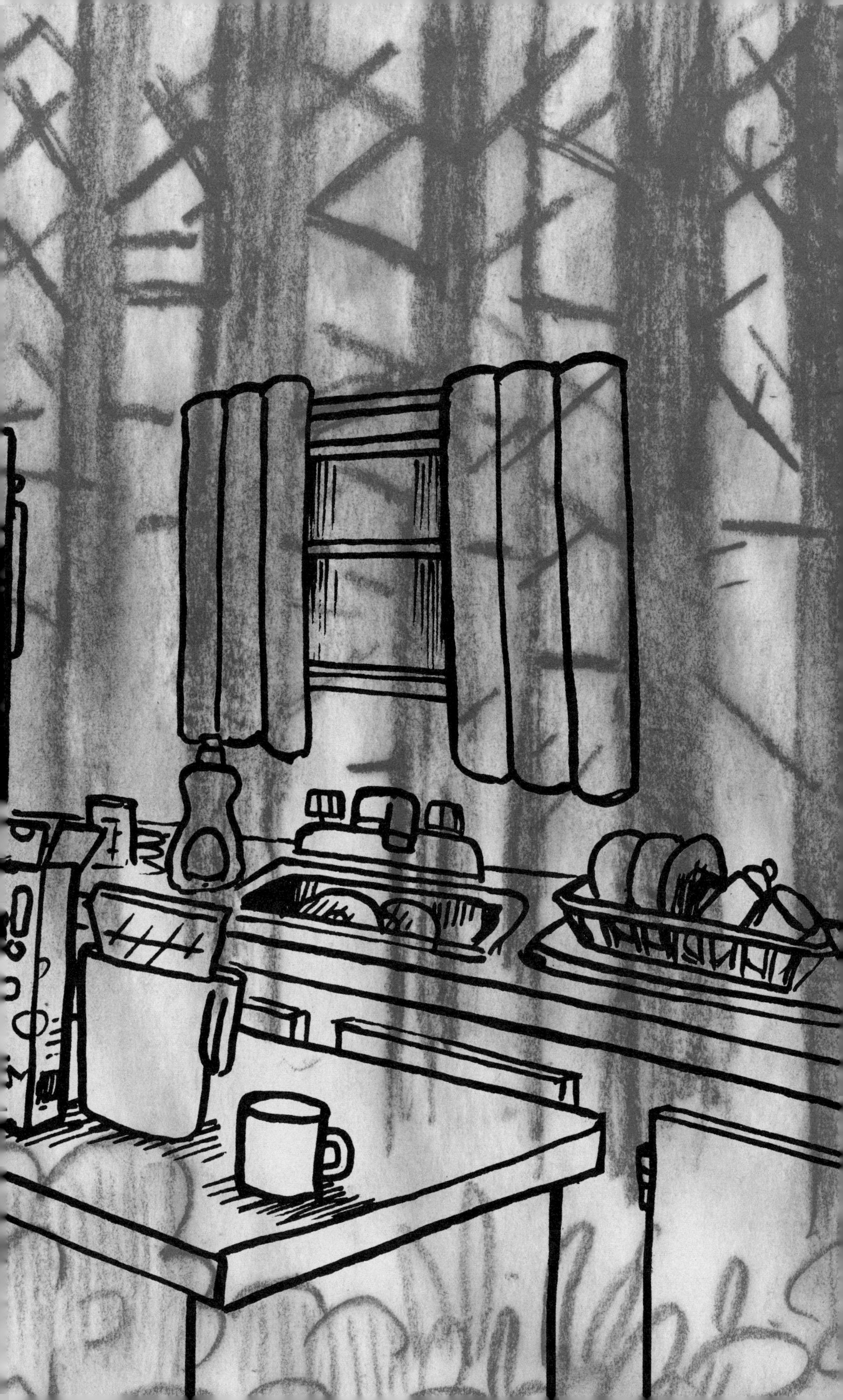

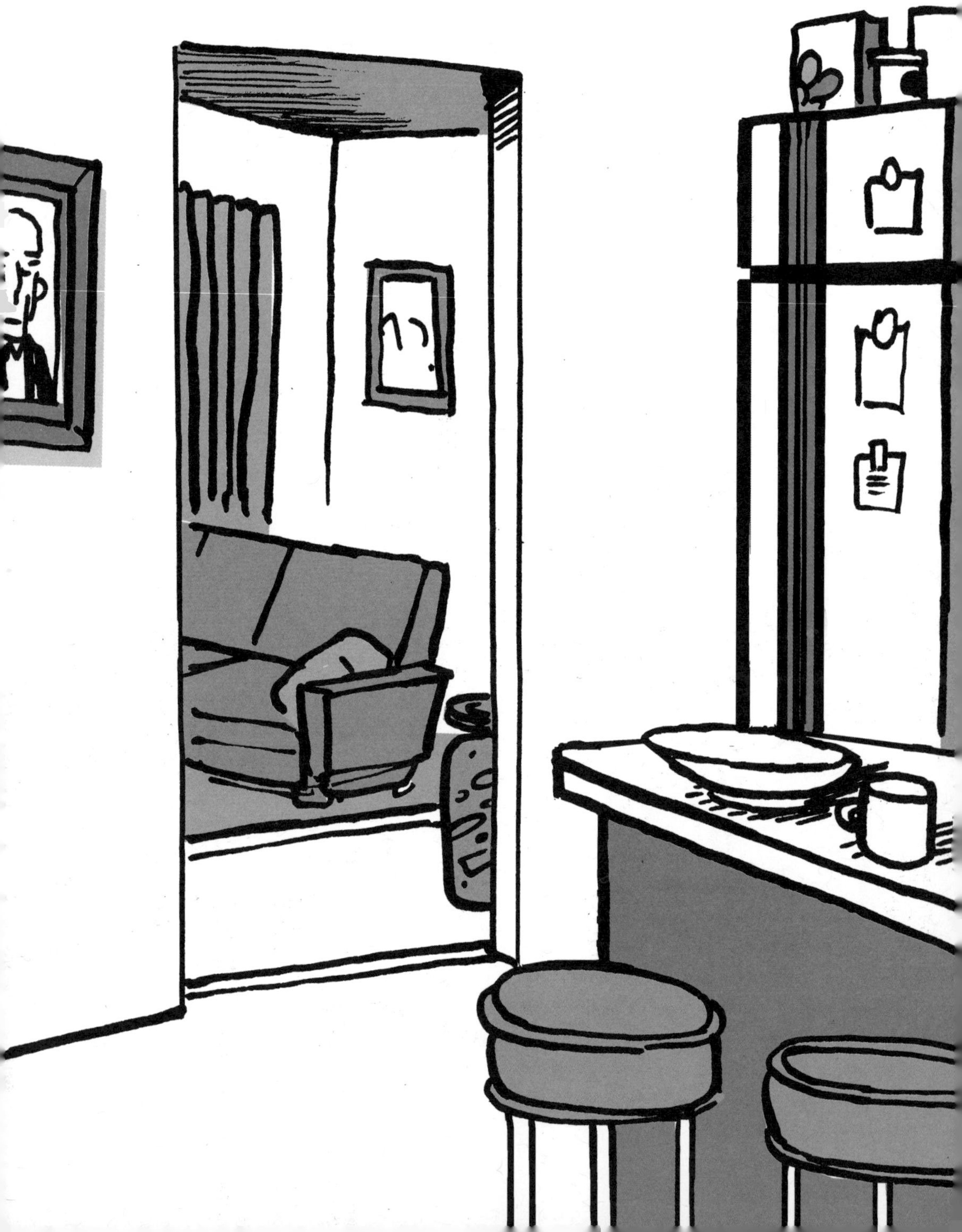

SCIENCE FICTION

BY JOE OLLMANN

CONUNDRUM PRESS

GREENWICH, NOVA SCOTIA

© Joe Ollmann, 2013

First Edition

Printed and bound in Canada by Gauvin

Library and Archives Canada Cataloguing in Publication

Ollmann, Joe, 1966-

    Science Fiction/ Joe Ollmann.

ISBN 978-1-894994-75-0

        1. Graphic novels. I. Title.

PN6733.056S35 2013   741.5'971   C2013-901304-0

Conundrum Press
Greenwich, Nova Scotia, Canada
www.conundrumpress.com

Conundrum Press acknowledges the financial assistance of the Canada
Council for the Arts and the Government of Canada through the Canada
Book Fund toward this Publication.

The author wishes to thank the Canada Council For the Arts for their
Generous Support.

Canada

Canada Council   Conseil des Arts
for the Arts   du Canada

OFUI

ORGANIZATION FOR UFO INVESTIGATION

"What is out there?" ©

U.F.O. QUESTIONAIRE

PLEASE ANSWER <u>ALL</u> QUESTIONS FULLY

"BLESSED ARE THEY THAT HAVE NOT SEEN AND YET HAVE BELIEVED."
- JOHN, 20:19

"AH, WHAT WILL IT TAKE TILL YOU BELIEVE IN ME? THE WAY THAT I BELIEVE IN YOU?"
- BILLY JOEL

THANKS TO:

ALL THESE NICE PEOPLE FOR THEIR CLOSE READINGS AND HELPFUL SUGGESTIONS ON IMPROVEMENTS: TAIEN NG-CHAN, BILLY MAVREAS, TOM DEVLIN, JULIA POHL-MIRANDA, AND PASCAL GIRARD, WHO ALSO CORRECTED INCIDENTAL FRENCH SIGNAGE MISTAKES. THANKS TO MURRAY LIGHTBURN FOR "BLACK-T"-CHECKING THE BOOK. THANKS AND LOVE TO MY MEAGHAN, LIZ AND SAM WHO HAVE ALL TAKEN THEIR TURN OVER THE YEARS SITTING DRAWING WITH THE OLD MAN. GRANDSONS WHO'S NAMES SHOULD APPEAR IN PRINT: OWEN, LUKE, AND SEAN.

TAIEN, MY DEAR OLD LOVE, THANKS FOR THE NEW TITLE SCIENCE FICTION.

THIS ONE'S FOR MY OLD FRIEND ANDY BROWN.

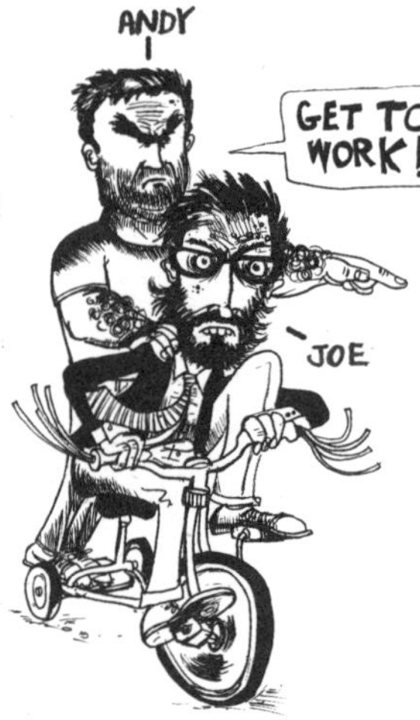

ANDY
GET TO WORK!
JOE

HAVE YOU BEEN ABDUCTED?
HERE ARE SOME QUESTIONS THAT YOU MIGHT WANT TO ASK YOURSELF. IT IS POSSIBLE YOU MAY BE AN ABDUCTEE.

1. HAVE YOU HAD MISSING OR LOST TIME?

2. HAVE YOU BEEN PARALYZED IN BED WITH A BEING IN YOUR ROOM?

3. DO YOU HAVE A STRONG MEMORY THAT MAKES NO SENSE BUT WILL NOT GO AWAY?

4. DO YOU HAVE MANY DREAMS OF UFO'S, BEAMS OF LIGHT, OR ALIEN BEINGS?

7. HAVE YOU AWAKENED WITH SORENESS IN YOUR GENITALS WHICH COULD NOT BE EXPLAINED?

9. DO YOU HAVE A STRONG SENSE OF HAVING A MISSION OR AN IMPORTANT TASK TO DO WITHOUT KNOWING WHERE THIS COMPULSION COMES FROM?

10. HAVE YOU HAD A FALSE PREGNANCY OR MISSING FETUS?

11. HAVE YOU AWAKENED IN ANOTHER PLACE THAN WHERE YOU WENT TO SLEEP OR DON'T REMEMBER GOING TO SLEEP?

12. HAVE YOU HAD DREAMS OF EYES LOOKING AT YOU OR DO YOU HAVE A FEAR OF EYES LOOKING AT YOU?

OFUI: Organization For UFO Investigation

13. DO YOU HAVE A STRONG AVERSION TO PICTURES OF ALIENS, OR ARE YOU DRAWN TO THEM?

14. DO YOU HAVE INEXPLICABLY STRONG FEARS OR PHOBIAS?

15. HAVE YOU HAD SELF-ESTEEM PROBLEMS MOST OF YOUR LIFE?

16. DO YOU HAVE AN EXTREME AVERSION TOWARDS THE SUB-JECT OF UFOS OR ALIENS?

17. HAVE YOU HAD CHRONIC SINUSITIS OR NASAL PROBLEMS?

18. DO YOU HAVE AN UNUSUAL FEAR OF DOCTORS OR MEDICAL TREATMENT?

19. DO YOU HAVE INSOMNIA?

20. DO YOU HAVE A VERY HARD TIME TRUSTING OTHERS?

21. DO YOU HAVE DREAMS OF DESTRUCTION OR CATASTROPHE?

22. DO YOU HAVE MANY OF THESE TRAITS BUT CANNOT REMEMBER ANYTHING ABOUT AN ALIEN ABDUCTION OR ALIEN ENCOUNTER?

23. DO YOU HAVE A FEELING THAT YOU ARE GOING CRAZY FOR THINKING ABOUT THESE THINGS?

24. USE THE SPACE PROVIDED TO ILLUSTRATE DETAILS OF YOUR ABDUCTION, THE BEINGS, OR THEIR SPACECRAFT.

THANK YOU.

Subject's Name: ------------------

OFUI: Organization For UFO Investigation

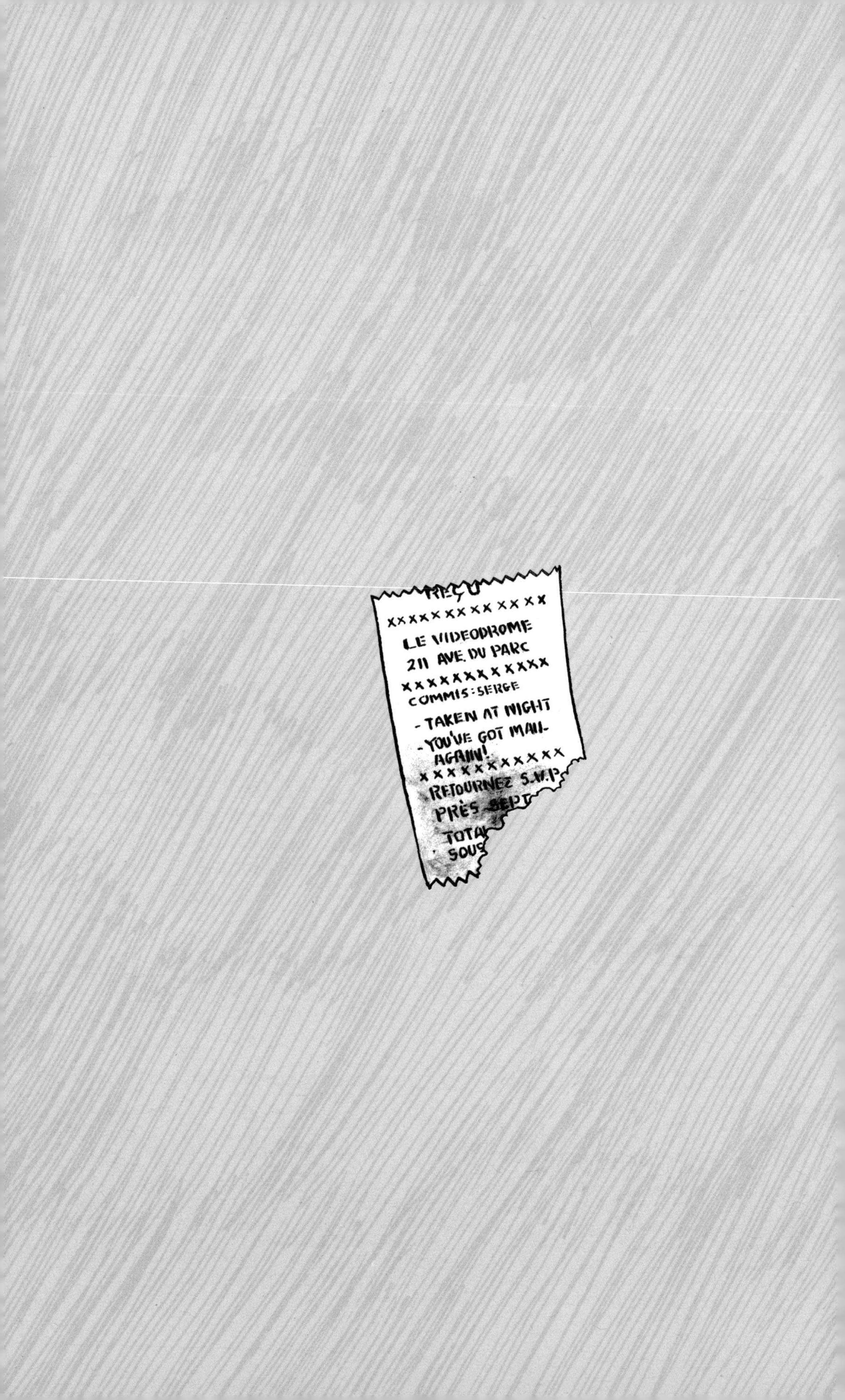
REÇU
XXXXXXXXXXXXXX
LE VIDEODROME
211 AVE. DU PARC
XXXXXXXXXXXX
COMMIS: SERGE
- TAKEN AT NIGHT
- YOU'VE GOT MAIL-
AGAIN!
XXXXXXXXXXXX
RETOURNEZ S.V.P.
PRÈS SEPT
TOTA
SOUS

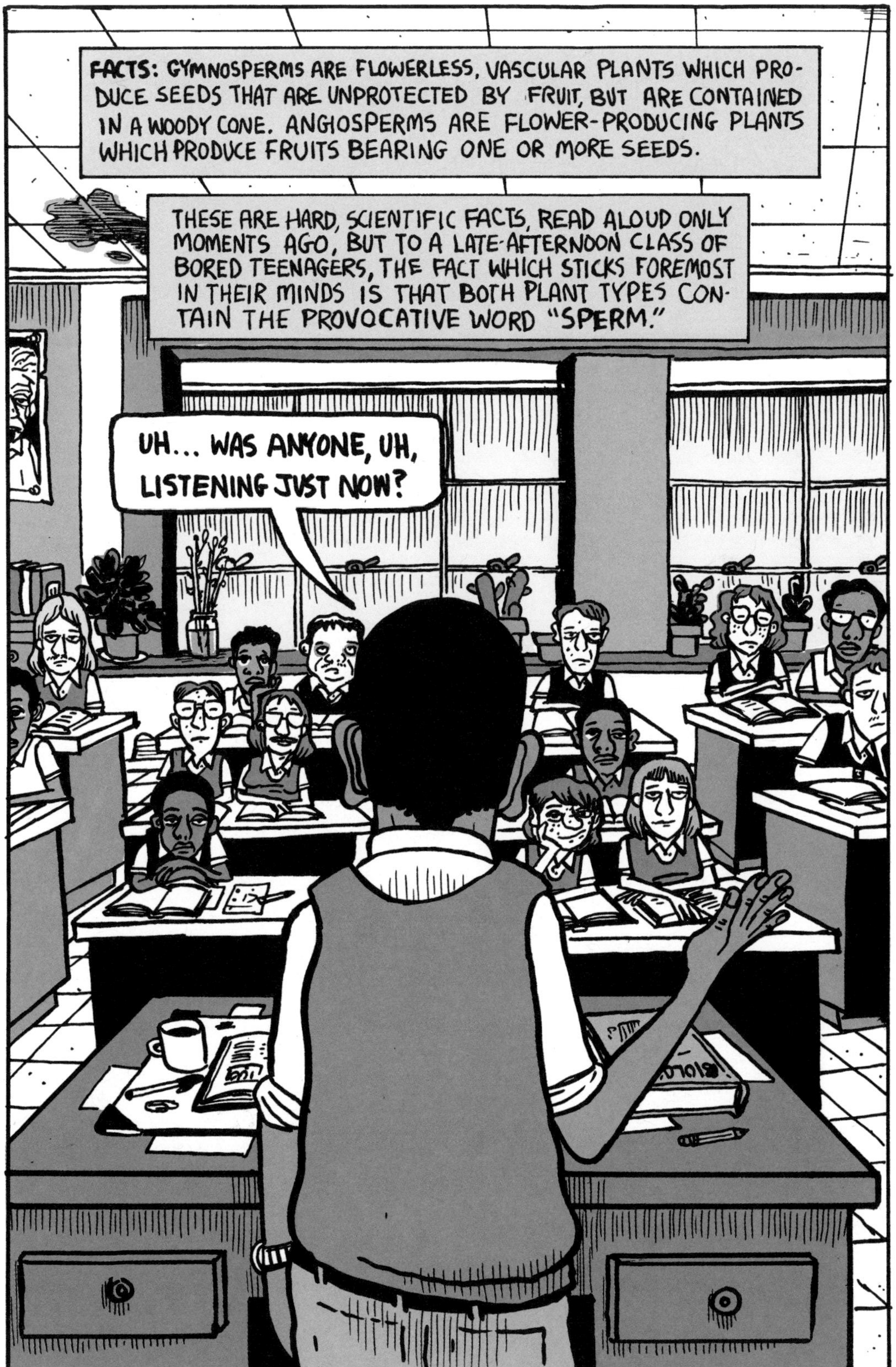
FACTS: GYMNOSPERMS ARE FLOWERLESS, VASCULAR PLANTS WHICH PRODUCE SEEDS THAT ARE UNPROTECTED BY FRUIT, BUT ARE CONTAINED IN A WOODY CONE. ANGIOSPERMS ARE FLOWER-PRODUCING PLANTS WHICH PRODUCE FRUITS BEARING ONE OR MORE SEEDS.
THESE ARE HARD, SCIENTIFIC FACTS, READ ALOUD ONLY MOMENTS AGO, BUT TO A LATE-AFTERNOON CLASS OF BORED TEENAGERS, THE FACT WHICH STICKS FOREMOST IN THEIR MINDS IS THAT BOTH PLANT TYPES CONTAIN THE PROVOCATIVE WORD "SPERM."
UH... WAS ANYONE, UH, LISTENING JUST NOW?

COME ON, PEOPLE! STAY WITH ME... ANGIOSPERM VERSUS GYMNOSPERM...

CELL WALL

MONOCO DICOT

MARK SETT IS A SERIOUS MAN. LIKE DICKENS' MR. GADGRIND, WHAT HE WANTS IS FACTS...

NO BAD IDEAS IN BRAIN STORMING... ANYONE?

MONOCO DICOT

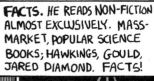

FACTS. HE READS NON-FICTION ALMOST EXCLUSIVELY. MASS-MARKET, POPULAR SCIENCE BOOKS; HAWKINGS, GOULD, JARED DIAMOND. FACTS!

NO ONE?

MONOCO DICOT

HE TEACHES BIOLOGY TO TEEN-AGERS AND HE IS OFTEN MILDLY DEPRESSED.

SERIOUSLY, JUST REPEAT BACK ANYTHING I JUST READ TO YOU TEN MINUTES AGO...

A PRAGMATIC AND RARELY A FRIVOLOUS MAN, MARK SUFFERS FOOLS TERSELY.

ANGIOSPERM? GYMNOSPERM?

CELL WALL   DICOT

ANGIOSPE

GY

.. HUH- HUH · HE SAID "SPERM" LIKE TWENTY TIMES... HUH-

OKAY GUYS, I KNOW "SPERM" IS A FUNNY, DIRTY WORD... BUT THIS STUFF WILL BE ON THE EXAM...

ALL-

OSPE N

SERIOUSLY- HE'S SPERM-CRAZY·· HUH- HUH-HUH···

MISTER OLSEN, WHAT'S SO FUNNY EXACTLY?

MONOCOT DICOT

ANGIOSPERM GYMNOSPERM

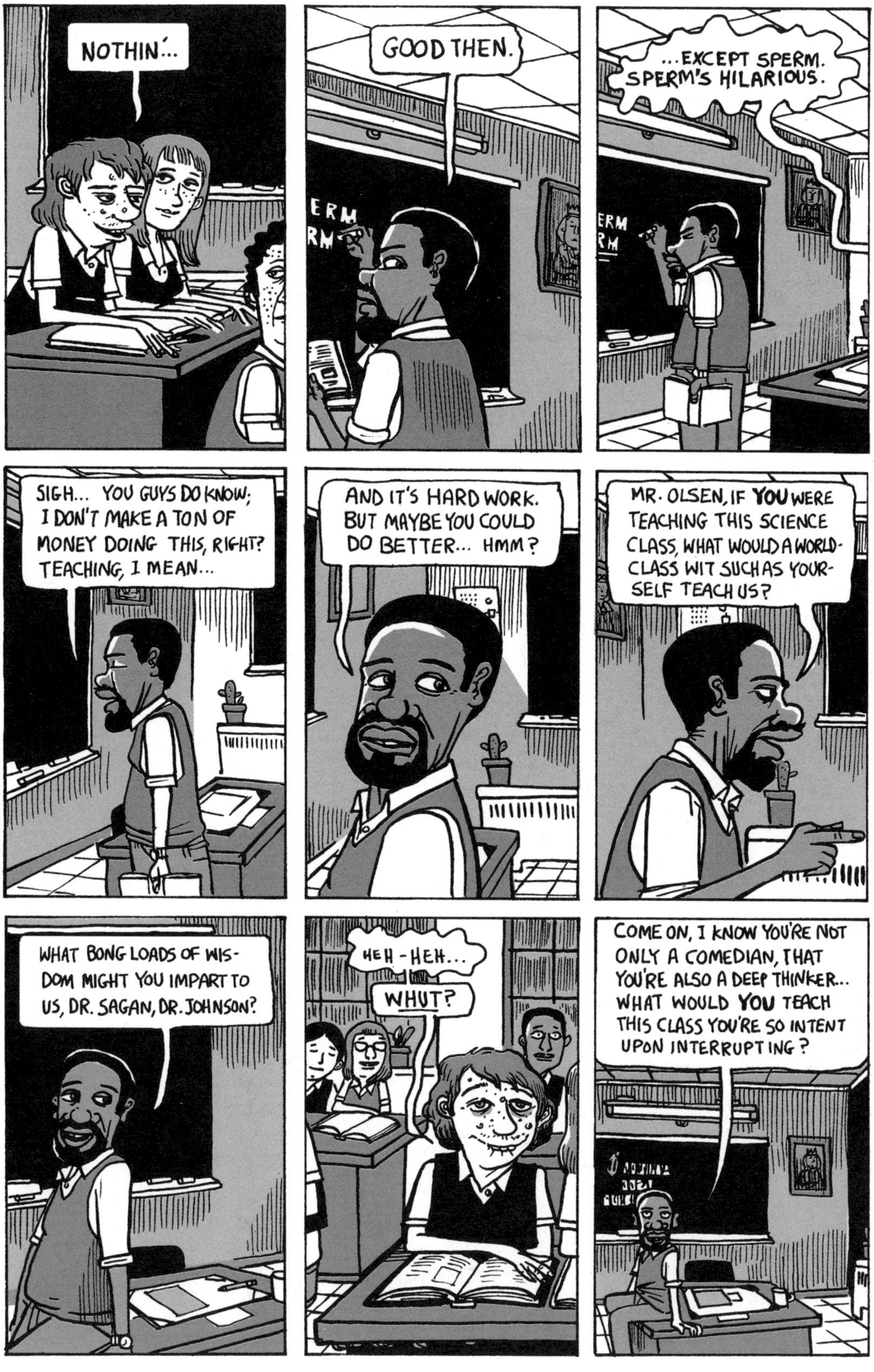
NOTHIN'...
GOOD THEN.
...EXCEPT SPERM. SPERM'S HILARIOUS.
SIGH... YOU GUYS DO KNOW; I DON'T MAKE A TON OF MONEY DOING THIS, RIGHT? TEACHING, I MEAN...
AND IT'S HARD WORK. BUT MAYBE YOU COULD DO BETTER... HMM?
MR. OLSEN, IF **YOU** WERE TEACHING THIS SCIENCE CLASS, WHAT WOULD A WORLD-CLASS WIT SUCH AS YOURSELF TEACH US?
WHAT BONG LOADS OF WISDOM MIGHT YOU IMPART TO US, DR. SAGAN, DR. JOHNSON?
HEH-HEH...
WHUT?
COME ON, I KNOW YOU'RE NOT ONLY A COMEDIAN, THAT YOU'RE ALSO A DEEP THINKER... WHAT WOULD **YOU** TEACH THIS CLASS YOU'RE SO INTENT UPON INTERRUPTING?

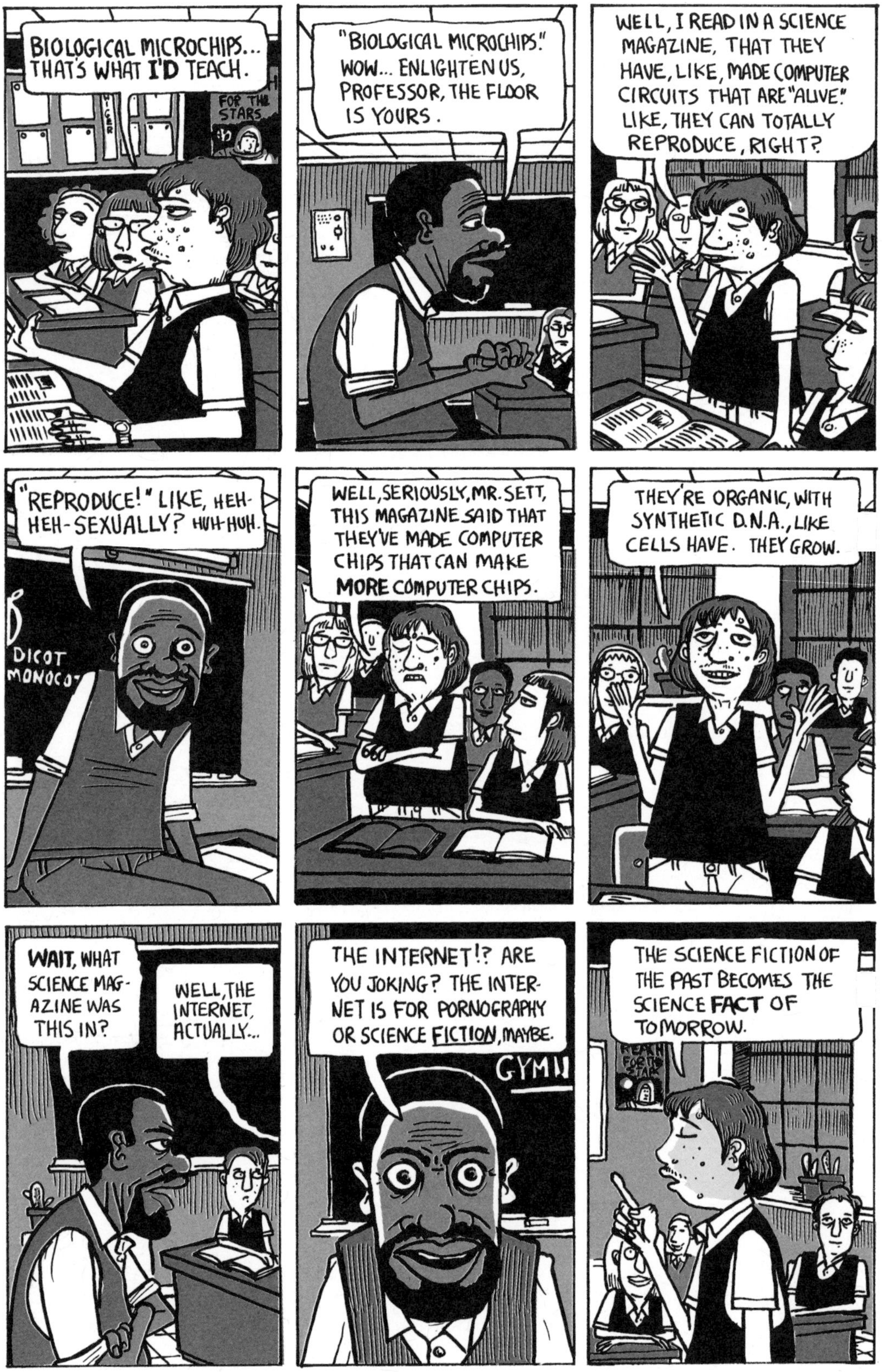
BIOLOGICAL MICROCHIPS... THAT'S WHAT I'D TEACH.
FOR THE STARS
"BIOLOGICAL MICROCHIPS." WOW... ENLIGHTEN US, PROFESSOR, THE FLOOR IS YOURS.
WELL, I READ IN A SCIENCE MAGAZINE, THAT THEY HAVE, LIKE, MADE COMPUTER CIRCUITS THAT ARE "ALIVE." LIKE, THEY CAN TOTALLY REPRODUCE, RIGHT?
"REPRODUCE!" LIKE, HEH-HEH-SEXUALLY? HUH-HUH.
DICOT
MONOCO-
WELL, SERIOUSLY, MR. SETT, THIS MAGAZINE SAID THAT THEY'VE MADE COMPUTER CHIPS THAT CAN MAKE MORE COMPUTER CHIPS.
THEY'RE ORGANIC, WITH SYNTHETIC D.N.A., LIKE CELLS HAVE. THEY GROW.
WAIT, WHAT SCIENCE MAGAZINE WAS THIS IN?
WELL, THE INTERNET, ACTUALLY...
THE INTERNET!? ARE YOU JOKING? THE INTERNET IS FOR PORNOGRAPHY OR SCIENCE FICTION, MAYBE.
GYM!!
THE SCIENCE FICTION OF THE PAST BECOMES THE SCIENCE FACT OF TOMORROW.
REACH FOR THE STAR

OH, MY GOD, NO, IT DOESN'T! IS THAT FROM STAR WARS OR SOMETHING? THIS IS A SCIENCE CLASS, OLSEN. LET'S STICK TO REALITY.

CAN SOMEONE TELL ME TWO DEFINING CHARACTERISTICS OF ANGIOSPERMS OR GYMNO-SPERMS, REMEMBERING THAT THE COMEDY PORTION OF OUR SHOW IS OVER...

CELL WALL
MONOCT
DICOT
ANGIO'
CYMN

COME ONNN!. GYMNO-SPERM? ANGIOSPERM? ANYONE? -SIGH- MISS LEE, PLEASE SAVE ME...

UH... GYMNOSPERMS ARE CON-IFEROUS, THEIR SEEDS HAVE NO FRUIT... ANGIOS HAVE FLOWERS AND FRUITS WITH ONE OR MORE SEEDS.

GREAT! ANY-ONE ELSE?

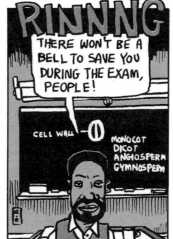

RINNNG

THERE WON'T BE A BELL TO SAVE YOU DURING THE EXAM, PEOPLE!

CELL WALL
MONOCOT
DICOT
ANGIOSPERM
GYMNOSPERM

READ THAT CHAPTER TONIGHT, BECAUSE I AM COMING BACK TO THIS TOMORROW.

KNOCK KNOCK, MARK...

TOK TOK

YOU GOT ANY TYLENOL?

OR, ALTERNATELY, CYANIDE?

HMM, NO CYANIDE, BUT I DO HAVE HOME-MADE ECSTACY.

OR ASPIRIN.

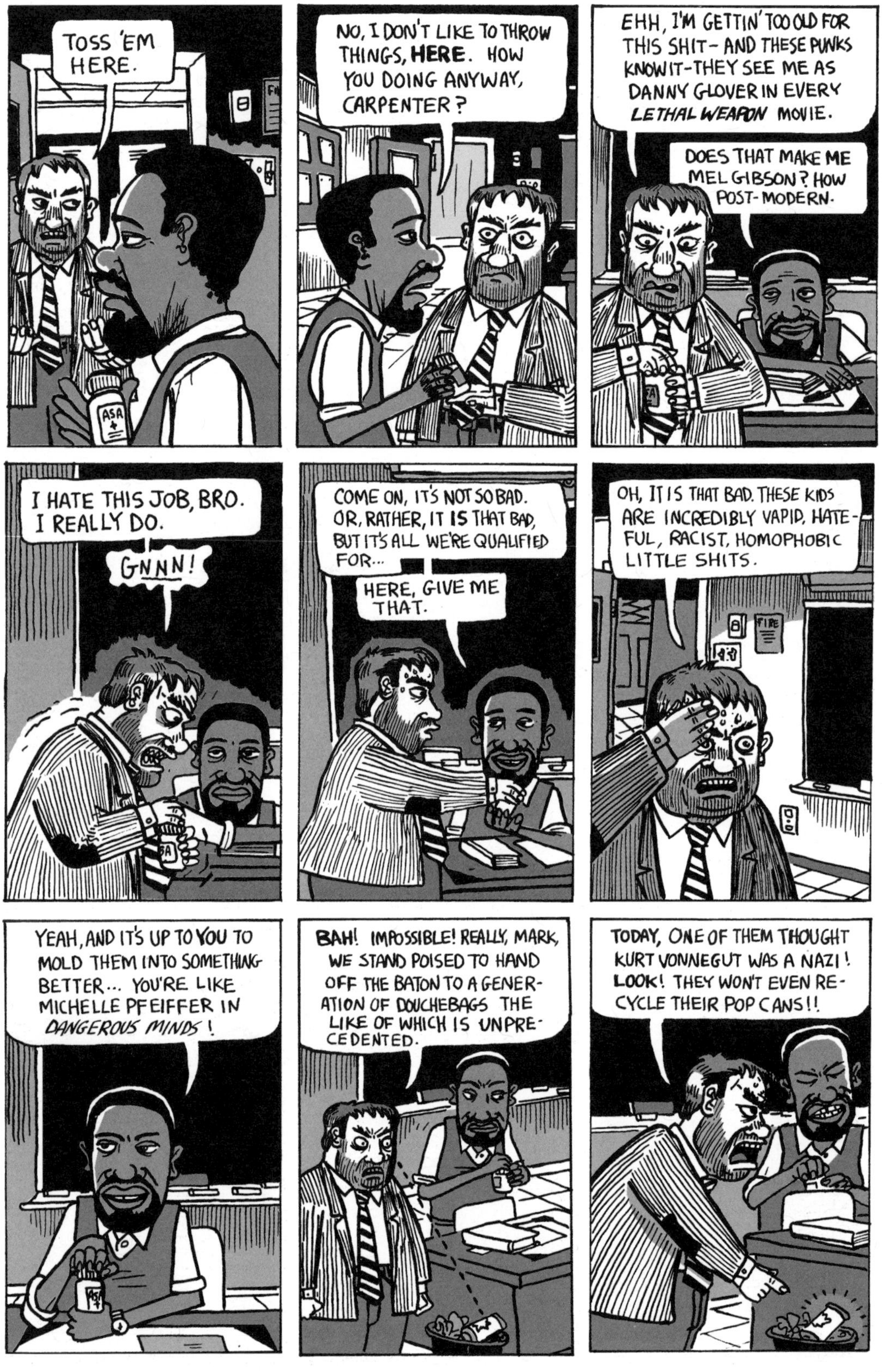
TOSS 'EM HERE.
NO, I DON'T LIKE TO THROW THINGS, **HERE**. HOW YOU DOING ANYWAY, CARPENTER?
EHH, I'M GETTIN' TOO OLD FOR THIS SHIT– AND THESE PUNKS KNOW IT–THEY SEE ME AS DANNY GLOVER IN EVERY *LETHAL WEAPON* MOVIE.
DOES THAT MAKE ME MEL GIBSON? HOW POST-MODERN.
I HATE THIS JOB, BRO. I REALLY DO.
GNNN!
COME ON, IT'S NOT SO BAD. OR, RATHER, IT **IS** THAT BAD, BUT IT'S ALL WE'RE QUALIFIED FOR...
HERE, GIVE ME THAT.
OH, IT IS THAT BAD. THESE KIDS ARE INCREDIBLY VAPID, HATEFUL, RACIST, HOMOPHOBIC LITTLE SHITS.
YEAH, AND IT'S UP TO **YOU** TO MOLD THEM INTO SOMETHING BETTER... YOU'RE LIKE MICHELLE PFEIFFER IN *DANGEROUS MINDS*!
BAH! IMPOSSIBLE! REALLY, MARK, WE STAND POISED TO HAND OFF THE BATON TO A GENERATION OF DOUCHEBAGS THE LIKE OF WHICH IS UNPRECEDENTED.
TODAY, ONE OF THEM THOUGHT KURT VONNEGUT WAS A NAZI! **LOOK**! THEY WON'T EVEN RECYCLE THEIR POP CANS!!

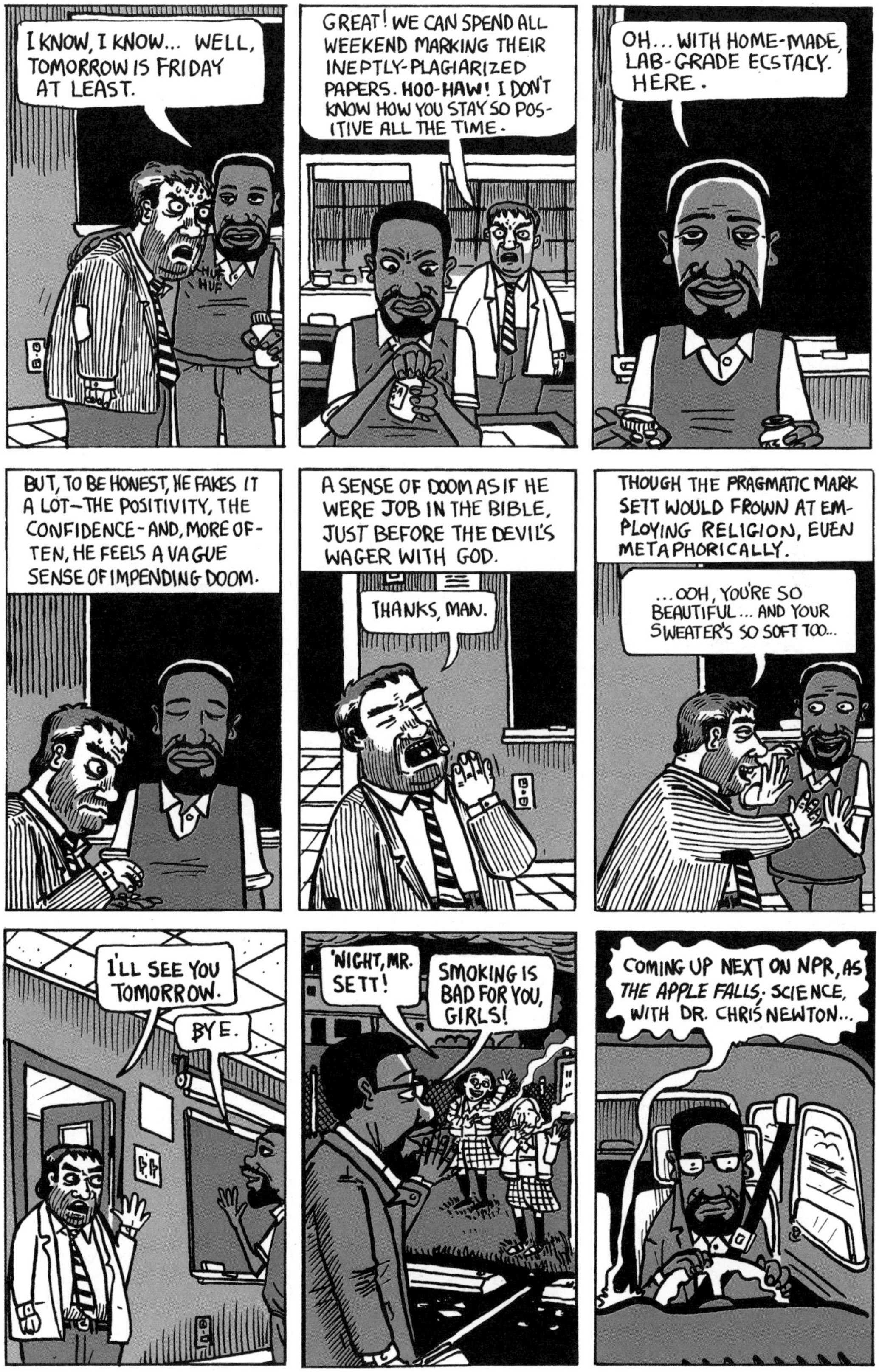
I KNOW, I KNOW... WELL, TOMORROW IS FRIDAY AT LEAST.
HUF HUF
GREAT! WE CAN SPEND ALL WEEKEND MARKING THEIR INEPTLY-PLAGIARIZED PAPERS. HOO-HAW! I DON'T KNOW HOW YOU STAY SO POSITIVE ALL THE TIME.
OH... WITH HOME-MADE, LAB-GRADE ECSTACY. HERE.
BUT, TO BE HONEST, HE FAKES IT A LOT—THE POSITIVITY, THE CONFIDENCE-AND, MORE OFTEN, HE FEELS A VAGUE SENSE OF IMPENDING DOOM.
A SENSE OF DOOM AS IF HE WERE JOB IN THE BIBLE, JUST BEFORE THE DEVIL'S WAGER WITH GOD.
THANKS, MAN.
THOUGH THE PRAGMATIC MARK SETT WOULD FROWN AT EMPLOYING RELIGION, EVEN METAPHORICALLY.
...OOH, YOU'RE SO BEAUTIFUL... AND YOUR SWEATER'S SO SOFT TOO...
I'LL SEE YOU TOMORROW.
BYE.
'NIGHT, MR. SETT!
SMOKING IS BAD FOR YOU, GIRLS!
COMING UP NEXT ON NPR, AS THE APPLE FALLS: SCIENCE, WITH DR. CHRIS NEWTON...

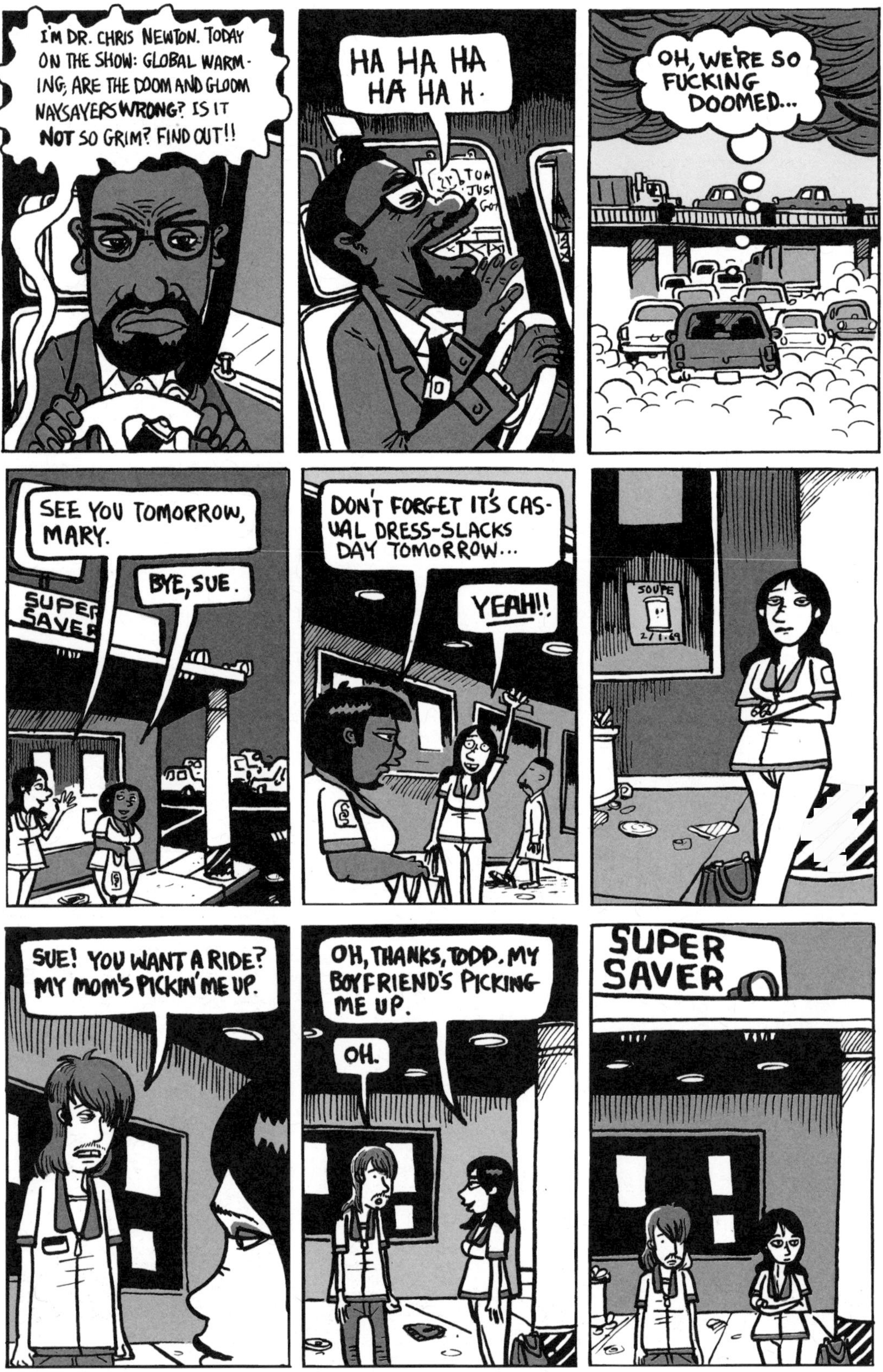
I'M DR. CHRIS NEWTON. TODAY ON THE SHOW: GLOBAL WARMING; ARE THE DOOM AND GLOOM NAYSAYERS WRONG? IS IT NOT SO GRIM? FIND OUT!!
HA HA HA HA HA H.
OH, WE'RE SO FUCKING DOOMED...
SEE YOU TOMORROW, MARY.
BYE, SUE.
SUPER SAVER
DON'T FORGET IT'S CASUAL DRESS-SLACKS DAY TOMORROW...
YEAH!!
SOUPE
2/1.69
SUE! YOU WANT A RIDE? MY MOM'S PICKIN' ME UP.
OH, THANKS, TODD. MY BOYFRIEND'S PICKING ME UP.
OH.
SUPER SAVER

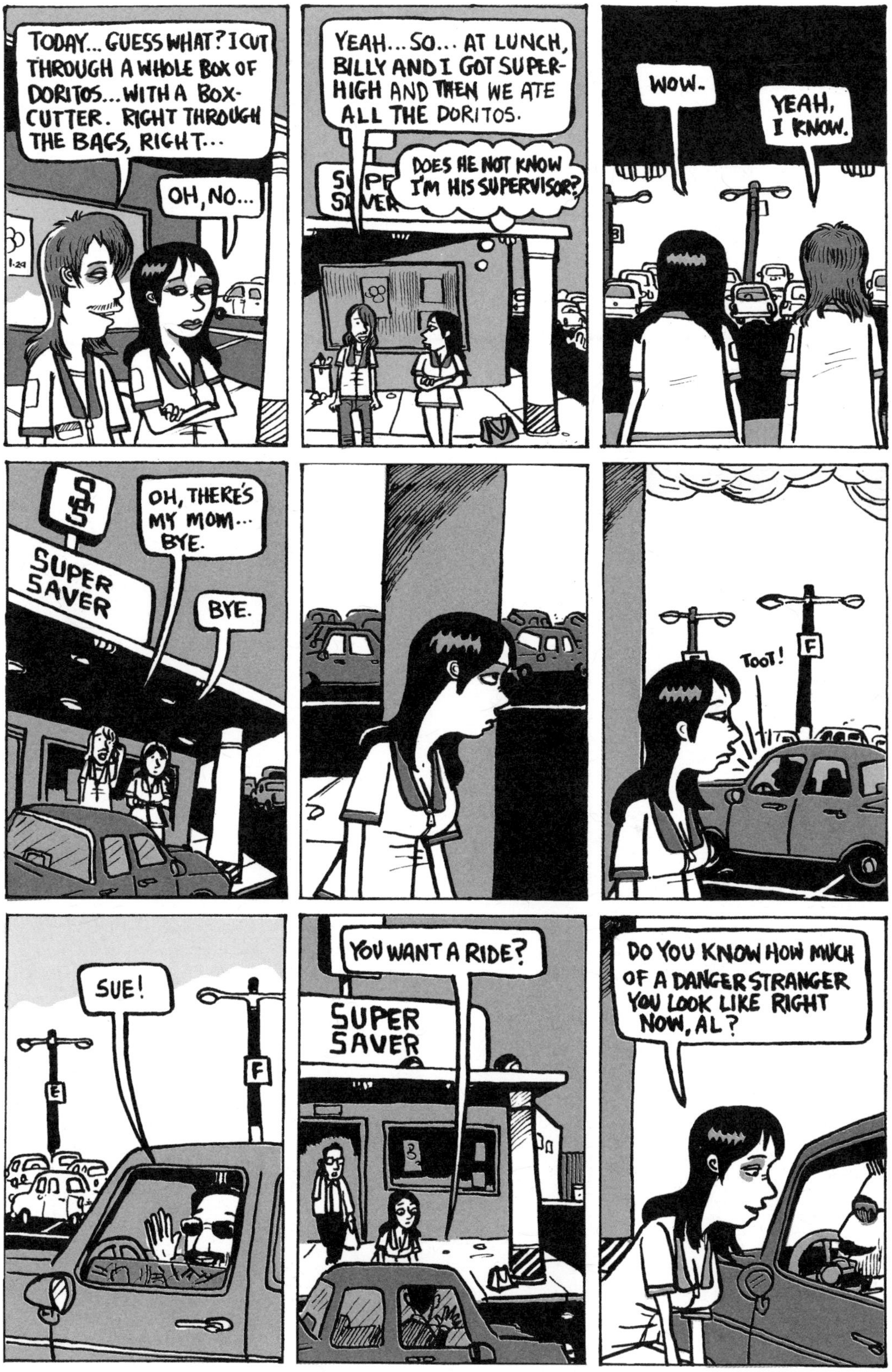
TODAY... GUESS WHAT? I CUT THROUGH A WHOLE BOX OF DORITOS... WITH A BOX-CUTTER. RIGHT THROUGH THE BAGS, RIGHT...
OH, NO...
YEAH... SO... AT LUNCH, BILLY AND I GOT SUPER-HIGH AND THEN WE ATE ALL THE DORITOS.
DOES HE NOT KNOW I'M HIS SUPERVISOR?
WOW.
YEAH, I KNOW.
SUPER SAVER
OH, THERE'S MY MOM... BYE.
BYE.
TOOT!
SUE!
YOU WANT A RIDE?
SUPER SAVER
DO YOU KNOW HOW MUCH OF A DANGER STRANGER YOU LOOK LIKE RIGHT NOW, AL?

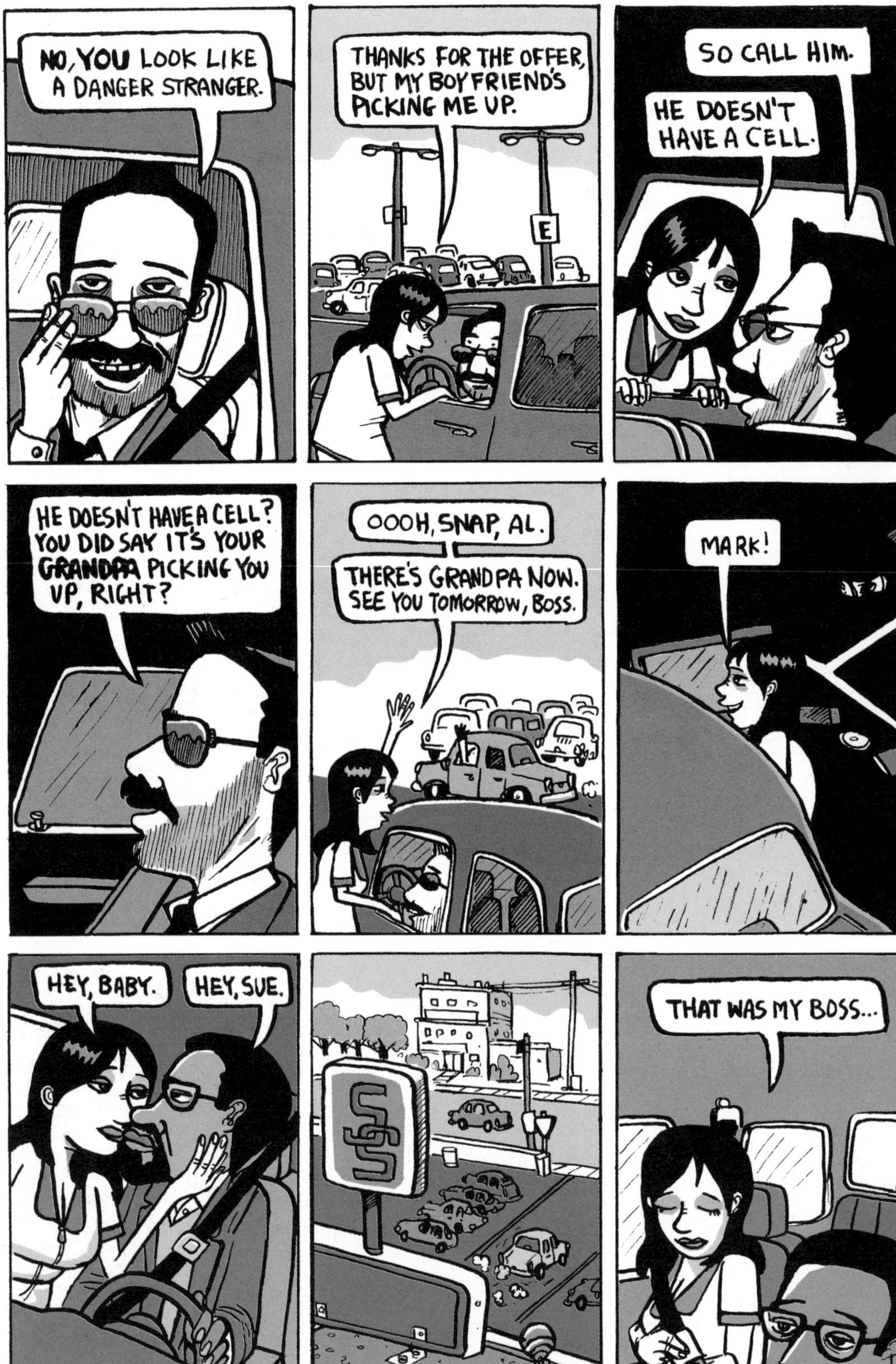
NO, YOU LOOK LIKE A DANGER STRANGER.
THANKS FOR THE OFFER, BUT MY BOYFRIEND'S PICKING ME UP.
E
SO CALL HIM.
HE DOESN'T HAVE A CELL.
HE DOESN'T HAVE A CELL? YOU DID SAY IT'S YOUR GRANDPA PICKING YOU UP, RIGHT?
OOOH, SNAP, AL.
THERE'S GRANDPA NOW. SEE YOU TOMORROW, BOSS.
MARK!
HEY, BABY.
HEY, SUE.
THAT WAS MY BOSS...

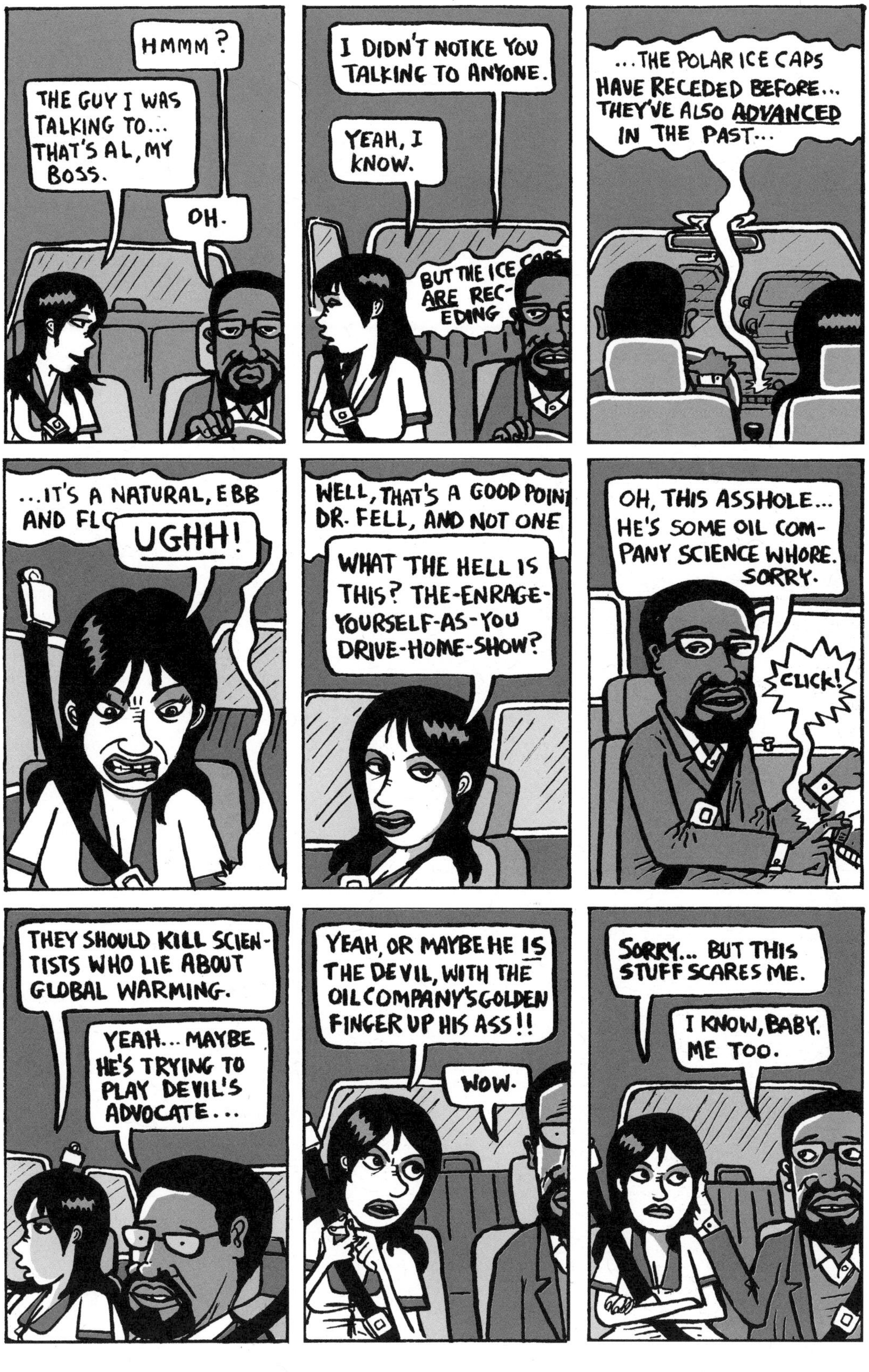
HMMM?
THE GUY I WAS TALKING TO... THAT'S AL, MY BOSS.
OH.
I DIDN'T NOTICE YOU TALKING TO ANYONE.
YEAH, I KNOW.
BUT THE ICE CAPS ARE REC-EDING
...THE POLAR ICE CAPS HAVE RECEDED BEFORE... THEY'VE ALSO ADVANCED IN THE PAST...
...IT'S A NATURAL, EBB AND FL
UGHH!
WELL, THAT'S A GOOD POINT DR. FELL, AND NOT ONE
WHAT THE HELL IS THIS? THE-ENRAGE-YOURSELF-AS-YOU DRIVE-HOME-SHOW?
OH, THIS ASSHOLE... HE'S SOME OIL COM-PANY SCIENCE WHORE. SORRY.
CLICK!
THEY SHOULD KILL SCIEN-TISTS WHO LIE ABOUT GLOBAL WARMING.
YEAH... MAYBE HE'S TRYING TO PLAY DEVIL'S ADVOCATE...
YEAH, OR MAYBE HE IS THE DEVIL, WITH THE OIL COMPANY'S GOLDEN FINGER UP HIS ASS!!
WOW.
SORRY... BUT THIS STUFF SCARES ME.
I KNOW, BABY. ME TOO.

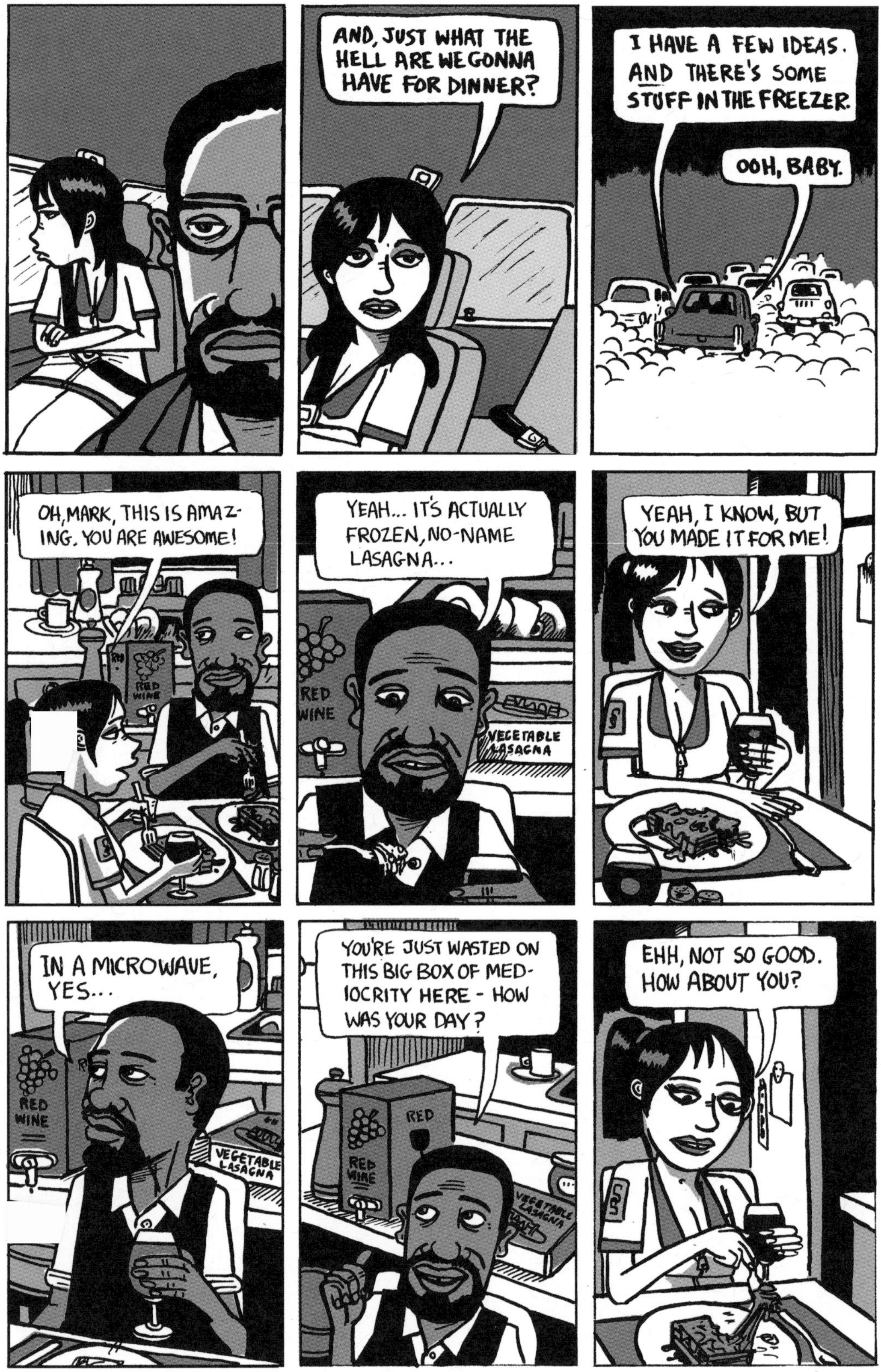
AND, JUST WHAT THE HELL ARE WE GONNA HAVE FOR DINNER?
I HAVE A FEW IDEAS. AND THERE'S SOME STUFF IN THE FREEZER.
OOH, BABY.
OH, MARK, THIS IS AMAZ-ING. YOU ARE AWESOME!
RED WINE
YEAH... IT'S ACTUALLY FROZEN, NO-NAME LASAGNA...
RED WINE
VEGETABLE LASAGNA
YEAH, I KNOW, BUT YOU MADE IT FOR ME!
IN A MICROWAVE, YES...
RED WINE
VEGETABLE LASAGNA
YOU'RE JUST WASTED ON THIS BIG BOX OF MED-IOCRITY HERE - HOW WAS YOUR DAY?
RED
RED WINE
VEGETABLE LASAGNA
EHH, NOT SO GOOD. HOW ABOUT YOU?

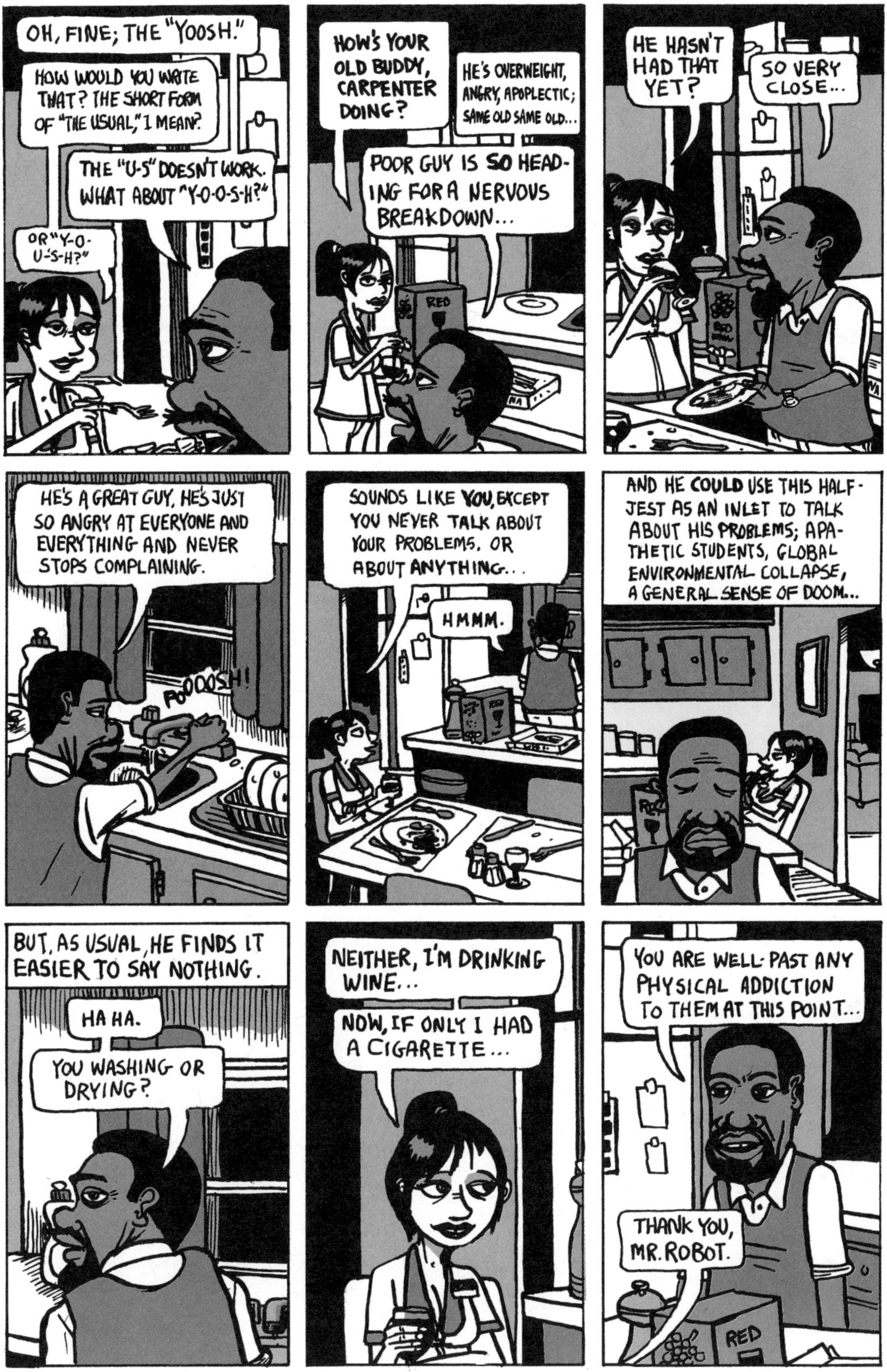
OH, FINE; THE "YOOSH."
HOW WOULD YOU WRITE THAT? THE SHORT FORM OF "THE USUAL," I MEAN?
THE "U-S" DOESN'T WORK. WHAT ABOUT "Y-O-O-S-H?"
OR "Y-O-U-S-H?"
HOW'S YOUR OLD BUDDY, CARPENTER DOING?
HE'S OVERWEIGHT, ANGRY, APOPLECTIC; SAME OLD SAME OLD...
POOR GUY IS SO HEADING FOR A NERVOUS BREAKDOWN...
HE HASN'T HAD THAT YET?
SO VERY CLOSE...
HE'S A GREAT GUY, HE'S JUST SO ANGRY AT EVERYONE AND EVERYTHING AND NEVER STOPS COMPLAINING.
FOOOOSH!
SOUNDS LIKE YOU, EXCEPT YOU NEVER TALK ABOUT YOUR PROBLEMS. OR ABOUT ANYTHING...
HMMM.
AND HE COULD USE THIS HALF-JEST AS AN INLET TO TALK ABOUT HIS PROBLEMS; APATHETIC STUDENTS, GLOBAL ENVIRONMENTAL COLLAPSE, A GENERAL SENSE OF DOOM...
BUT, AS USUAL, HE FINDS IT EASIER TO SAY NOTHING.
HA HA.
YOU WASHING OR DRYING?
NEITHER, I'M DRINKING WINE...
NOW, IF ONLY I HAD A CIGARETTE...
YOU ARE WELL-PAST ANY PHYSICAL ADDICTION TO THEM AT THIS POINT...
THANK YOU, MR. ROBOT.

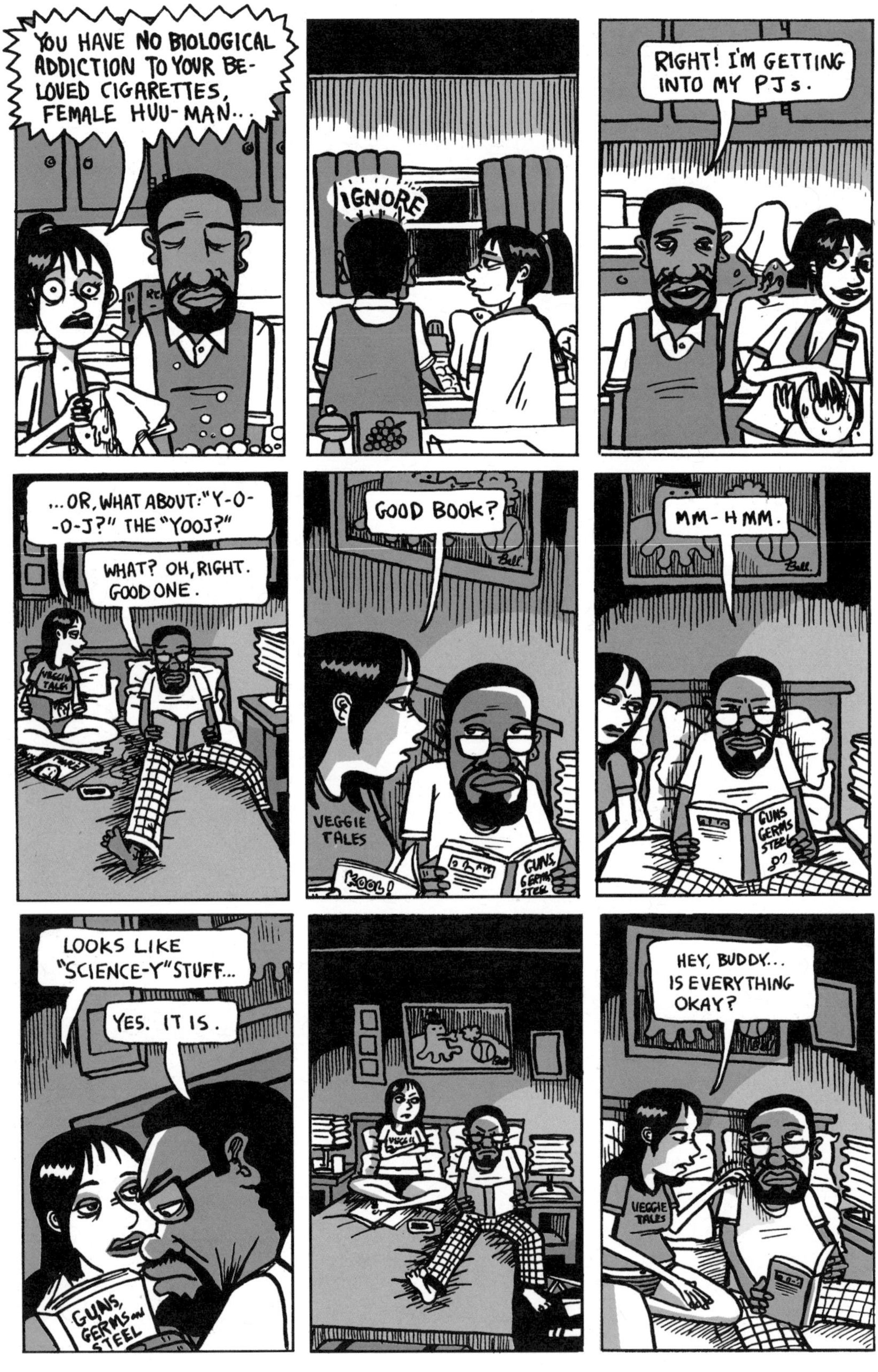
YOU HAVE NO BIOLOGICAL ADDICTION TO YOUR BE-LOVED CIGARETTES, FEMALE HUU-MAN...
IGNORE
RIGHT! I'M GETTING INTO MY PJs.
...OR, WHAT ABOUT: "Y-O-O-J?" THE "YOOJ?"
WHAT? OH, RIGHT. GOOD ONE.
GOOD BOOK?
MM-HMM.
LOOKS LIKE "SCIENCE-Y" STUFF...
YES. IT IS.
HEY, BUDDY... IS EVERYTHING OKAY?

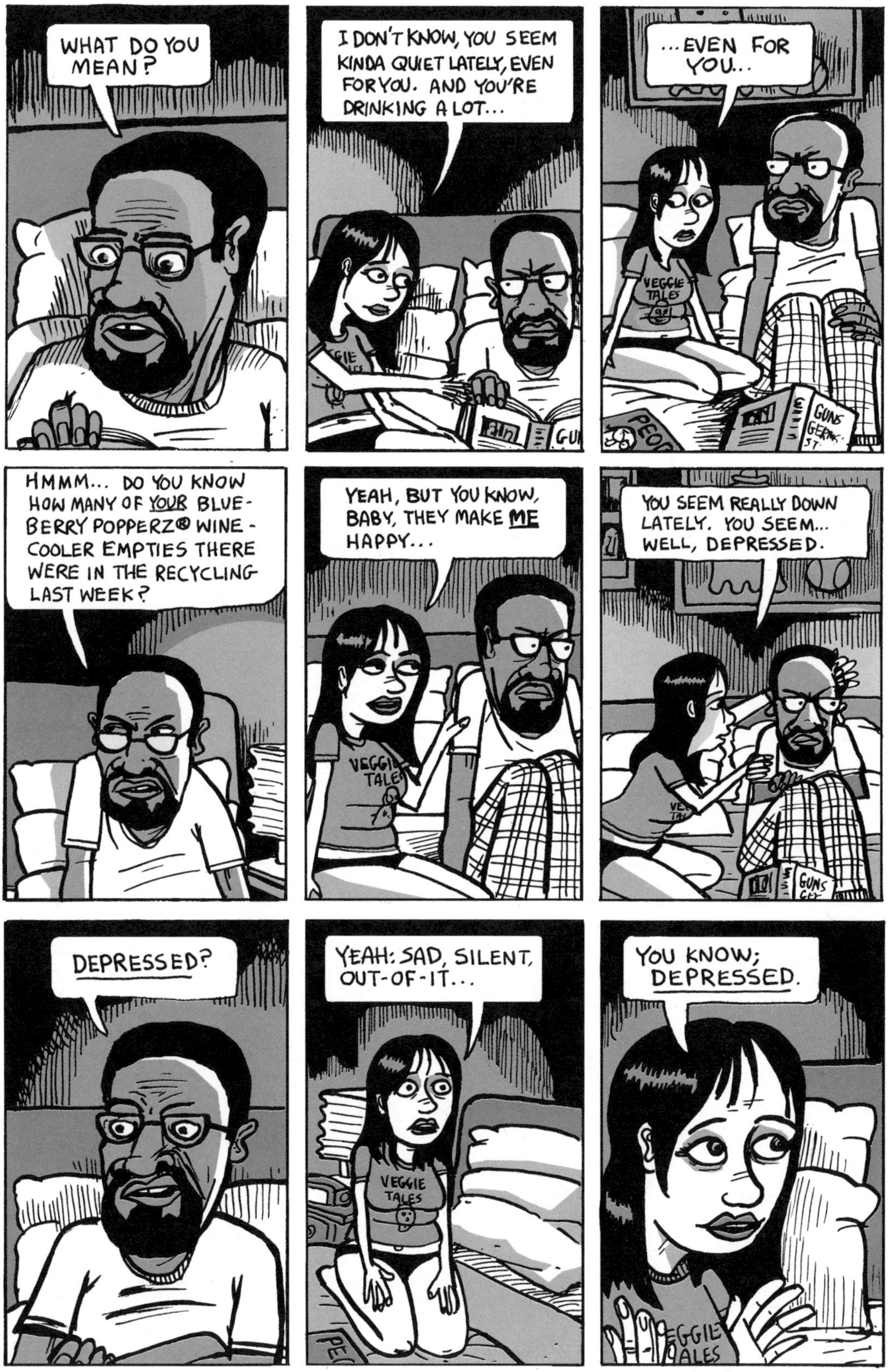
WHAT DO YOU MEAN?
I DON'T KNOW, YOU SEEM KINDA QUIET LATELY, EVEN FOR YOU. AND YOU'RE DRINKING A LOT...
...EVEN FOR YOU...
HMMM... DO YOU KNOW HOW MANY OF YOUR BLUE-BERRY POPPERZ® WINE-COOLER EMPTIES THERE WERE IN THE RECYCLING LAST WEEK?
YEAH, BUT YOU KNOW, BABY, THEY MAKE ME HAPPY...
YOU SEEM REALLY DOWN LATELY. YOU SEEM... WELL, DEPRESSED.
DEPRESSED?
YEAH: SAD, SILENT, OUT-OF-IT...
YOU KNOW; DEPRESSED.

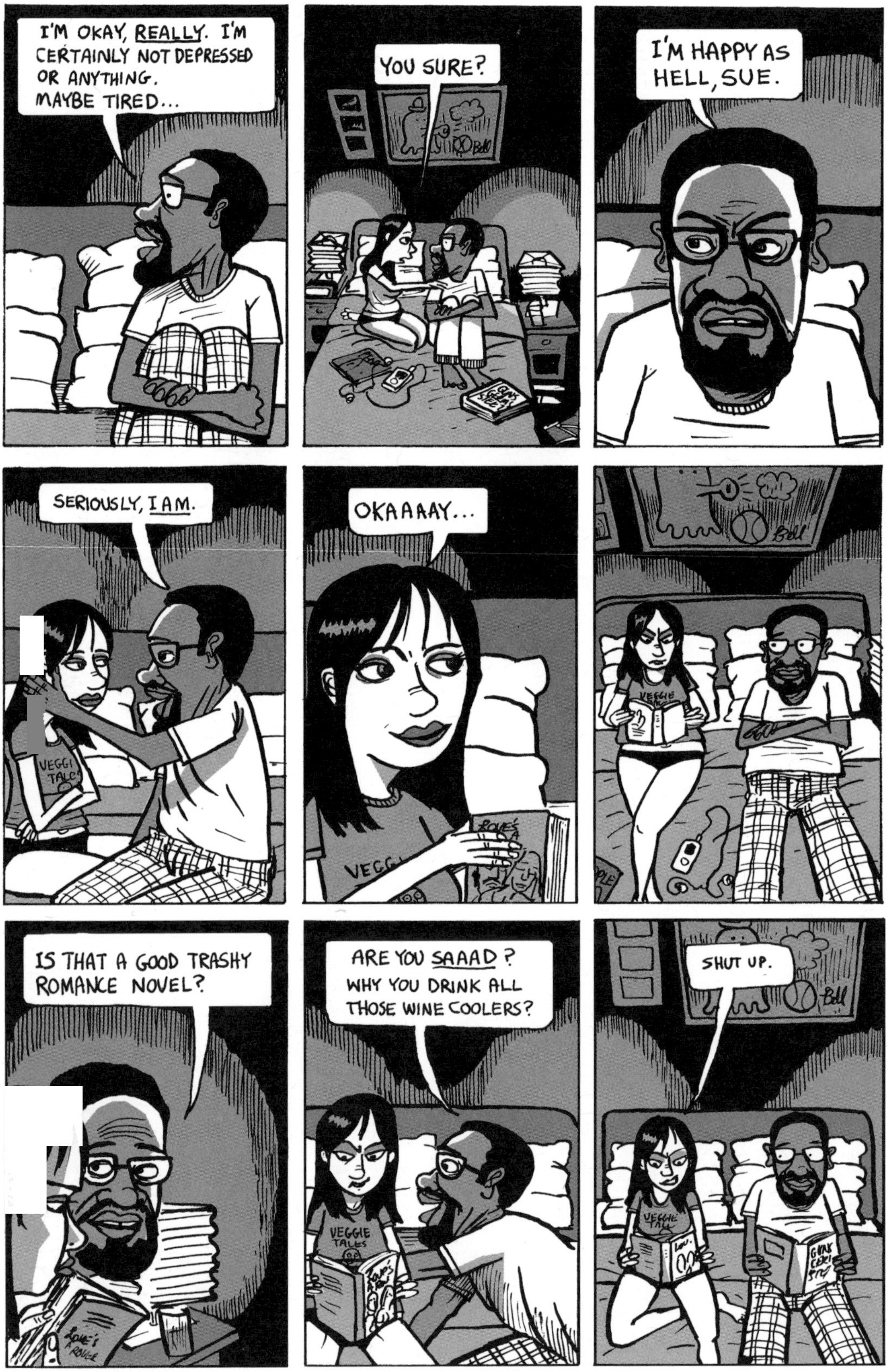
I'M OKAY, REALLY. I'M CERTAINLY NOT DEPRESSED OR ANYTHING. MAYBE TIRED...
YOU SURE?
I'M HAPPY AS HELL, SUE.
SERIOUSLY, I AM.
OKAAAAY...
IS THAT A GOOD TRASHY ROMANCE NOVEL?
ARE YOU SAAAD? WHY YOU DRINK ALL THOSE WINE COOLERS?
SHUT UP.

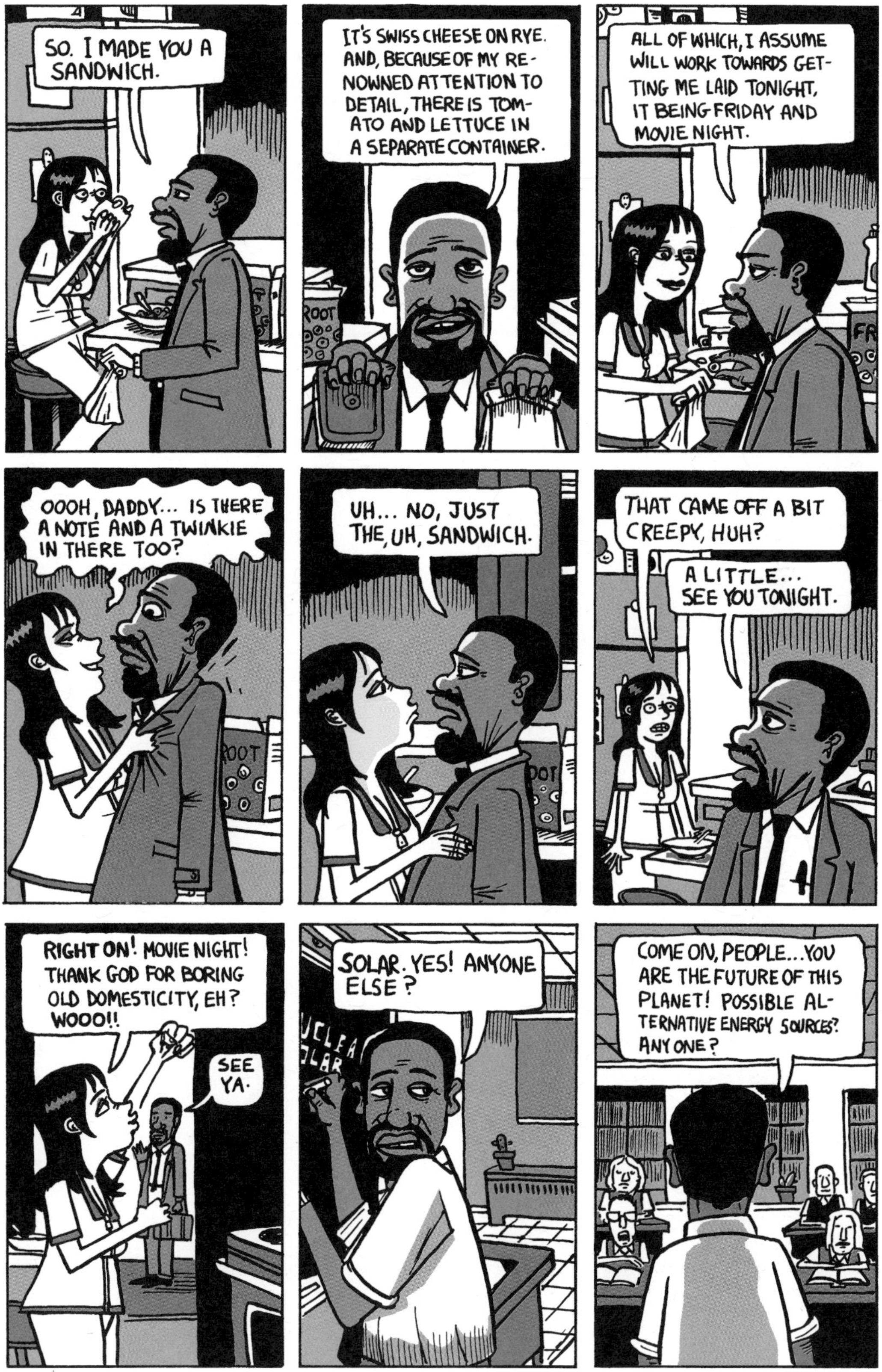
SO. I MADE YOU A SANDWICH.
IT'S SWISS CHEESE ON RYE. AND, BECAUSE OF MY RENOWNED ATTENTION TO DETAIL, THERE IS TOMATO AND LETTUCE IN A SEPARATE CONTAINER.
ALL OF WHICH, I ASSUME WILL WORK TOWARDS GETTING ME LAID TONIGHT, IT BEING FRIDAY AND MOVIE NIGHT.
OOOH, DADDY... IS THERE A NOTE AND A TWINKIE IN THERE TOO?
UH... NO, JUST THE, UH, SANDWICH.
THAT CAME OFF A BIT CREEPY, HUH?
A LITTLE... SEE YOU TONIGHT.
RIGHT ON! MOVIE NIGHT! THANK GOD FOR BORING OLD DOMESTICITY, EH? WOOO!!
SEE YA.
SOLAR. YES! ANYONE ELSE?
COME ON, PEOPLE... YOU ARE THE FUTURE OF THIS PLANET! POSSIBLE ALTERNATIVE ENERGY SOURCES? ANY ONE?

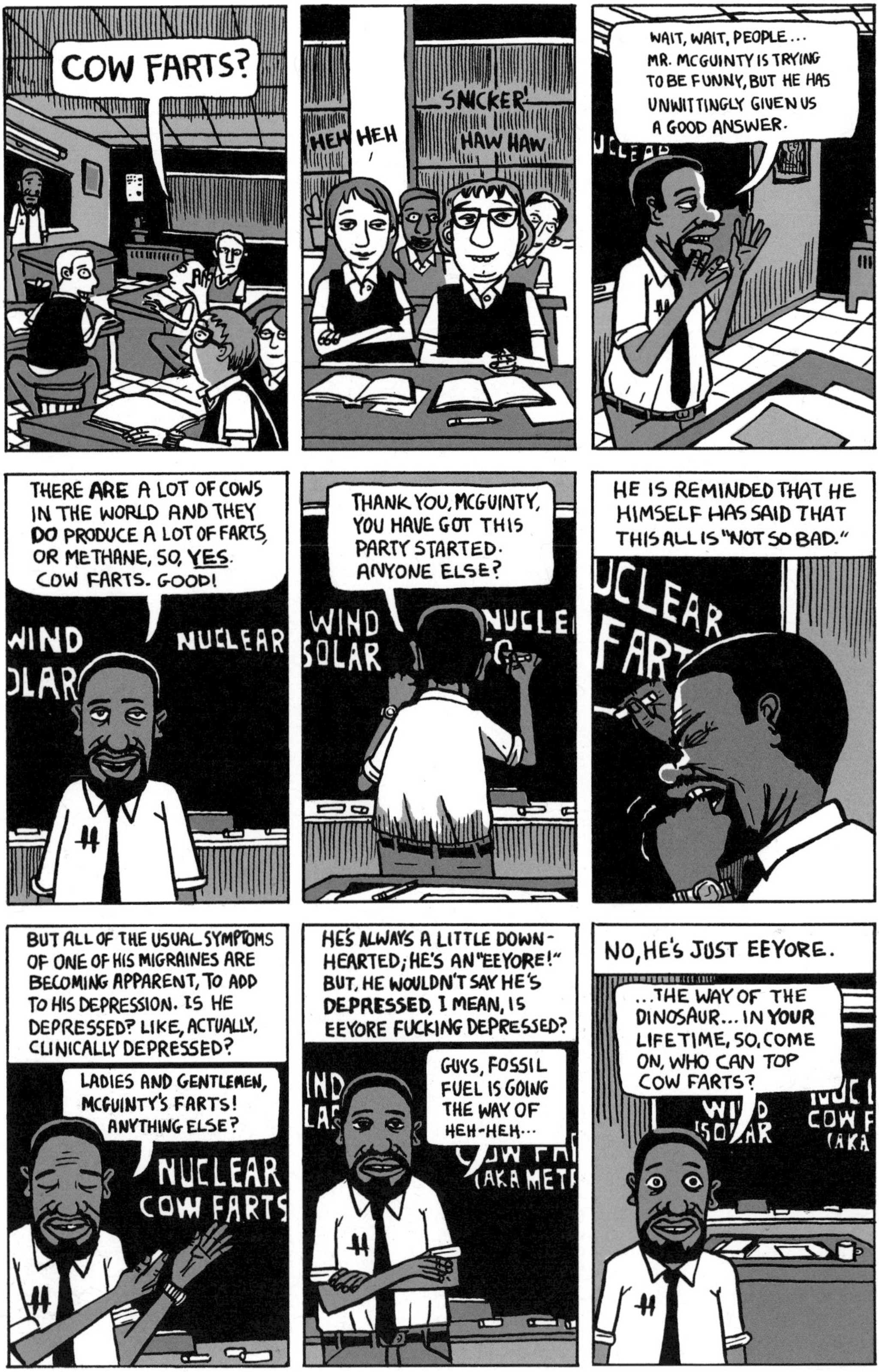
COW FARTS?
HEH HEH
SNICKER!
HAW HAW
WAIT, WAIT, PEOPLE... MR. MCGUINTY IS TRYING TO BE FUNNY, BUT HE HAS UNWITTINGLY GIVEN US A GOOD ANSWER.
THERE ARE A LOT OF COWS IN THE WORLD AND THEY DO PRODUCE A LOT OF FARTS, OR METHANE, SO, YES. COW FARTS. GOOD!
WIND
NUCLEAR
THANK YOU, MCGUINTY, YOU HAVE GOT THIS PARTY STARTED. ANYONE ELSE?
HE IS REMINDED THAT HE HIMSELF HAS SAID THAT THIS ALL IS "NOT SO BAD."
BUT ALL OF THE USUAL SYMPTOMS OF ONE OF HIS MIGRAINES ARE BECOMING APPARENT, TO ADD TO HIS DEPRESSION. IS HE DEPRESSED? LIKE, ACTUALLY, CLINICALLY DEPRESSED?
LADIES AND GENTLEMEN, MCGUINTY'S FARTS! ANYTHING ELSE?
NUCLEAR
COW FARTS
HE'S ALWAYS A LITTLE DOWN-HEARTED; HE'S AN "EEYORE!" BUT, HE WOULDN'T SAY HE'S DEPRESSED, I MEAN, IS EEYORE FUCKING DEPRESSED?
GUYS, FOSSIL FUEL IS GOING THE WAY OF HEH-HEH...
NO, HE'S JUST EEYORE.
...THE WAY OF THE DINOSAUR... IN YOUR LIFETIME, SO, COME ON, WHO CAN TOP COW FARTS?

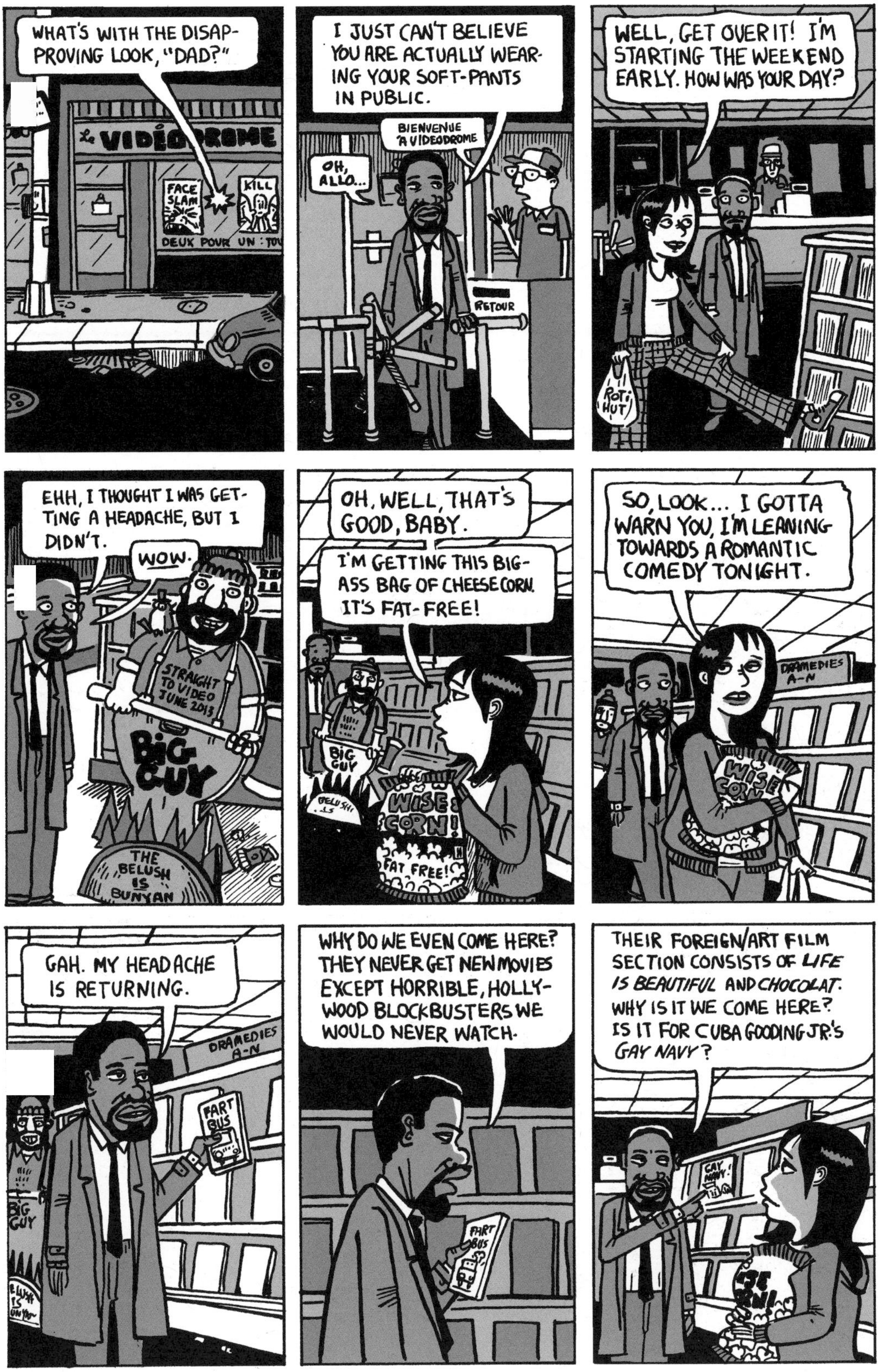
WHAT'S WITH THE DISAPPROVING LOOK, "DAD?"
Le VIDÉODROME
FACE SLAM
KILL
DEUX POUR UN : TOU
I JUST CAN'T BELIEVE YOU ARE ACTUALLY WEARING YOUR SOFT-PANTS IN PUBLIC.
BIENVENUE 'A VIDEODROME
OH, ALLO...
RETOUR
WELL, GET OVER IT! I'M STARTING THE WEEKEND EARLY. HOW WAS YOUR DAY?
ROTI HUT
EHH, I THOUGHT I WAS GETTING A HEADACHE, BUT I DIDN'T.
WOW.
STRAIGHT TO VIDEO JUNE 2013
BIG GUY
THE BELUSH IS BUNYAN
OH, WELL, THAT'S GOOD, BABY.
I'M GETTING THIS BIG-ASS BAG OF CHEESE CORN. IT'S FAT-FREE!
WISE CORN!
FAT FREE!
SO, LOOK... I GOTTA WARN YOU, I'M LEANING TOWARDS A ROMANTIC COMEDY TONIGHT.
DRAMEDIES A-N
GAH. MY HEADACHE IS RETURNING.
DRAMEDIES A-N
FART BUS
WHY DO WE EVEN COME HERE? THEY NEVER GET NEW MOVIES EXCEPT HORRIBLE, HOLLYWOOD BLOCKBUSTERS WE WOULD NEVER WATCH.
FART BUS
THEIR FOREIGN/ART FILM SECTION CONSISTS OF *LIFE IS BEAUTIFUL* AND *CHOCOLAT*. WHY IS IT WE COME HERE? IS IT FOR CUBA GOODING JR.'S *GAY NAVY*?
GAY NAVY!

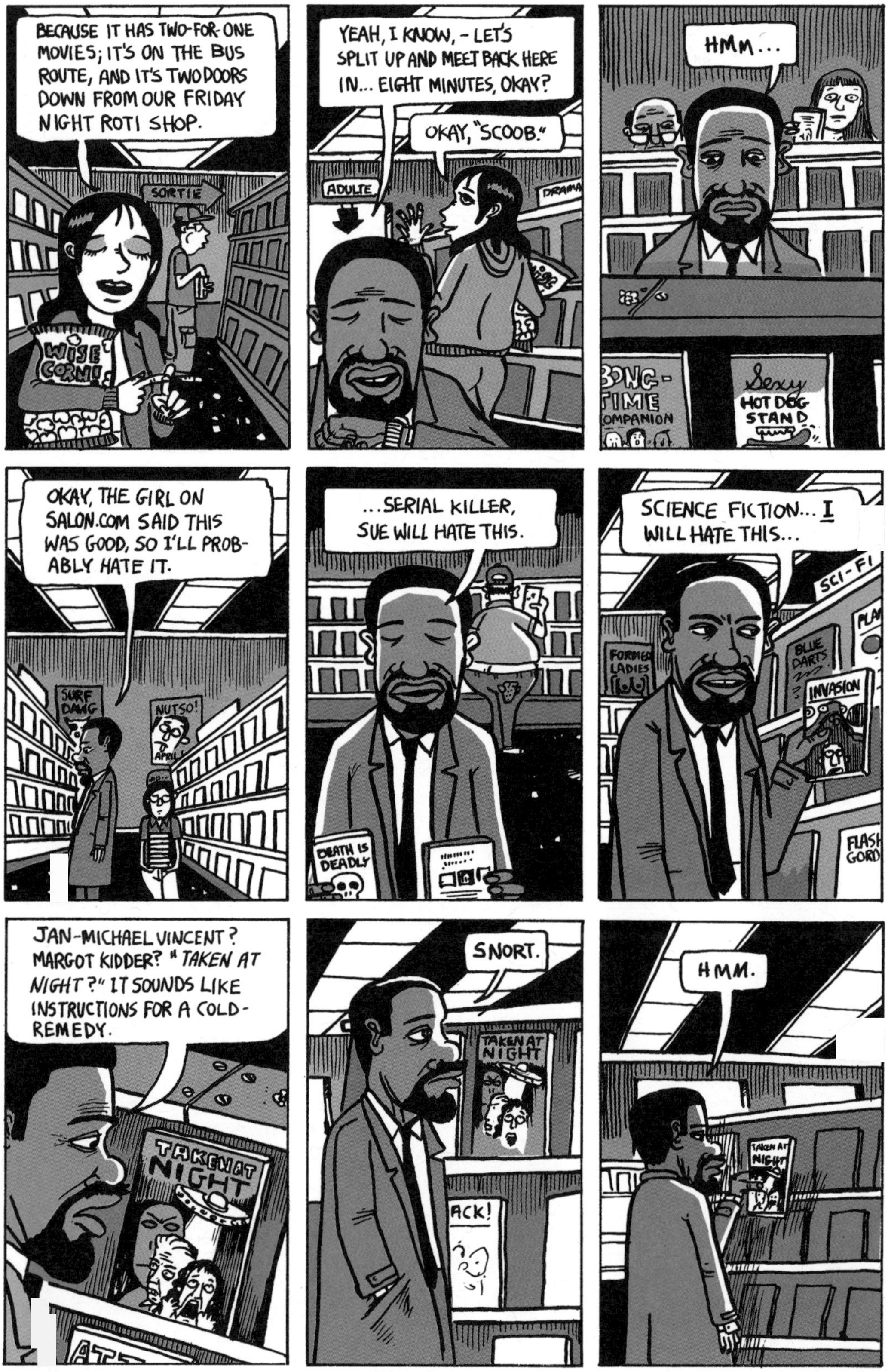
BECAUSE IT HAS TWO-FOR-ONE MOVIES; IT'S ON THE BUS ROUTE, AND IT'S TWO DOORS DOWN FROM OUR FRIDAY NIGHT ROTI SHOP.
SORTIE
WISE CORN
YEAH, I KNOW, - LET'S SPLIT UP AND MEET BACK HERE IN... EIGHT MINUTES, OKAY?
OKAY, "SCOOB."
ADULTE
DRAMA
HMM...
BONG-TIME COMPANION
Sexy HOT DOG STAND
OKAY, THE GIRL ON SALON.COM SAID THIS WAS GOOD, SO I'LL PROBABLY HATE IT.
SURF DAWG
NUTSO!
...SERIAL KILLER, SUE WILL HATE THIS.
DEATH IS DEADLY
SCIENCE FICTION... I WILL HATE THIS...
SCI-FI
FORMER LADIES
BLUE DARTS
INVASION
FLASH GORD
JAN-MICHAEL VINCENT? MARGOT KIDDER? "TAKEN AT NIGHT?" IT SOUNDS LIKE INSTRUCTIONS FOR A COLD-REMEDY.
TAKEN AT NIGHT
SNORT.
TAKEN AT NIGHT
ACK!
HMM.
TAKEN AT NIGHT

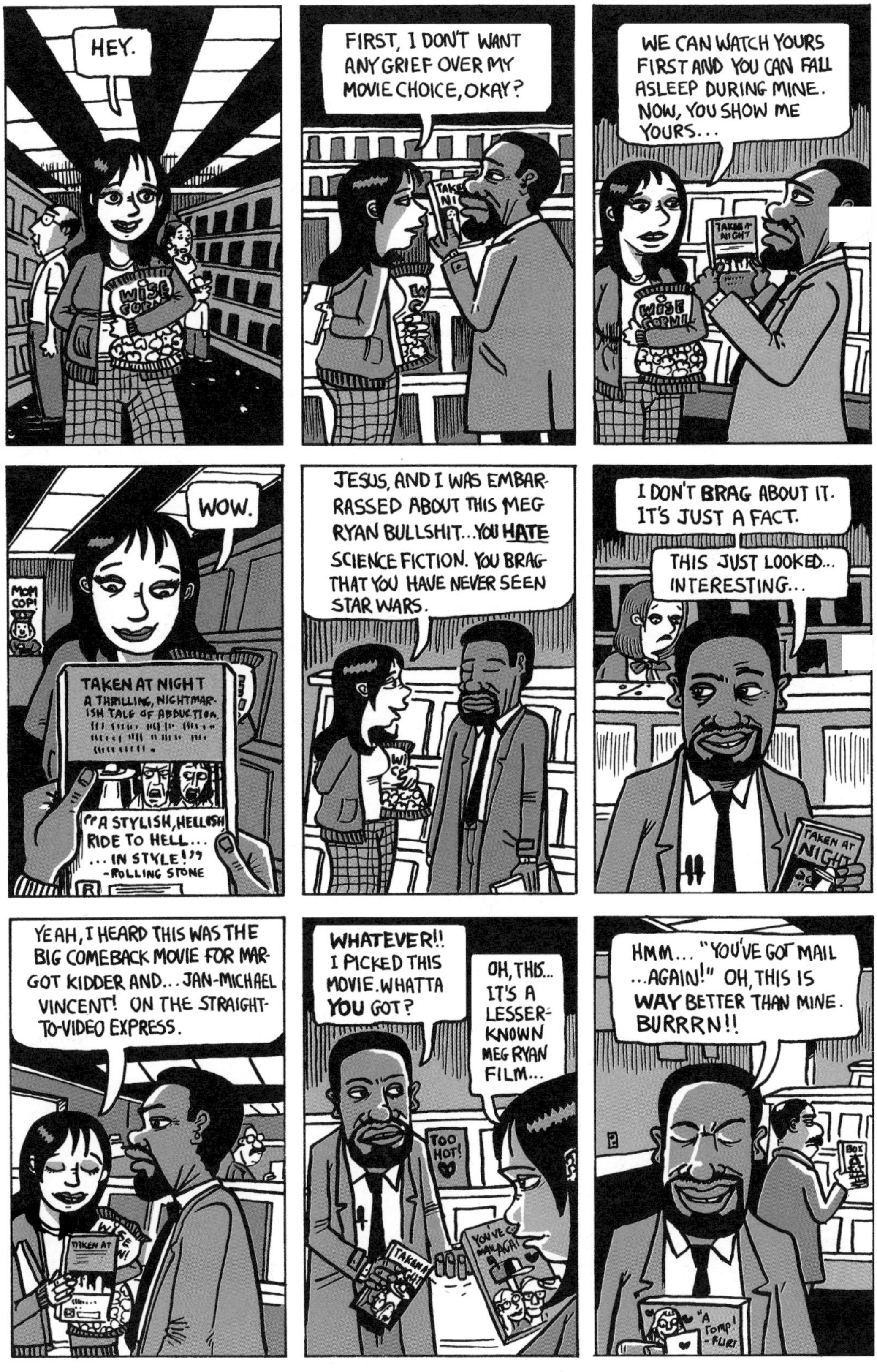
HEY.
FIRST, I DON'T WANT ANY GRIEF OVER MY MOVIE CHOICE, OKAY?
WE CAN WATCH YOURS FIRST AND YOU CAN FALL ASLEEP DURING MINE. NOW, YOU SHOW ME YOURS...
WOW.
TAKEN AT NIGHT
A THRILLING, NIGHTMARISH TALE OF ABDUCTION.
"A STYLISH, HELLISH RIDE TO HELL... ...IN STYLE!" -ROLLING STONE
MOM COP!
JESUS, AND I WAS EMBARRASSED ABOUT THIS MEG RYAN BULLSHIT... YOU HATE SCIENCE FICTION. YOU BRAG THAT YOU HAVE NEVER SEEN STAR WARS.
I DON'T BRAG ABOUT IT. IT'S JUST A FACT.
THIS JUST LOOKED... INTERESTING...
TAKEN AT NIGHT
YEAH, I HEARD THIS WAS THE BIG COMEBACK MOVIE FOR MARGOT KIDDER AND... JAN-MICHAEL VINCENT! ON THE STRAIGHT-TO-VIDEO EXPRESS.
WHATEVER!! I PICKED THIS MOVIE. WHATTA YOU GOT?
OH, THIS... IT'S A LESSER-KNOWN MEG RYAN FILM...
TOO HOT!
HMM... "YOU'VE GOT MAIL ...AGAIN!" OH, THIS IS WAY BETTER THAN MINE. BURRRN!!
"A ROMP!" -FLIRT

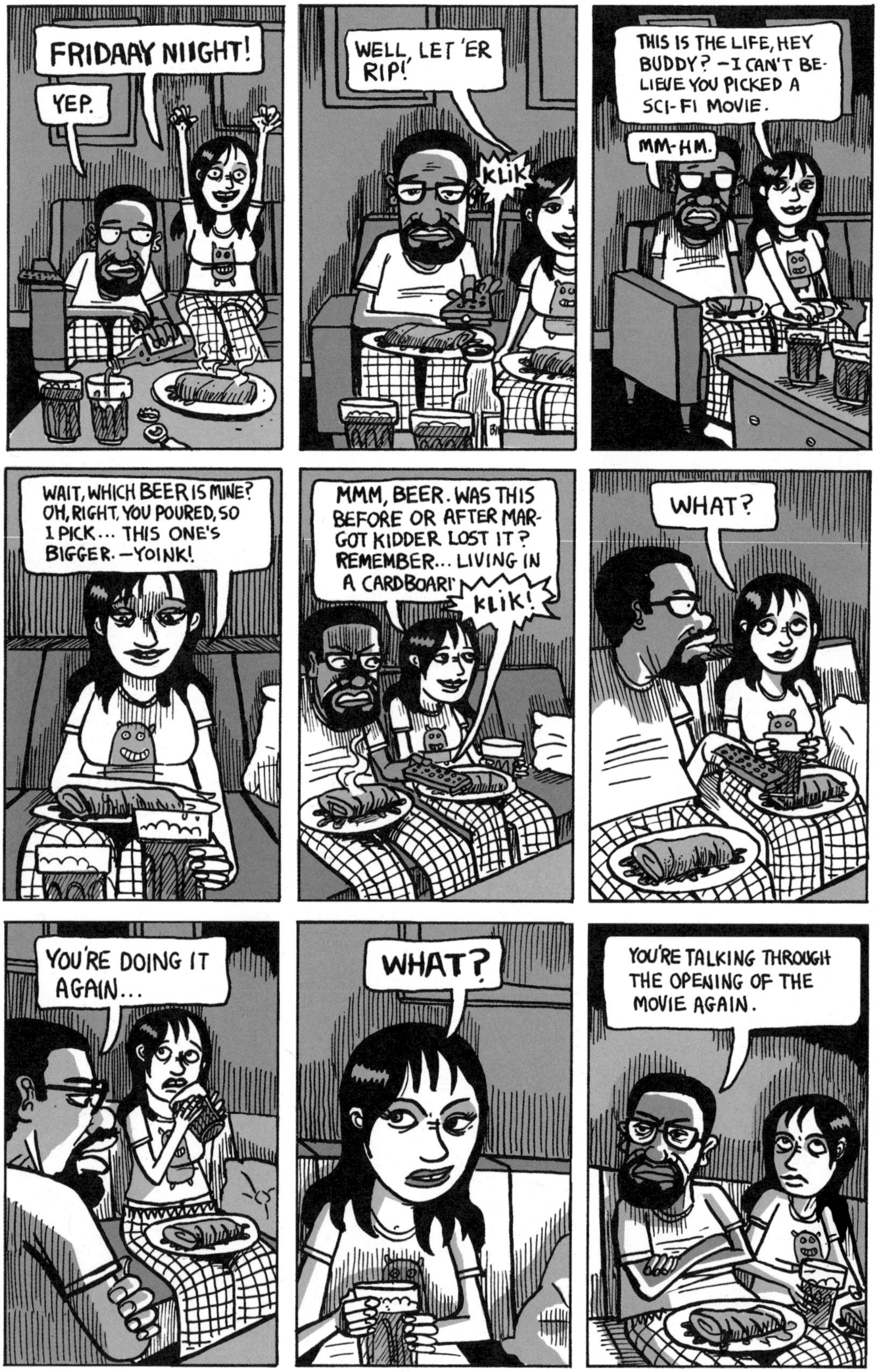
FRIDAAY NIIGHT!
YEP.
WELL, LET 'ER RIP!
KLIK
THIS IS THE LIFE, HEY BUDDY? —I CAN'T BE-LIEVE YOU PICKED A SCI-FI MOVIE.
MM-HM.
WAIT, WHICH BEER IS MINE? OH, RIGHT, YOU POURED, SO I PICK... THIS ONE'S BIGGER. —YOINK!
MMM, BEER. WAS THIS BEFORE OR AFTER MAR-GOT KIDDER LOST IT? REMEMBER... LIVING IN A CARDBOARI'
KLIK!
WHAT?
YOU'RE DOING IT AGAIN...
WHAT?
YOU'RE TALKING THROUGH THE OPENING OF THE MOVIE AGAIN.

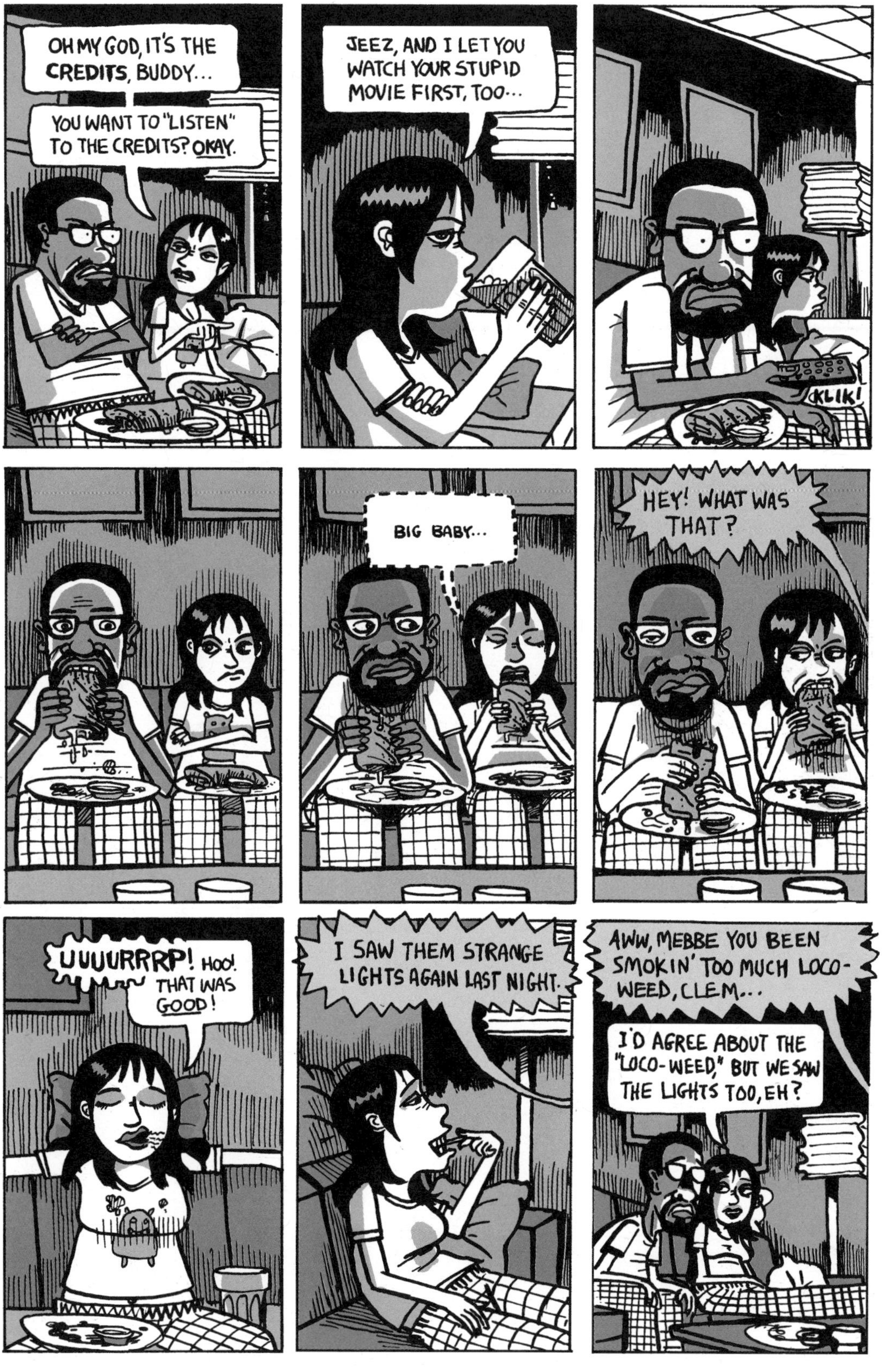
OH MY GOD, IT'S THE **CREDITS**, BUDDY...
YOU WANT TO "LISTEN" TO THE CREDITS? OKAY.
JEEZ, AND I LET YOU WATCH YOUR STUPID MOVIE FIRST, TOO...
KLIK!
BIG BABY...
HEY! WHAT WAS THAT?
UUUURRRP! HOO! THAT WAS GOOD!
I SAW THEM STRANGE LIGHTS AGAIN LAST NIGHT.
AWW, MEBBE YOU BEEN SMOKIN' TOO MUCH LOCO-WEED, CLEM...
I'D AGREE ABOUT THE "LOCO-WEED," BUT WE SAW THE LIGHTS TOO, EH?

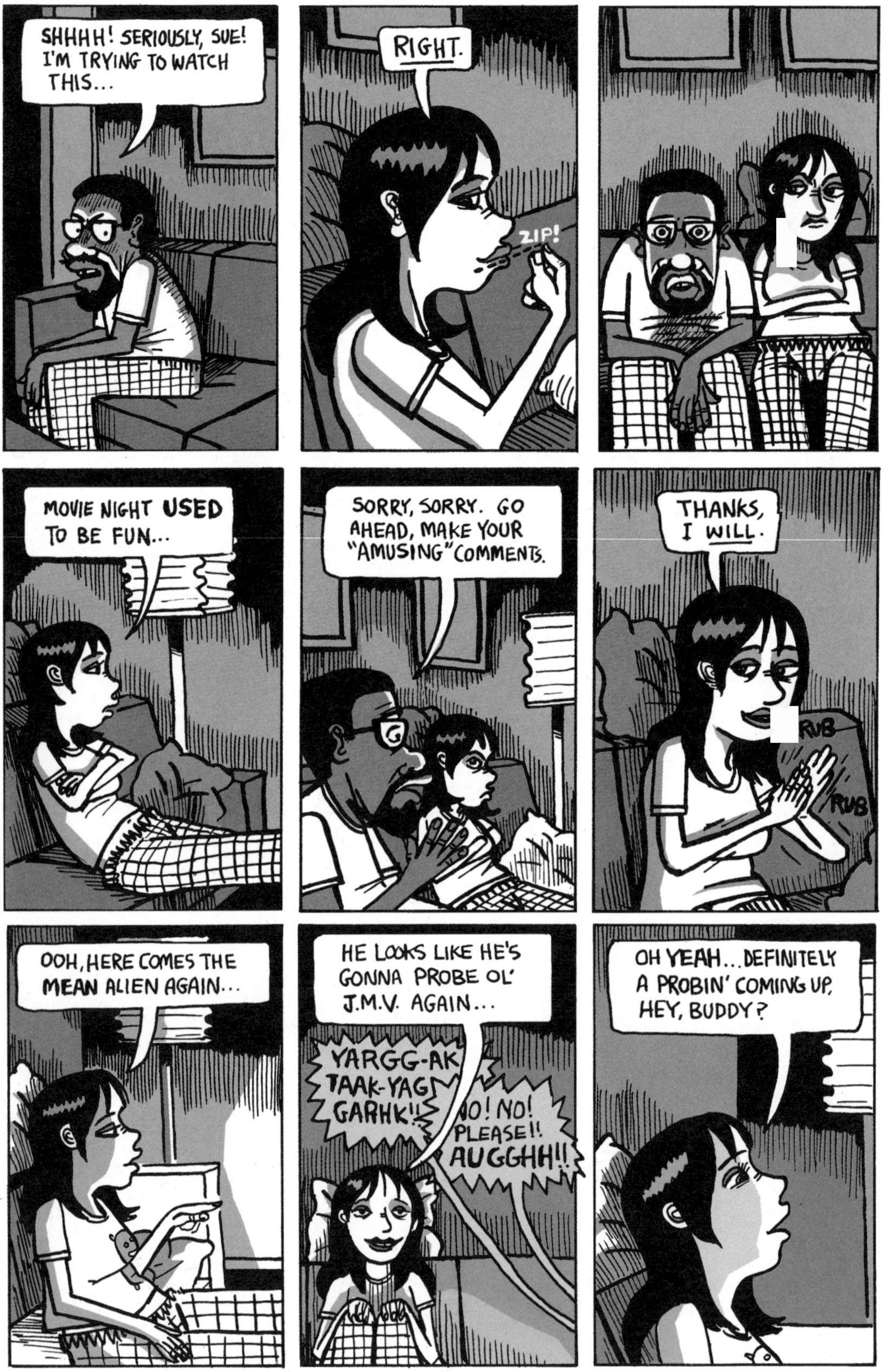
SHHHH! SERIOUSLY, SUE! I'M TRYING TO WATCH THIS...
RIGHT.
ZIP!
MOVIE NIGHT USED TO BE FUN...
SORRY, SORRY. GO AHEAD, MAKE YOUR "AMUSING" COMMENTS.
THANKS, I WILL.
RUB
RUB
OOH, HERE COMES THE MEAN ALIEN AGAIN...
HE LOOKS LIKE HE'S GONNA PROBE OL' J.M.V. AGAIN...
YARGG-AK TAAK-YAG GARHK!!
NO! NO! PLEASE!! AUGGHH!!
OH YEAH... DEFINITELY A PROBIN' COMING UP, HEY, BUDDY?

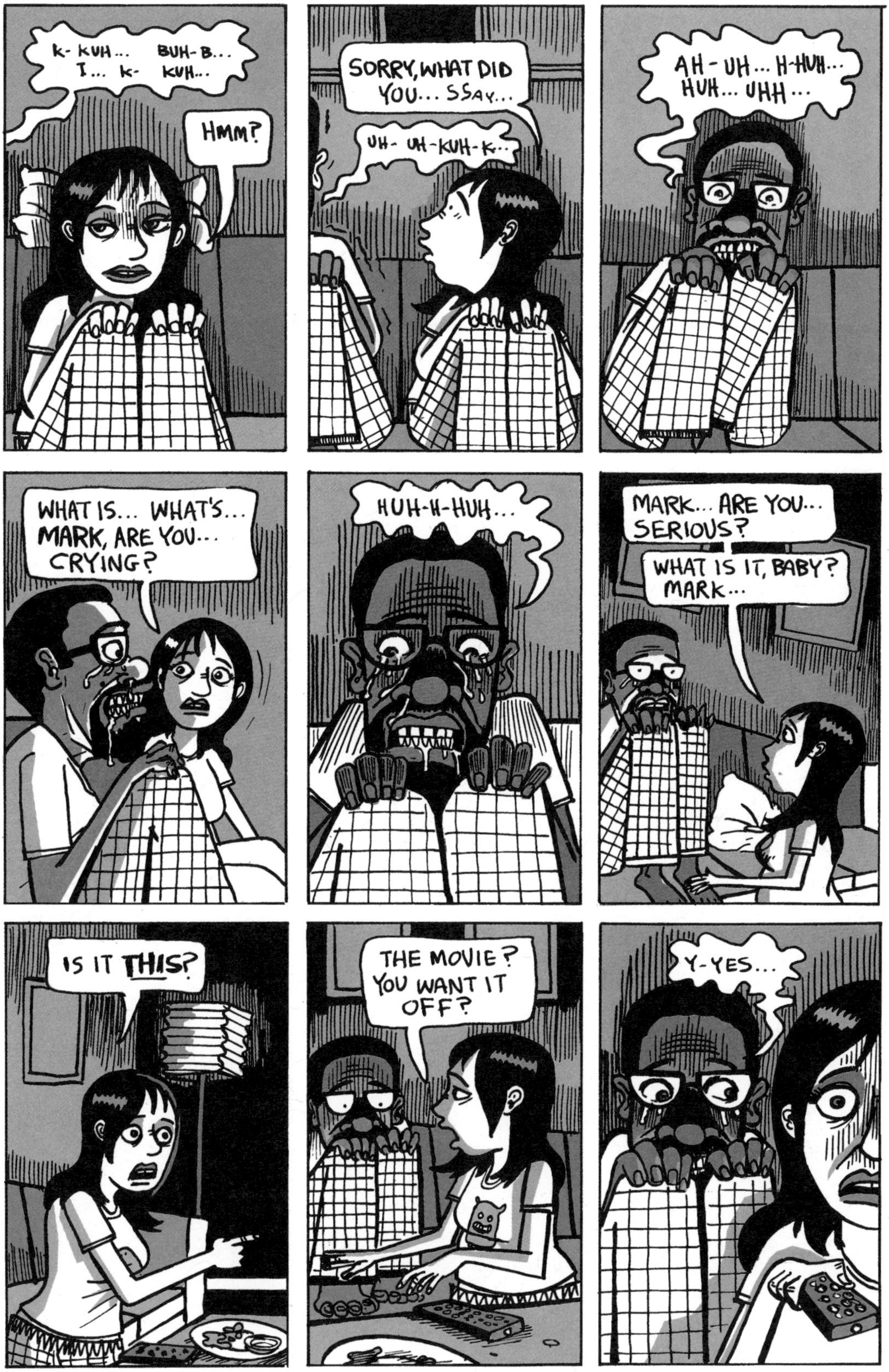
K- KUH... BUH- B... I... K- KUH...
HMM?
SORRY, WHAT DID YOU... SSAY...
UH- UH-KUH-K...
AH- UH... H-HUH... HUH... UHH...
WHAT IS... WHAT'S... MARK, ARE YOU... CRYING?
HUH-H-HUH...
MARK... ARE YOU... SERIOUS?
WHAT IS IT, BABY? MARK...
IS IT THIS?
THE MOVIE? YOU WANT IT OFF?
Y-YES...

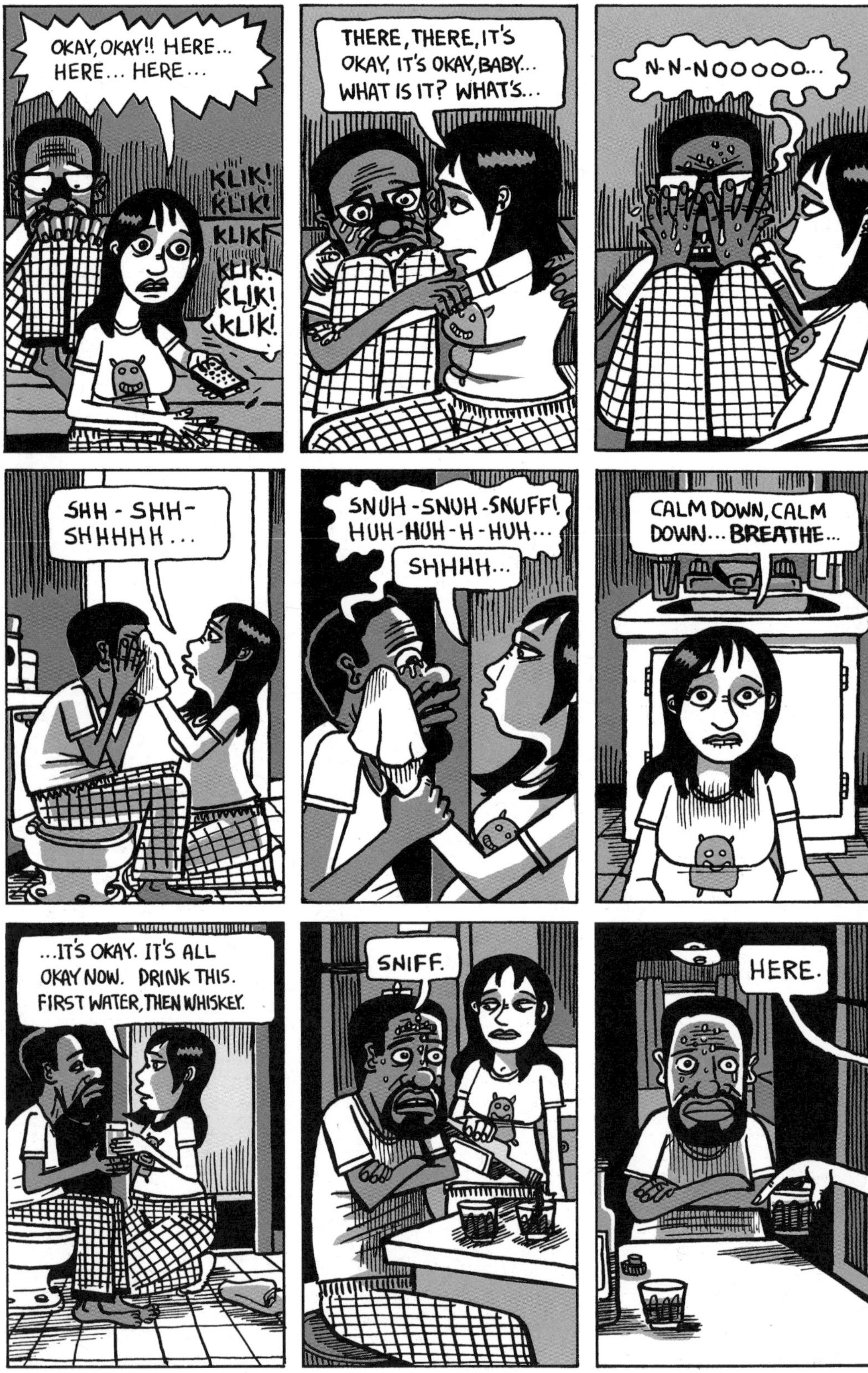
OKAY, OKAY!! HERE... HERE... HERE...
KLIK! KLIK! KLIK KLIK! KLIK! KLIK!
THERE, THERE, IT'S OKAY, IT'S OKAY, BABY... WHAT IS IT? WHAT'S...
N-N-NOOOOO...
SHH - SHH - SHHHHH...
SNUH - SNUH - SNUFF! HUH - HUH - H - HUH...
SHHHH...
CALM DOWN, CALM DOWN... BREATHE...
...IT'S OKAY. IT'S ALL OKAY NOW. DRINK THIS. FIRST WATER, THEN WHISKEY.
SNIFF.
HERE.

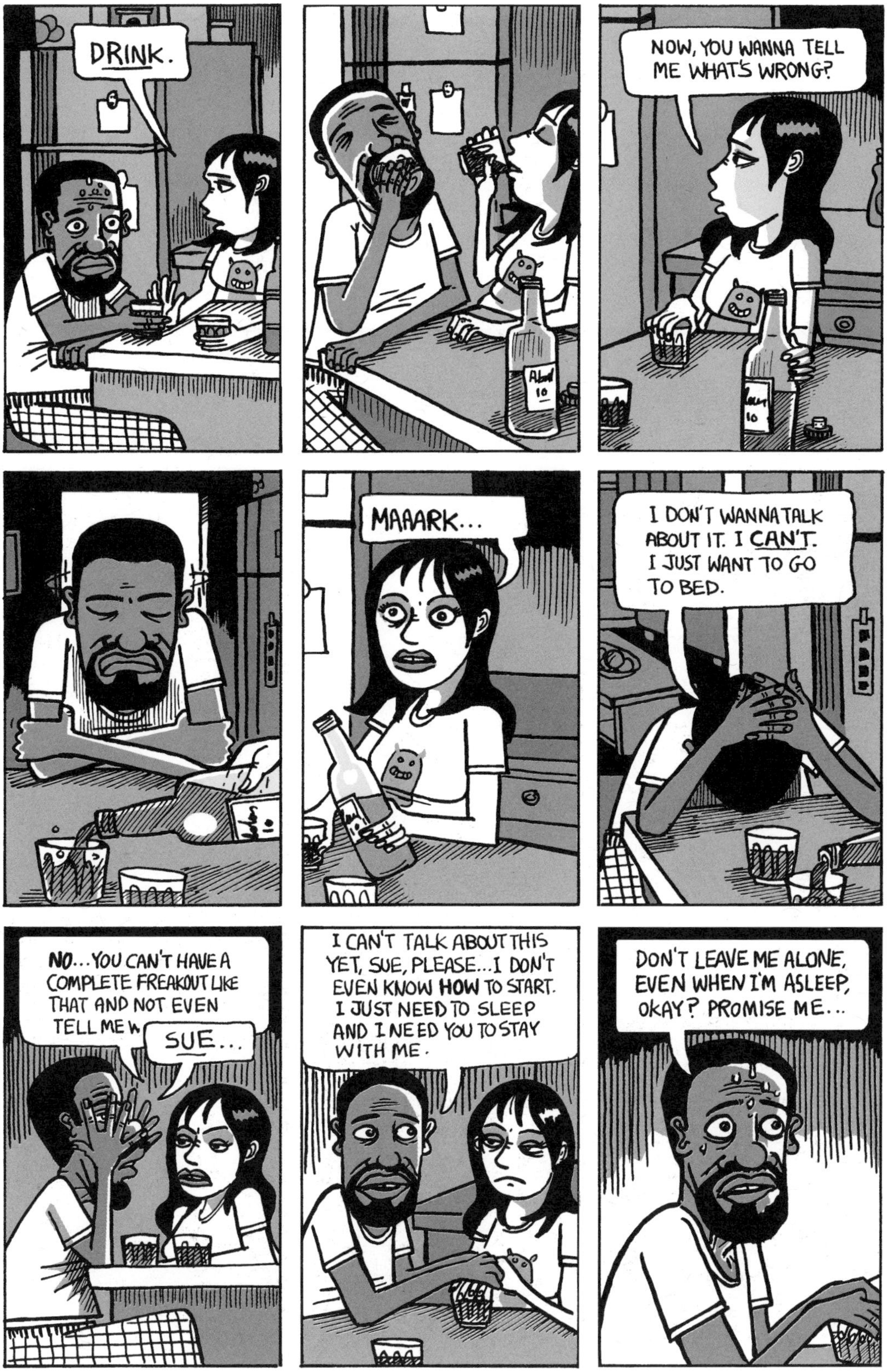
DRINK.
NOW, YOU WANNA TELL ME WHAT'S WRONG?
MAAARK...
I DON'T WANNA TALK ABOUT IT. I CAN'T. I JUST WANT TO GO TO BED.
NO...YOU CAN'T HAVE A COMPLETE FREAKOUT LIKE THAT AND NOT EVEN TELL ME W
SUE...
I CAN'T TALK ABOUT THIS YET, SUE, PLEASE...I DON'T EVEN KNOW HOW TO START. I JUST NEED TO SLEEP AND I NEED YOU TO STAY WITH ME.
DON'T LEAVE ME ALONE, EVEN WHEN I'M ASLEEP, OKAY? PROMISE ME...

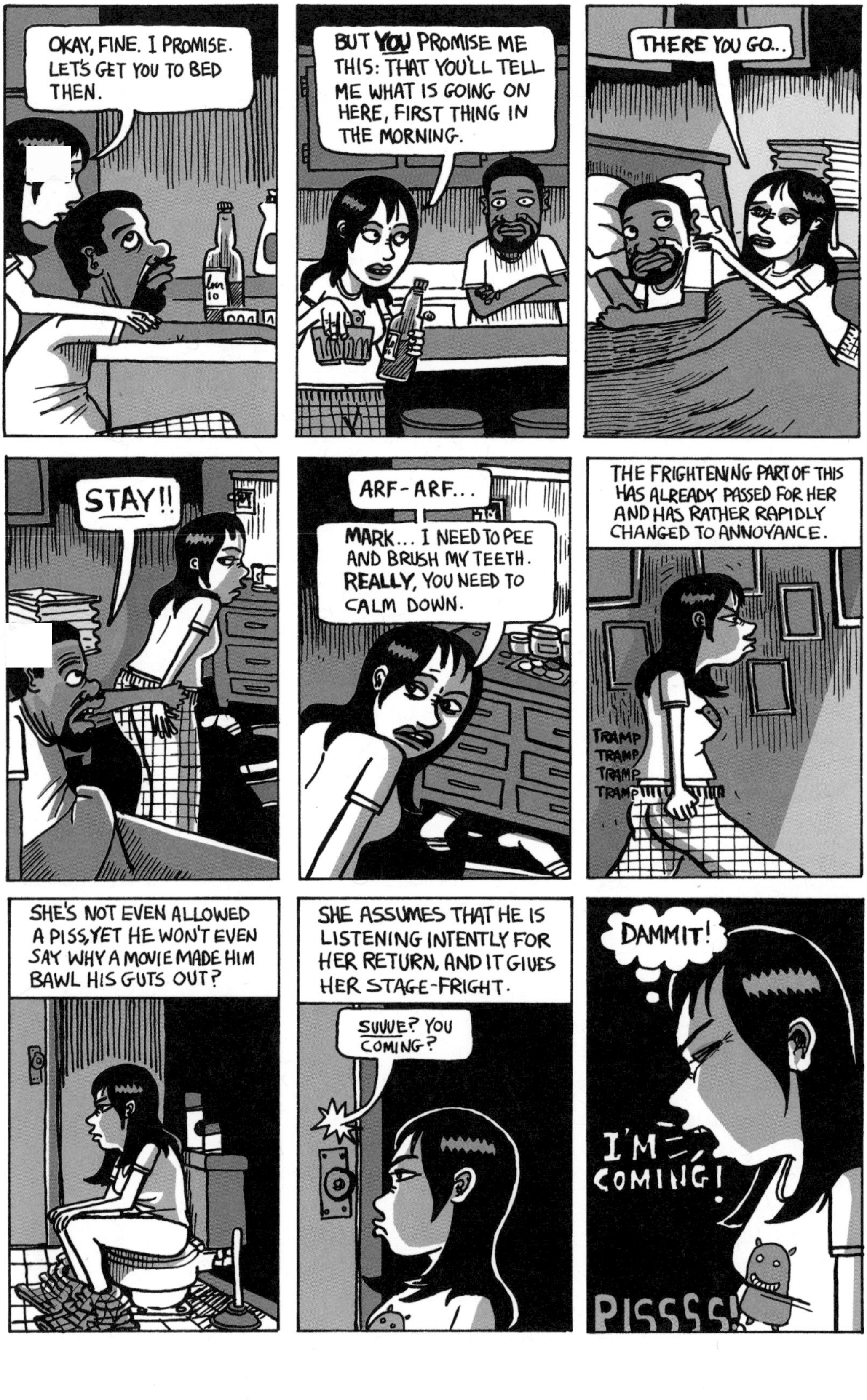

OKAY, FINE. I PROMISE. LET'S GET YOU TO BED THEN.
BUT YOU PROMISE ME THIS: THAT YOU'LL TELL ME WHAT IS GOING ON HERE, FIRST THING IN THE MORNING.
THERE YOU GO..
STAY!!
ARF-ARF...
MARK... I NEED TO PEE AND BRUSH MY TEETH. REALLY, YOU NEED TO CALM DOWN.
THE FRIGHTENING PART OF THIS HAS ALREADY PASSED FOR HER AND HAS RATHER RAPIDLY CHANGED TO ANNOYANCE.
TRAMP TRAMP TRAMP TRAMP
SHE'S NOT EVEN ALLOWED A PISS, YET HE WON'T EVEN SAY WHY A MOVIE MADE HIM BAWL HIS GUTS OUT?
SHE ASSUMES THAT HE IS LISTENING INTENTLY FOR HER RETURN, AND IT GIVES HER STAGE-FRIGHT.
SUUUE? YOU COMING?
DAMMIT!
I'M COMING!
PISSSS!

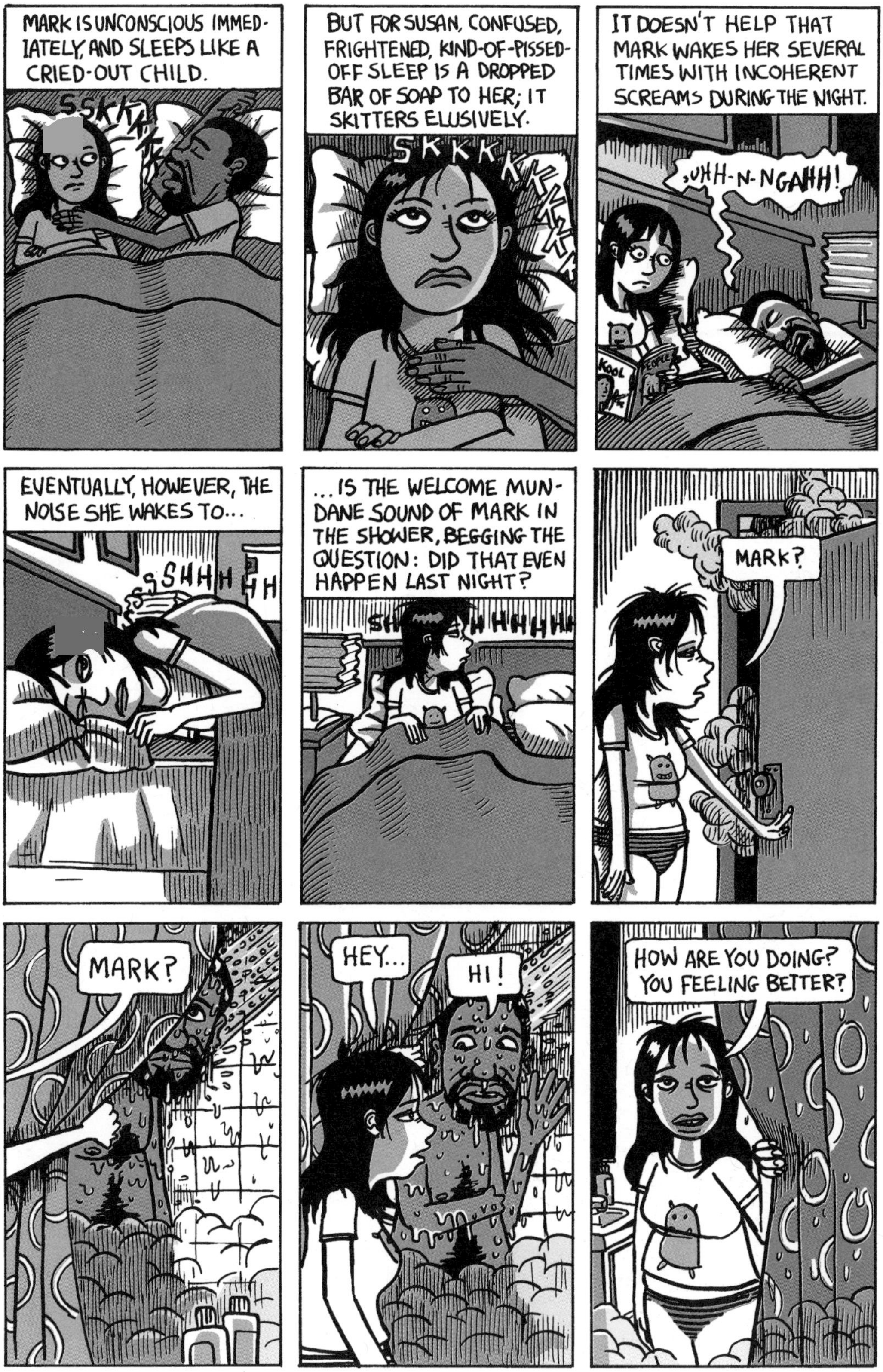
MARK IS UNCONSCIOUS IMMEDIATELY, AND SLEEPS LIKE A CRIED-OUT CHILD.
SSKKKKK
BUT FOR SUSAN, CONFUSED, FRIGHTENED, KIND-OF-PISSED-OFF SLEEP IS A DROPPED BAR OF SOAP TO HER; IT SKITTERS ELUSIVELY.
SKKKKKKKKK
IT DOESN'T HELP THAT MARK WAKES HER SEVERAL TIMES WITH INCOHERENT SCREAMS DURING THE NIGHT.
UHH-N-NGAHH!
KOOL
PEOPLE
EVENTUALLY, HOWEVER, THE NOISE SHE WAKES TO...
SSHHHHHH
...IS THE WELCOME MUNDANE SOUND OF MARK IN THE SHOWER, BEGGING THE QUESTION: DID THAT EVEN HAPPEN LAST NIGHT?
SHHHHHHH
MARK?
MARK?
HEY...
HI!
HOW ARE YOU DOING? YOU FEELING BETTER?

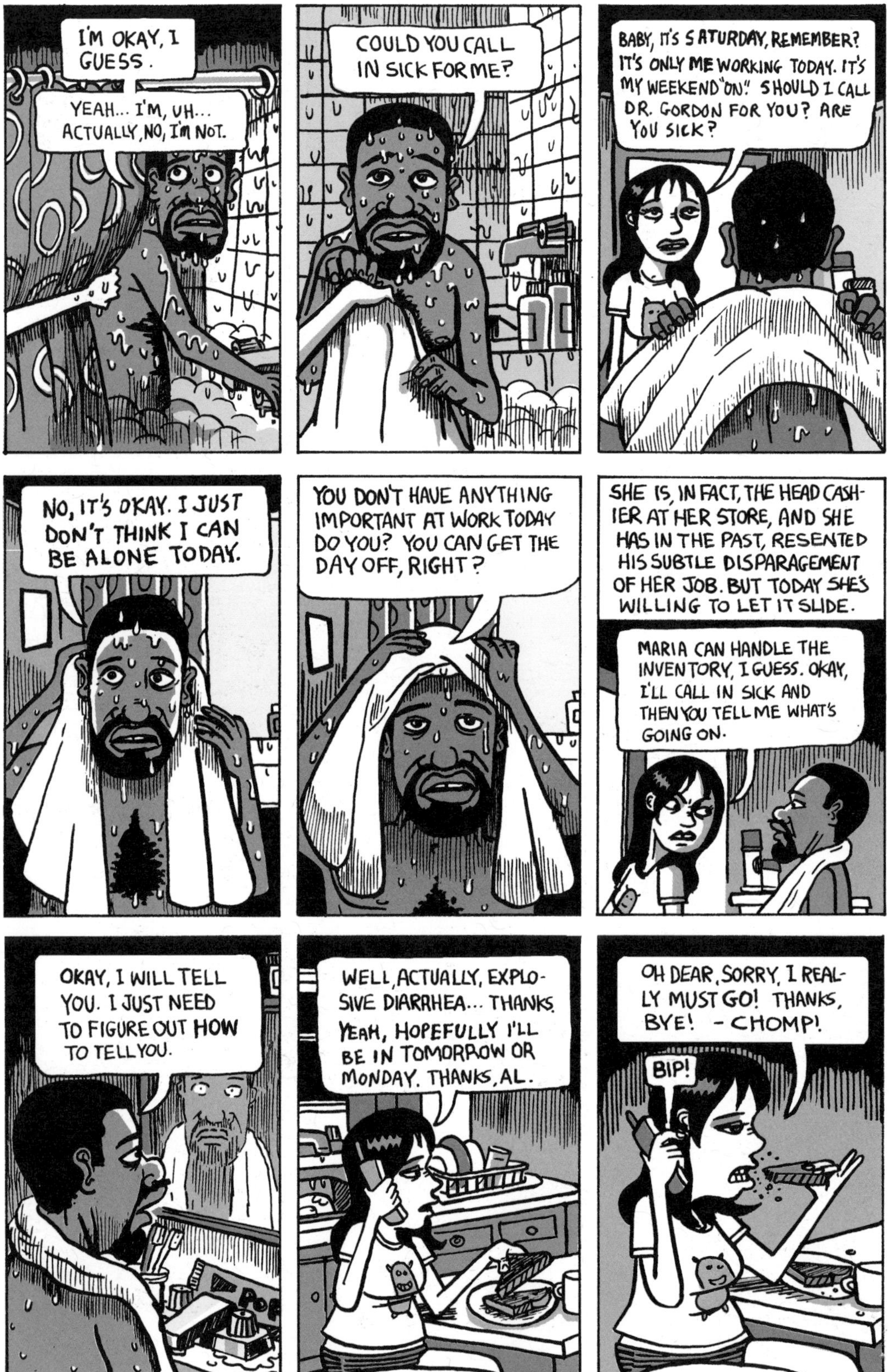
I'M OKAY, I GUESS.
YEAH... I'M, UH... ACTUALLY, NO, I'M NOT.
COULD YOU CALL IN SICK FOR ME?
BABY, IT'S SATURDAY, REMEMBER? IT'S ONLY ME WORKING TODAY. IT'S MY WEEKEND "ON." SHOULD I CALL DR. GORDON FOR YOU? ARE YOU SICK?
NO, IT'S OKAY. I JUST DON'T THINK I CAN BE ALONE TODAY.
YOU DON'T HAVE ANYTHING IMPORTANT AT WORK TODAY DO YOU? YOU CAN GET THE DAY OFF, RIGHT?
SHE IS, IN FACT, THE HEAD CASHIER AT HER STORE, AND SHE HAS IN THE PAST, RESENTED HIS SUBTLE DISPARAGEMENT OF HER JOB. BUT TODAY SHE'S WILLING TO LET IT SLIDE.
MARIA CAN HANDLE THE INVENTORY, I GUESS. OKAY, I'LL CALL IN SICK AND THEN YOU TELL ME WHAT'S GOING ON.
OKAY, I WILL TELL YOU. I JUST NEED TO FIGURE OUT HOW TO TELL YOU.
WELL, ACTUALLY, EXPLOSIVE DIARRHEA... THANKS. YEAH, HOPEFULLY I'LL BE IN TOMORROW OR MONDAY. THANKS, AL.
OH DEAR, SORRY, I REALLY MUST GO! THANKS, BYE! - CHOMP!
BIP!

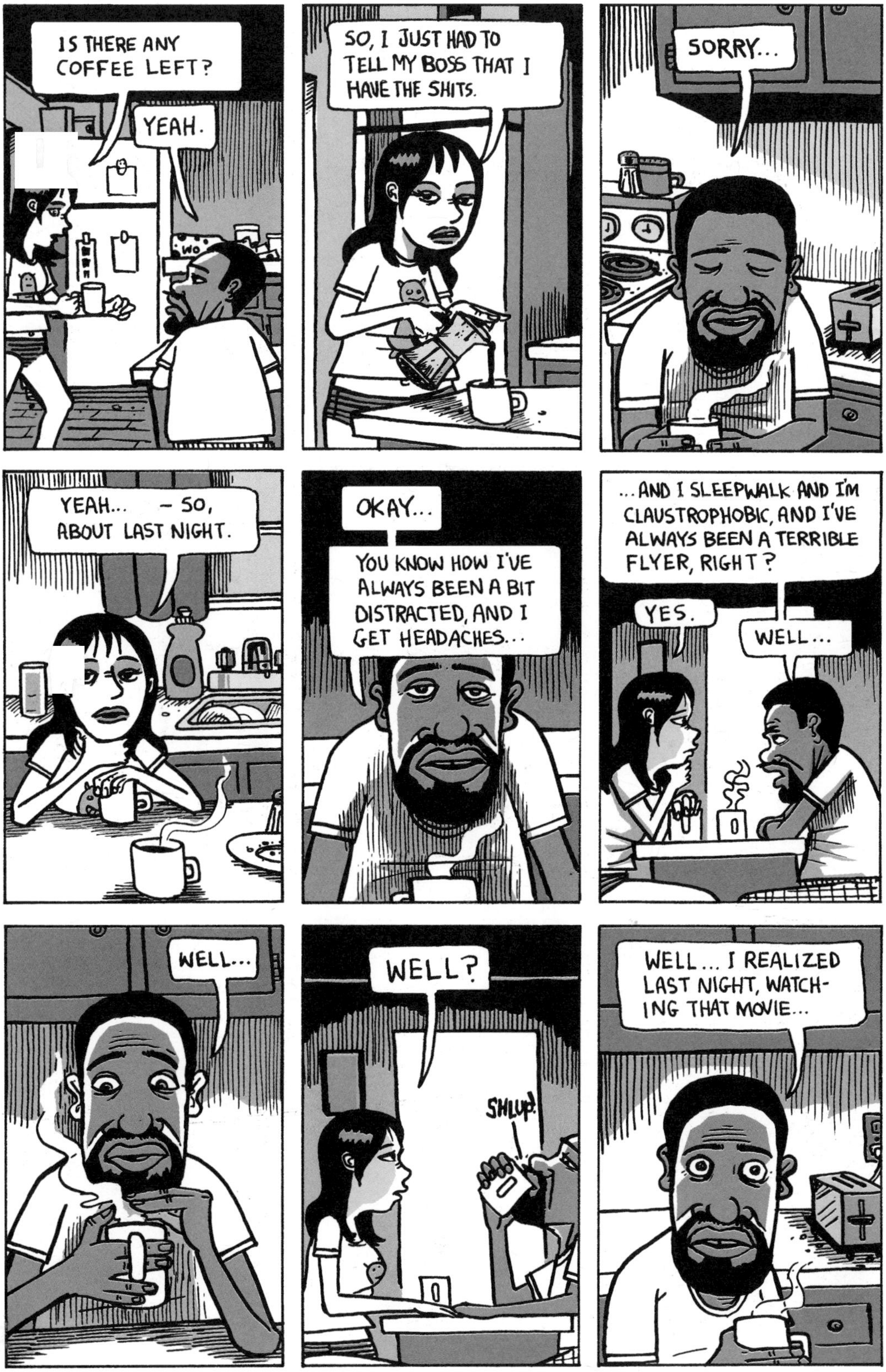
IS THERE ANY COFFEE LEFT?
YEAH.
SO, I JUST HAD TO TELL MY BOSS THAT I HAVE THE SHITS.
SORRY...
YEAH... - SO, ABOUT LAST NIGHT.
OKAY...
YOU KNOW HOW I'VE ALWAYS BEEN A BIT DISTRACTED, AND I GET HEADACHES...
...AND I SLEEPWALK AND I'M CLAUSTROPHOBIC, AND I'VE ALWAYS BEEN A TERRIBLE FLYER, RIGHT?
YES.
WELL...
WELL...
WELL?
SHLUP!
WELL... I REALIZED LAST NIGHT, WATCH-ING THAT MOVIE...

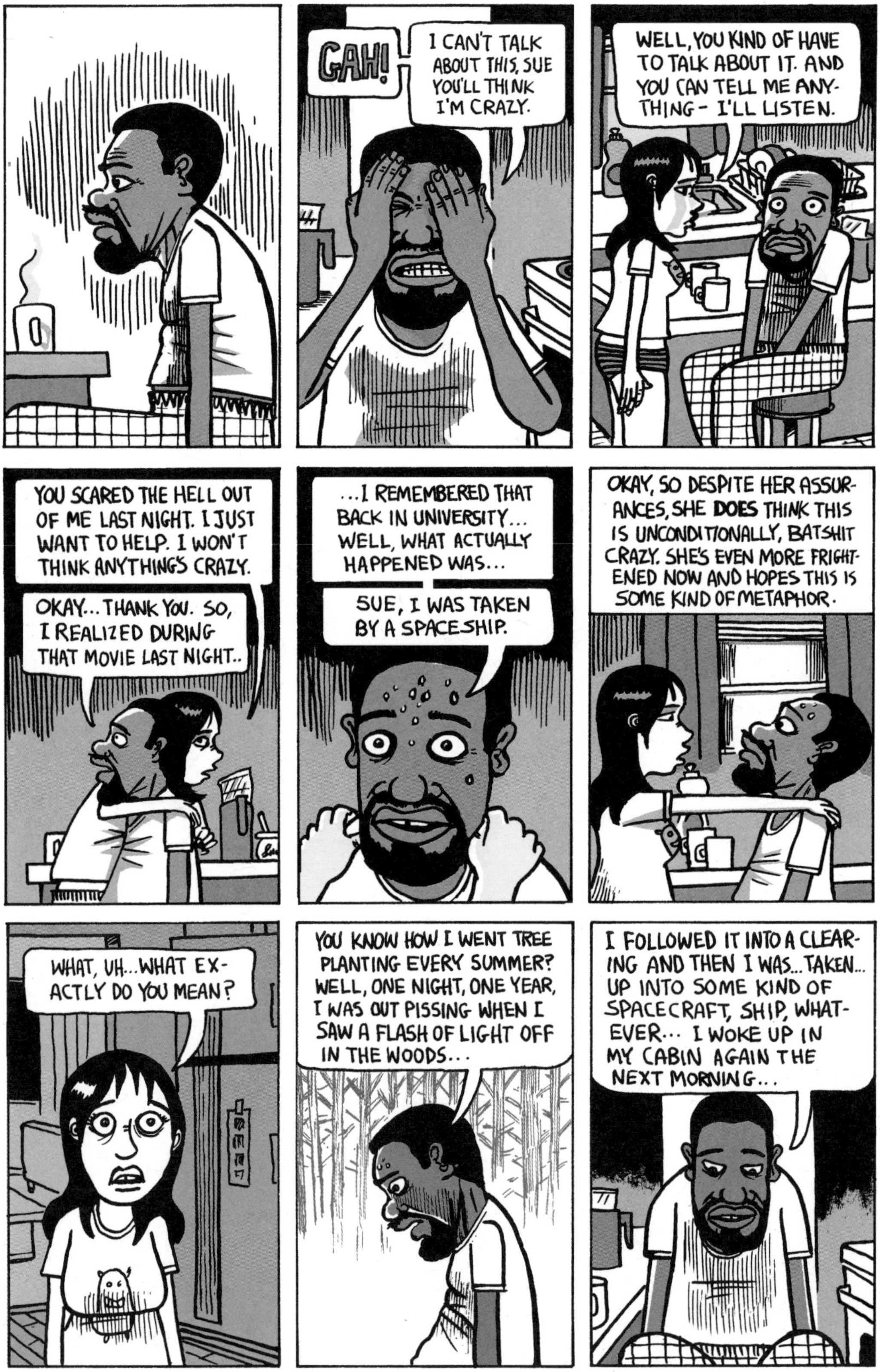
GAH!
I CAN'T TALK ABOUT THIS, SUE YOU'LL THINK I'M CRAZY.
WELL, YOU KIND OF HAVE TO TALK ABOUT IT. AND YOU CAN TELL ME ANYTHING - I'LL LISTEN.
YOU SCARED THE HELL OUT OF ME LAST NIGHT. I JUST WANT TO HELP. I WON'T THINK ANYTHING'S CRAZY.
OKAY... THANK YOU. SO, I REALIZED DURING THAT MOVIE LAST NIGHT..
...I REMEMBERED THAT BACK IN UNIVERSITY... WELL, WHAT ACTUALLY HAPPENED WAS...
SUE, I WAS TAKEN BY A SPACESHIP.
OKAY, SO DESPITE HER ASSURANCES, SHE DOES THINK THIS IS UNCONDITIONALLY, BATSHIT CRAZY. SHE'S EVEN MORE FRIGHTENED NOW AND HOPES THIS IS SOME KIND OF METAPHOR.
WHAT, UH... WHAT EXACTLY DO YOU MEAN?
YOU KNOW HOW I WENT TREE PLANTING EVERY SUMMER? WELL, ONE NIGHT, ONE YEAR, I WAS OUT PISSING WHEN I SAW A FLASH OF LIGHT OFF IN THE WOODS...
I FOLLOWED IT INTO A CLEARING AND THEN I WAS... TAKEN... UP INTO SOME KIND OF SPACECRAFT, SHIP, WHATEVER... I WOKE UP IN MY CABIN AGAIN THE NEXT MORNING...

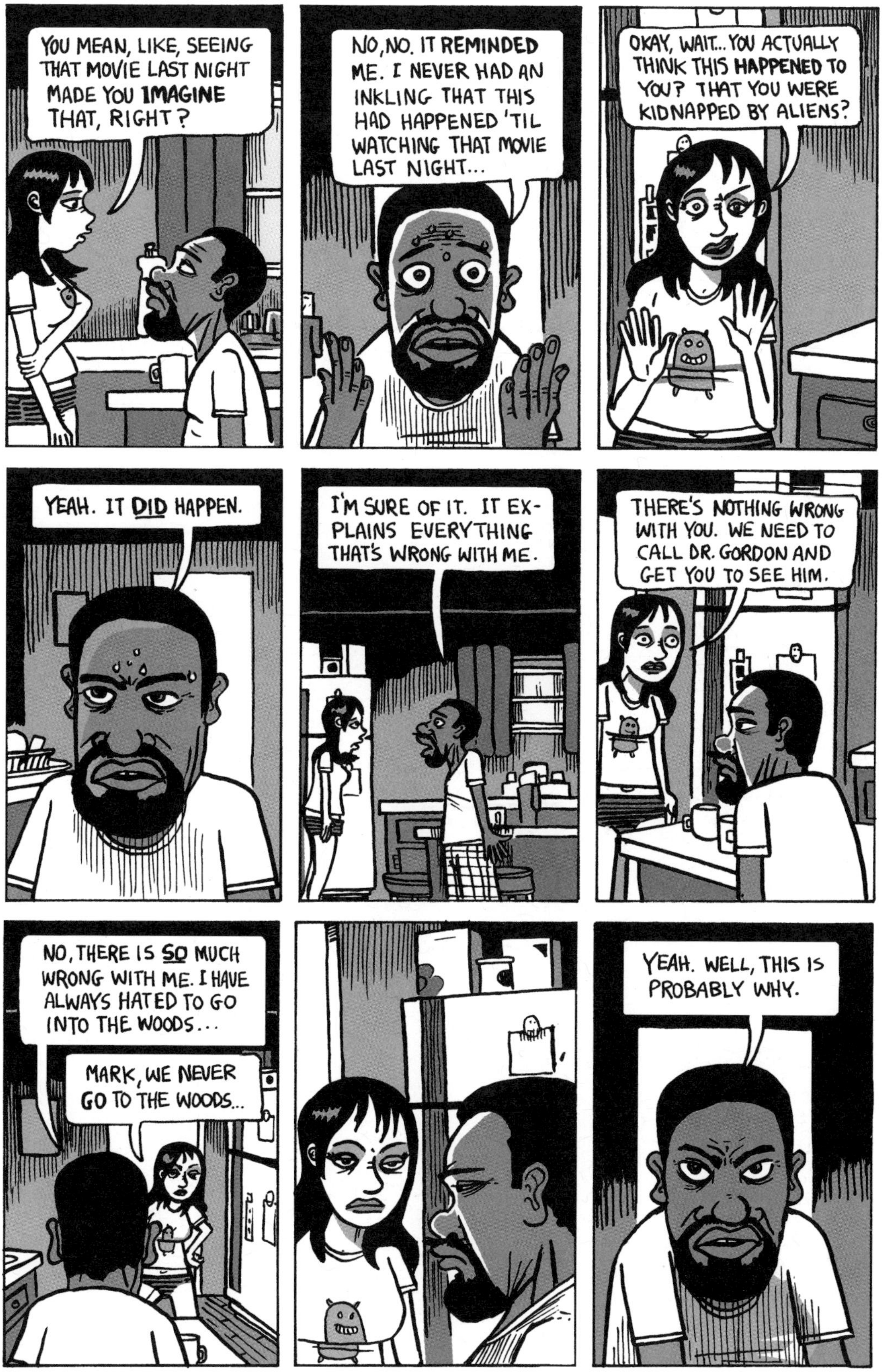
YOU MEAN, LIKE, SEEING THAT MOVIE LAST NIGHT MADE YOU **IMAGINE** THAT, RIGHT?
NO, NO. IT **REMINDED** ME. I NEVER HAD AN INKLING THAT THIS HAD HAPPENED 'TIL WATCHING THAT MOVIE LAST NIGHT...
OKAY, WAIT... YOU ACTUALLY THINK THIS **HAPPENED** TO YOU? THAT YOU WERE KIDNAPPED BY ALIENS?
YEAH. IT DID HAPPEN.
I'M SURE OF IT. IT EXPLAINS EVERYTHING THAT'S WRONG WITH ME.
THERE'S NOTHING WRONG WITH YOU. WE NEED TO CALL DR. GORDON AND GET YOU TO SEE HIM.
NO, THERE IS SO MUCH WRONG WITH ME. I HAVE ALWAYS HATED TO GO INTO THE WOODS...
MARK, WE NEVER GO TO THE WOODS...
YEAH. WELL, THIS IS PROBABLY WHY.

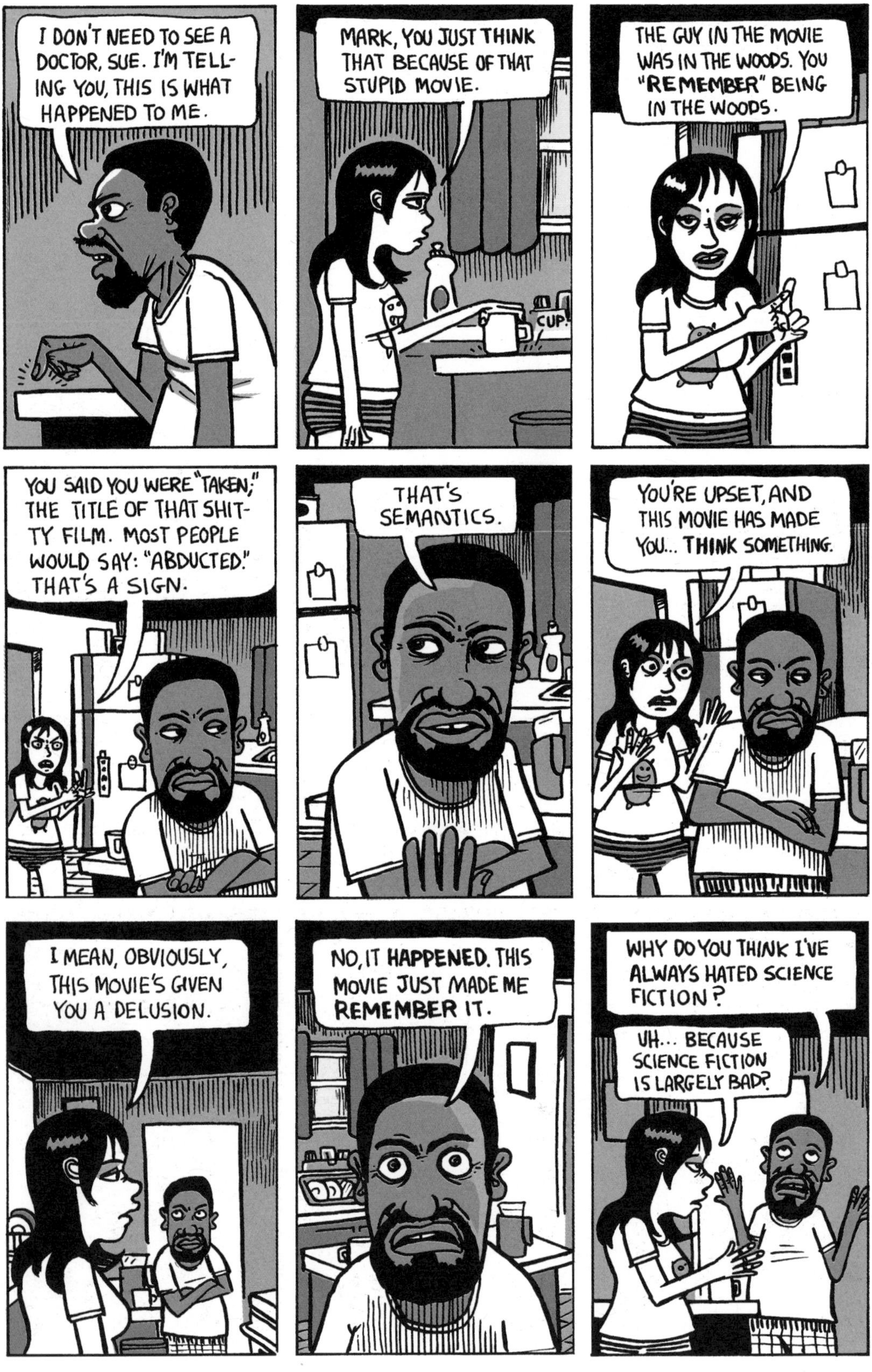
I DON'T NEED TO SEE A DOCTOR, SUE. I'M TELLING YOU, THIS IS WHAT HAPPENED TO ME.
MARK, YOU JUST THINK THAT BECAUSE OF THAT STUPID MOVIE.
CUP!
THE GUY IN THE MOVIE WAS IN THE WOODS. YOU "REMEMBER" BEING IN THE WOODS.
YOU SAID YOU WERE "TAKEN;" THE TITLE OF THAT SHITTY FILM. MOST PEOPLE WOULD SAY: "ABDUCTED." THAT'S A SIGN.
THAT'S SEMANTICS.
YOU'RE UPSET, AND THIS MOVIE HAS MADE YOU... THINK SOMETHING.
I MEAN, OBVIOUSLY, THIS MOVIE'S GIVEN YOU A DELUSION.
NO, IT HAPPENED. THIS MOVIE JUST MADE ME REMEMBER IT.
WHY DO YOU THINK I'VE ALWAYS HATED SCIENCE FICTION?
UH... BECAUSE SCIENCE FICTION IS LARGELY BAD?

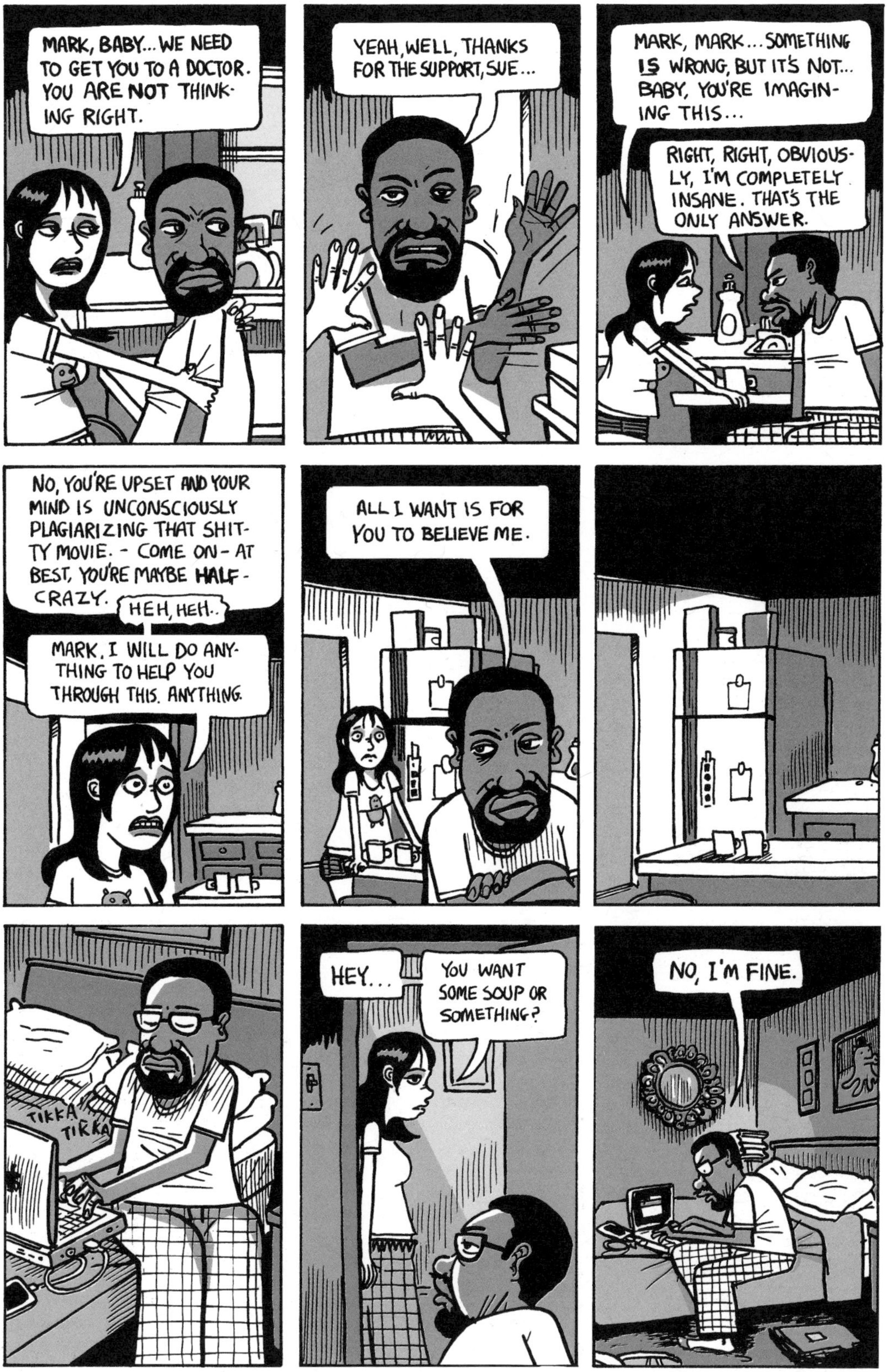
MARK, BABY... WE NEED TO GET YOU TO A DOCTOR. YOU ARE NOT THINKING RIGHT.
YEAH, WELL, THANKS FOR THE SUPPORT, SUE...
MARK, MARK... SOMETHING IS WRONG, BUT IT'S NOT... BABY, YOU'RE IMAGINING THIS...
RIGHT, RIGHT, OBVIOUSLY, I'M COMPLETELY INSANE. THAT'S THE ONLY ANSWER.
NO, YOU'RE UPSET AND YOUR MIND IS UNCONSCIOUSLY PLAGIARIZING THAT SHITTY MOVIE. - COME ON - AT BEST, YOU'RE MAYBE HALF-CRAZY.
HEH, HEH..
MARK, I WILL DO ANYTHING TO HELP YOU THROUGH THIS. ANYTHING.
ALL I WANT IS FOR YOU TO BELIEVE ME.
TIKKA TIKKA
HEY...
YOU WANT SOME SOUP OR SOMETHING?
NO, I'M FINE.

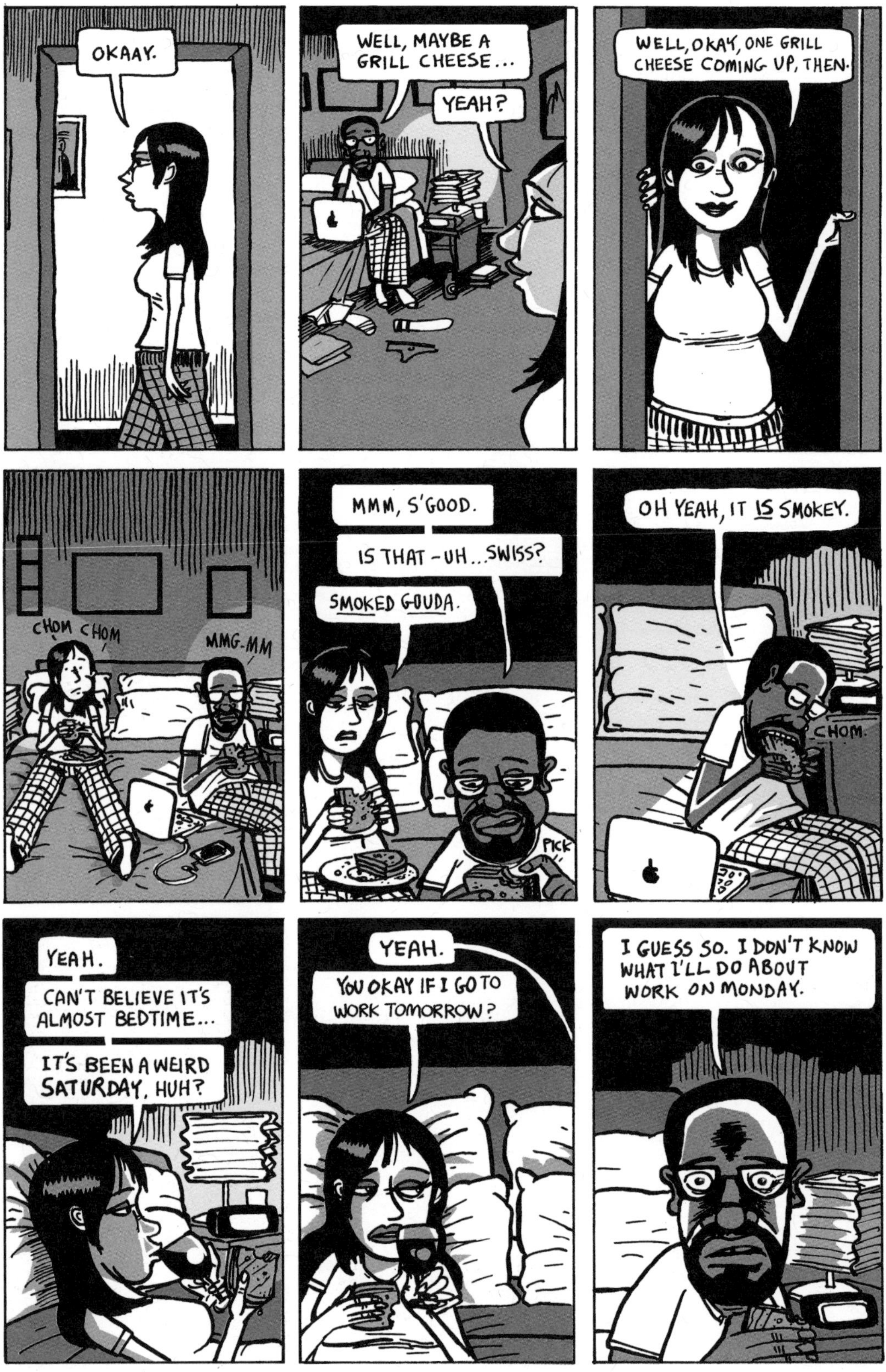
OKAAY.
WELL, MAYBE A GRILL CHEESE...
YEAH?
WELL, OKAY, ONE GRILL CHEESE COMING UP, THEN.
CHOM CHOM
MMG-MM
MMM, S'GOOD.
IS THAT - UH... SWISS?
SMOKED GOUDA.
PICK
OH YEAH, IT IS SMOKEY.
CHOM.
YEAH.
CAN'T BELIEVE IT'S ALMOST BEDTIME...
IT'S BEEN A WEIRD SATURDAY, HUH?
YEAH.
YOU OKAY IF I GO TO WORK TOMORROW?
I GUESS SO. I DON'T KNOW WHAT I'LL DO ABOUT WORK ON MONDAY.

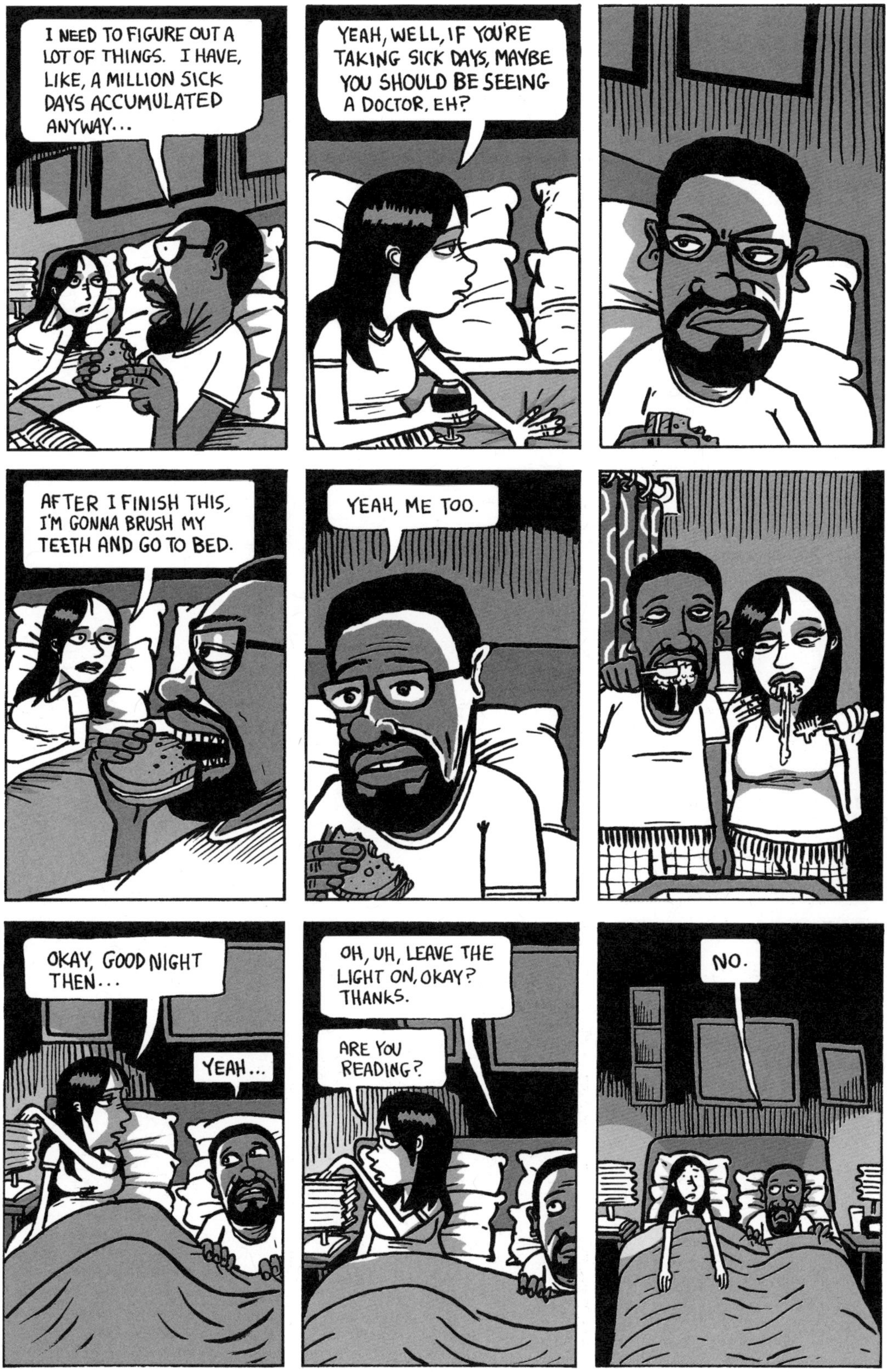
I NEED TO FIGURE OUT A LOT OF THINGS. I HAVE, LIKE, A MILLION SICK DAYS ACCUMULATED ANYWAY...
YEAH, WELL, IF YOU'RE TAKING SICK DAYS, MAYBE YOU SHOULD BE SEEING A DOCTOR, EH?
AFTER I FINISH THIS, I'M GONNA BRUSH MY TEETH AND GO TO BED.
YEAH, ME TOO.
OKAY, GOOD NIGHT THEN...
YEAH...
OH, UH, LEAVE THE LIGHT ON, OKAY? THANKS.
ARE YOU READING?
NO.

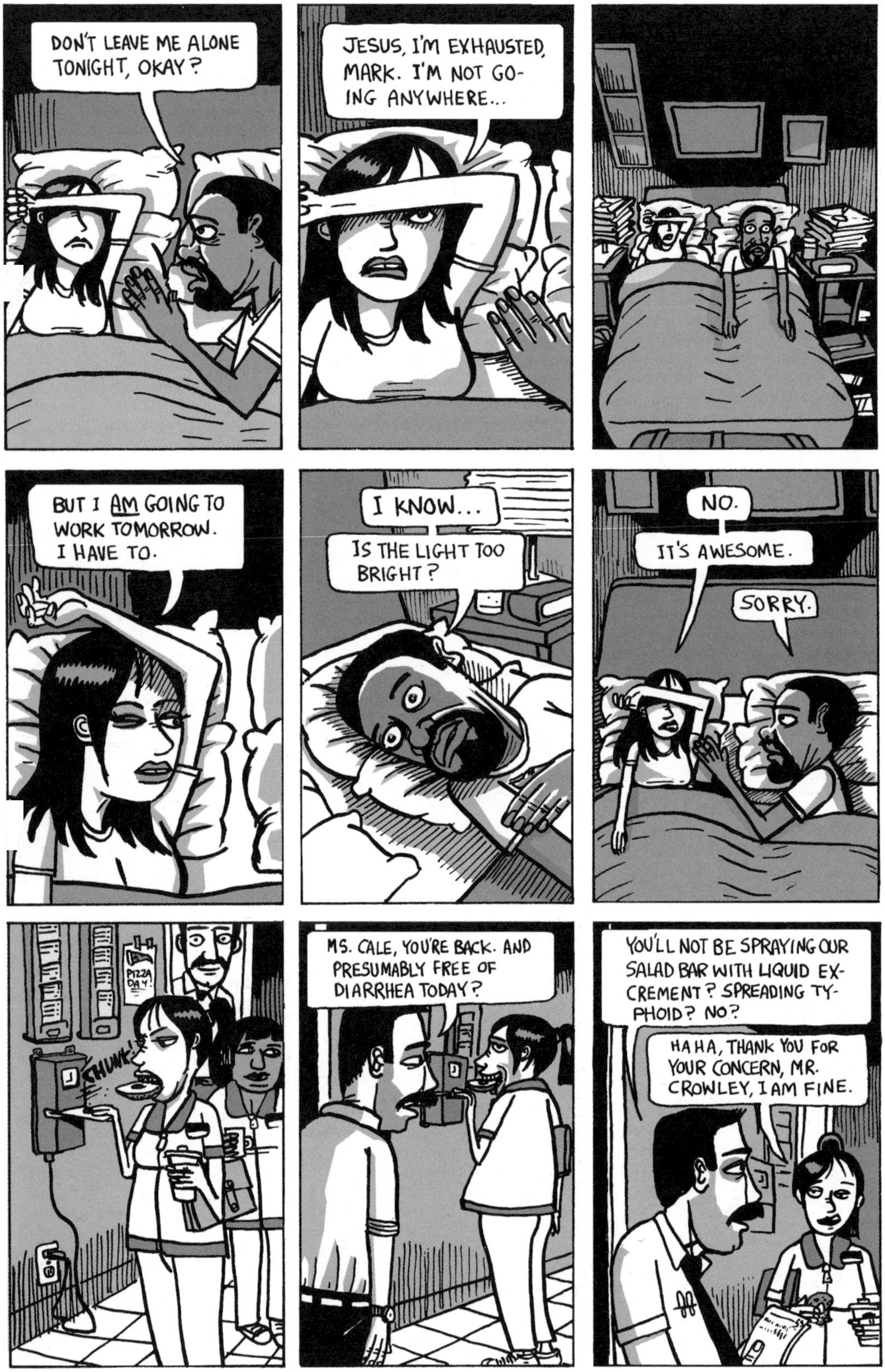
DON'T LEAVE ME ALONE TONIGHT, OKAY?
JESUS, I'M EXHAUSTED, MARK. I'M NOT GO-ING ANYWHERE...
BUT I AM GOING TO WORK TOMORROW. I HAVE TO.
I KNOW...
IS THE LIGHT TOO BRIGHT?
NO.
IT'S AWESOME.
SORRY.
PIZZA DAY!
THUNK!
MS. CALE, YOU'RE BACK. AND PRESUMABLY FREE OF DIARRHEA TODAY?
YOU'LL NOT BE SPRAYING OUR SALAD BAR WITH LIQUID EX-CREMENT? SPREADING TY-PHOID? NO?
HA HA, THANK YOU FOR YOUR CONCERN, MR. CROWLEY, I AM FINE.

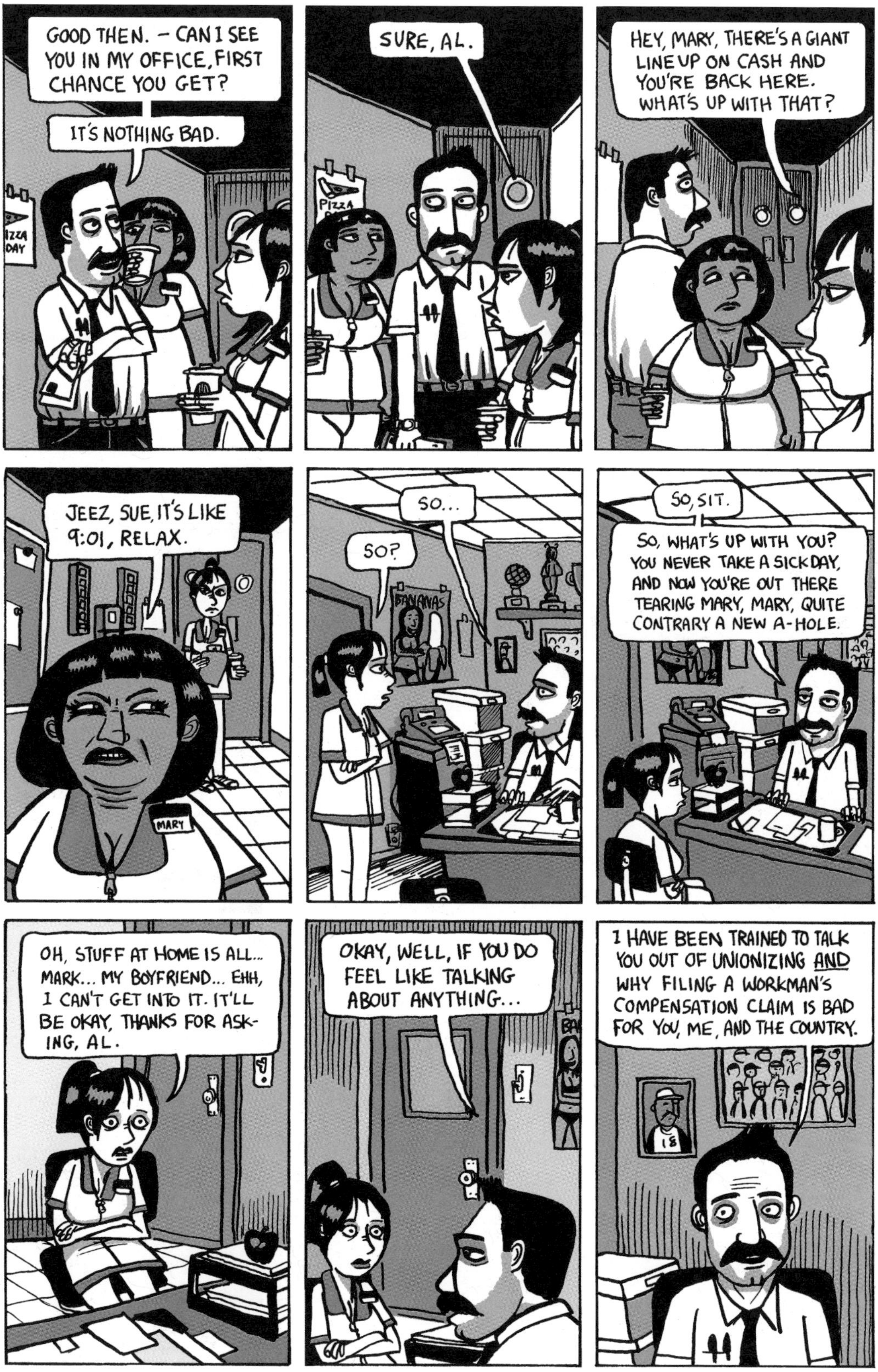
GOOD THEN. – CAN I SEE YOU IN MY OFFICE, FIRST CHANCE YOU GET?
IT'S NOTHING BAD.
PIZZA DAY
SURE, AL.
PIZZA
HEY, MARY, THERE'S A GIANT LINE UP ON CASH AND YOU'RE BACK HERE. WHAT'S UP WITH THAT?
JEEZ, SUE, IT'S LIKE 9:01, RELAX.
MARY
SO...
SO?
BANANAS
SO, SIT.
SO, WHAT'S UP WITH YOU? YOU NEVER TAKE A SICK DAY, AND NOW YOU'RE OUT THERE TEARING MARY, MARY, QUITE CONTRARY A NEW A-HOLE.
OH, STUFF AT HOME IS ALL... MARK... MY BOYFRIEND... EHH, I CAN'T GET INTO IT. IT'LL BE OKAY, THANKS FOR ASK-ING, AL.
OKAY, WELL, IF YOU DO FEEL LIKE TALKING ABOUT ANYTHING...
I HAVE BEEN TRAINED TO TALK YOU OUT OF UNIONIZING AND WHY FILING A WORKMAN'S COMPENSATION CLAIM IS BAD FOR YOU, ME, AND THE COUNTRY.
18

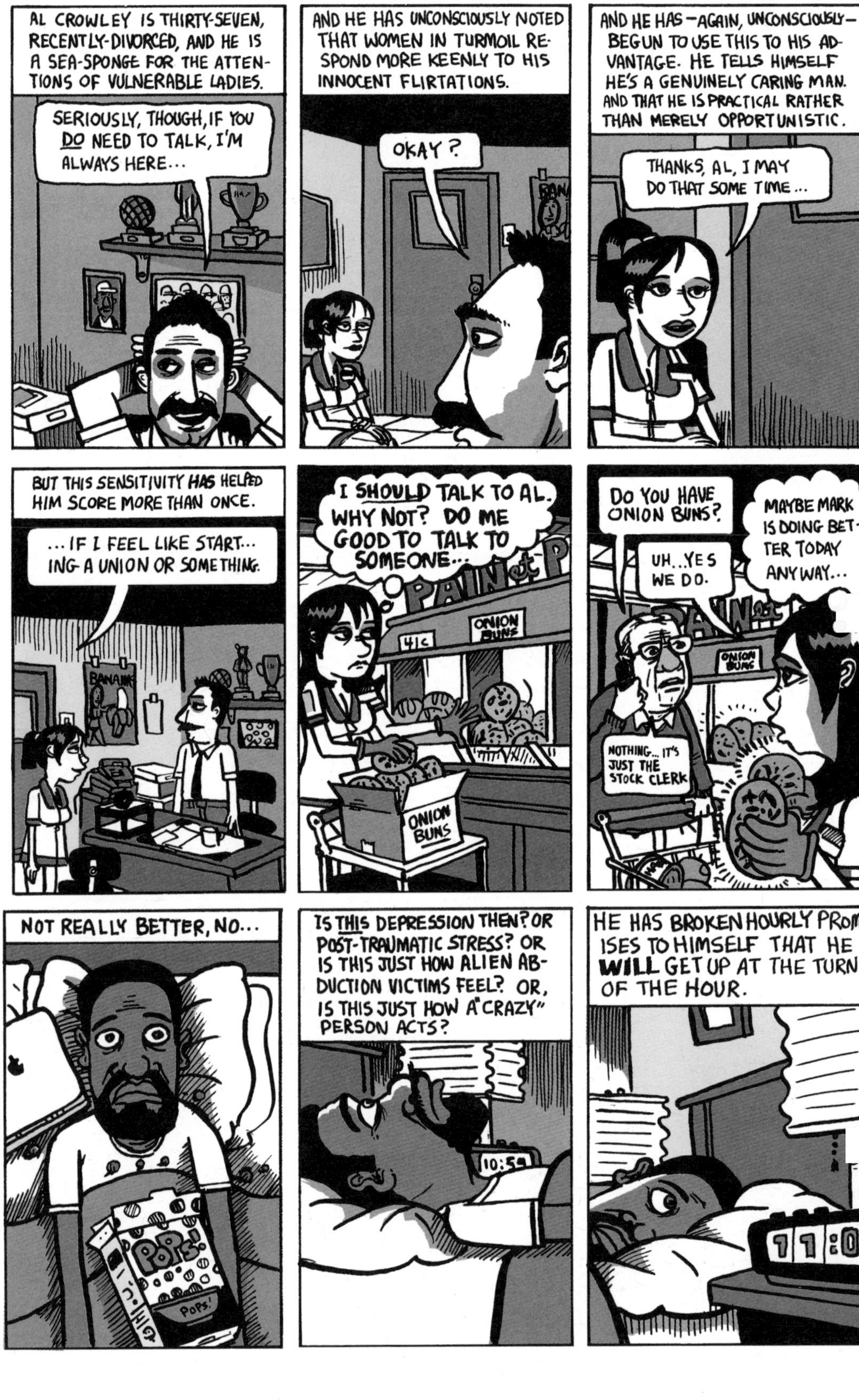
AL CROWLEY IS THIRTY-SEVEN, RECENTLY-DIVORCED, AND HE IS A SEA-SPONGE FOR THE ATTENTIONS OF VULNERABLE LADIES.
SERIOUSLY, THOUGH, IF YOU DO NEED TO TALK, I'M ALWAYS HERE...
AND HE HAS UNCONSCIOUSLY NOTED THAT WOMEN IN TURMOIL RESPOND MORE KEENLY TO HIS INNOCENT FLIRTATIONS.
OKAY?
AND HE HAS—AGAIN, UNCONSCIOUSLY—BEGUN TO USE THIS TO HIS ADVANTAGE. HE TELLS HIMSELF HE'S A GENUINELY CARING MAN. AND THAT HE IS PRACTICAL RATHER THAN MERELY OPPORTUNISTIC.
THANKS, AL, I MAY DO THAT SOME TIME...
BUT THIS SENSITIVITY HAS HELPED HIM SCORE MORE THAN ONCE.
...IF I FEEL LIKE STARTING A UNION OR SOMETHING.
I SHOULD TALK TO AL. WHY NOT? DO ME GOOD TO TALK TO SOMEONE...
ONION BUNS
ONION BUNS
DO YOU HAVE ONION BUNS?
UH...YES WE DO.
MAYBE MARK IS DOING BETTER TODAY ANYWAY...
ONION BUNS
NOTHING... IT'S JUST THE STOCK CLERK
NOT REALLY BETTER, NO...
POPS!
IS THIS DEPRESSION THEN? OR POST-TRAUMATIC STRESS? OR IS THIS JUST HOW ALIEN ABDUCTION VICTIMS FEEL? OR, IS THIS JUST HOW A "CRAZY" PERSON ACTS?
10:59
HE HAS BROKEN HOURLY PROMISES TO HIMSELF THAT HE WILL GET UP AT THE TURN OF THE HOUR.
11:0

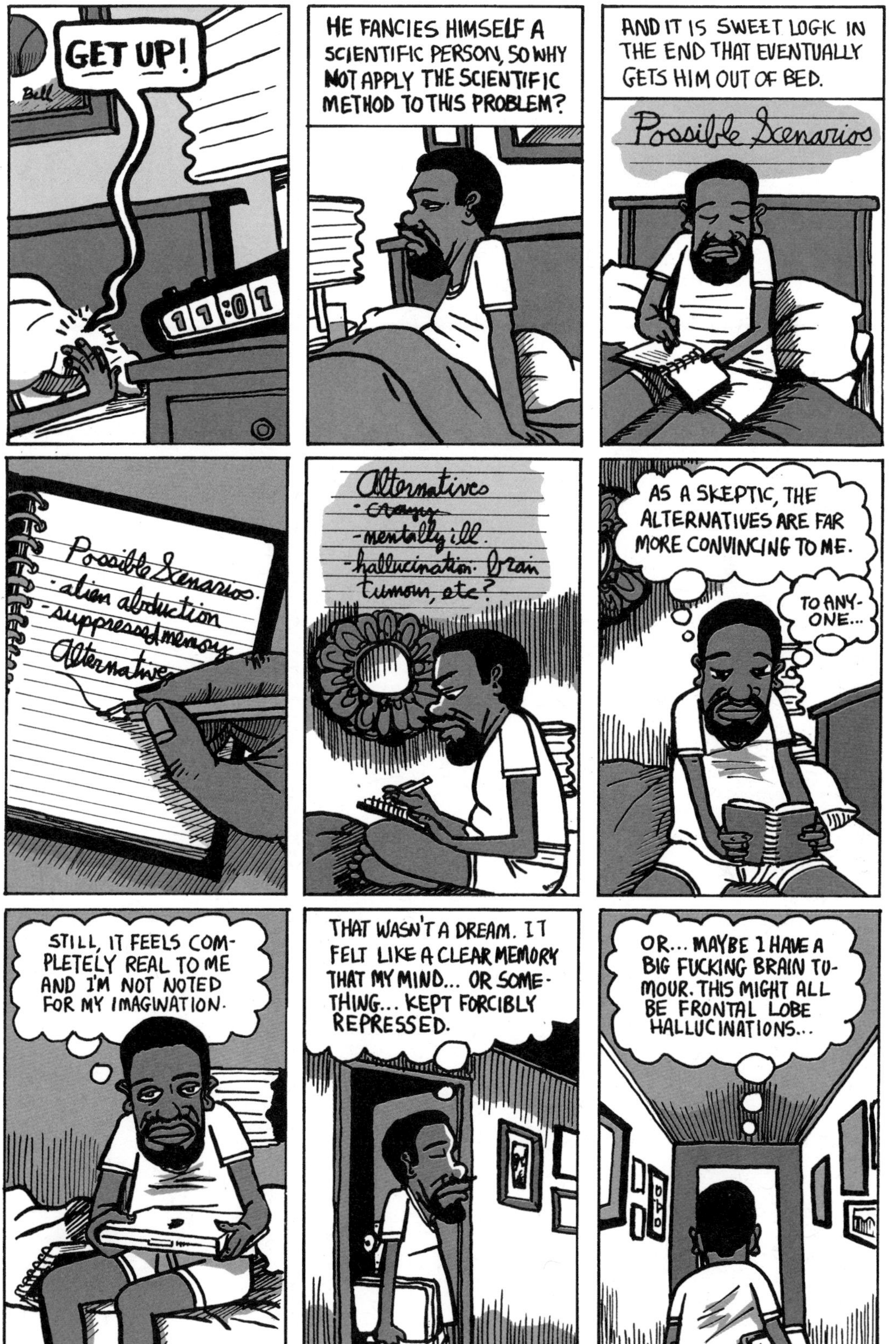
GET UP!
HE FANCIES HIMSELF A SCIENTIFIC PERSON, SO WHY NOT APPLY THE SCIENTIFIC METHOD TO THIS PROBLEM?
AND IT IS SWEET LOGIC IN THE END THAT EVENTUALLY GETS HIM OUT OF BED.
Possible Scenarios
Possible Scenarios.
-alien abduction
-suppressed memory
Alternatives
Alternatives
-crazy
-mentally ill.
-hallucination. brain tumour, etc?
AS A SKEPTIC, THE ALTERNATIVES ARE FAR MORE CONVINCING TO ME.
TO ANYONE...
STILL, IT FEELS COMPLETELY REAL TO ME AND I'M NOT NOTED FOR MY IMAGINATION.
THAT WASN'T A DREAM. IT FELT LIKE A CLEAR MEMORY THAT MY MIND... OR SOMETHING... KEPT FORCIBLY REPRESSED.
OR... MAYBE I HAVE A BIG FUCKING BRAIN TUMOUR. THIS MIGHT ALL BE FRONTAL LOBE HALLUCINATIONS...

YEAH... BUT WITH NO OTHER SYMPTOMS THOUGH... I MEAN, HEADACHES, YES. MIGRAINES, TECHNICALLY...

JUST BECAUSE I'M NOT PULLING OFF GRAND MAL SEIZURES DOESN'T PRECLUDE THE POSSIBILITY THAT A BIG OL' BRAIN TUMOUR...

...ISN'T PUSHING ON THE RIGHT LOBES TO MAKE ME BELIEVE I WAS TAKEN BY ALIENS WHILE I TOOK A PEE IN THE WOODS...

GOD, THAT SOUNDS SO FUCKING CRAZY.

BUT I'D **SWEAR** IT IS ABSOLUTELY TRUE.

THERE MUST BE CREDIBLE SCIENTIFIC RESEARCH INTO A PHENOMENA AS WIDESPREAD AS THIS SEEMS TO BE... DIDN'T CARL SAGAN OR THAT FRENCH GUY, JACQUES VALLÉE LOOK INTO THIS STUFF?

Googl

nd scientific research of UFO

Google Search   I'm Feelin Luck

TYPE   TYPE
   TYPE.

GOOD GOD...

THE INTERNET IS NO PLACE TO BE DOING RESEARCH, HE REMINDS HIMSELF. ANY ASSHOLE WITH A MODEM AND AN AGENDA IS AN EXPERT.

HE WOULD CASTIGATE HIS STUDENTS FOR THIS KIND OF GULLIBILITY.

PFFF.

THIS IS SHAKY, UNSCIENTIFIC GROUND. SHIT, THIS IS QUICKSAND, EVEN TO A BELIEVER.

THESE ARE SAD, CRAZY PEOPLE.

AND NOW, TECHNICALLY, I'M ONE OF THEM.

"ALIEN ABDUCTION, ALIEN AUTOPSIES, CATTLE MUTILATIONS, THE BERMUDA TRIANGLE..."

...THE SAD, PATHETIC CHECKLIST OF THE CONSPIRACY THEORIST.

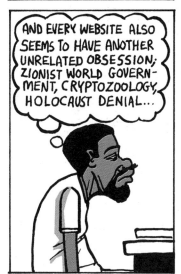

AND EVERY WEBSITE ALSO SEEMS TO HAVE ANOTHER UNRELATED OBSESSION; ZIONIST WORLD GOVERNMENT, CRYPTOZOOLOGY, HOLOCAUST DENIAL...

...OR AMWAY SALES.

JESUS, MARK, YOU'RE IN THE MIDST OF SOME ESTEEMED "COLLEAGUES" HERE.

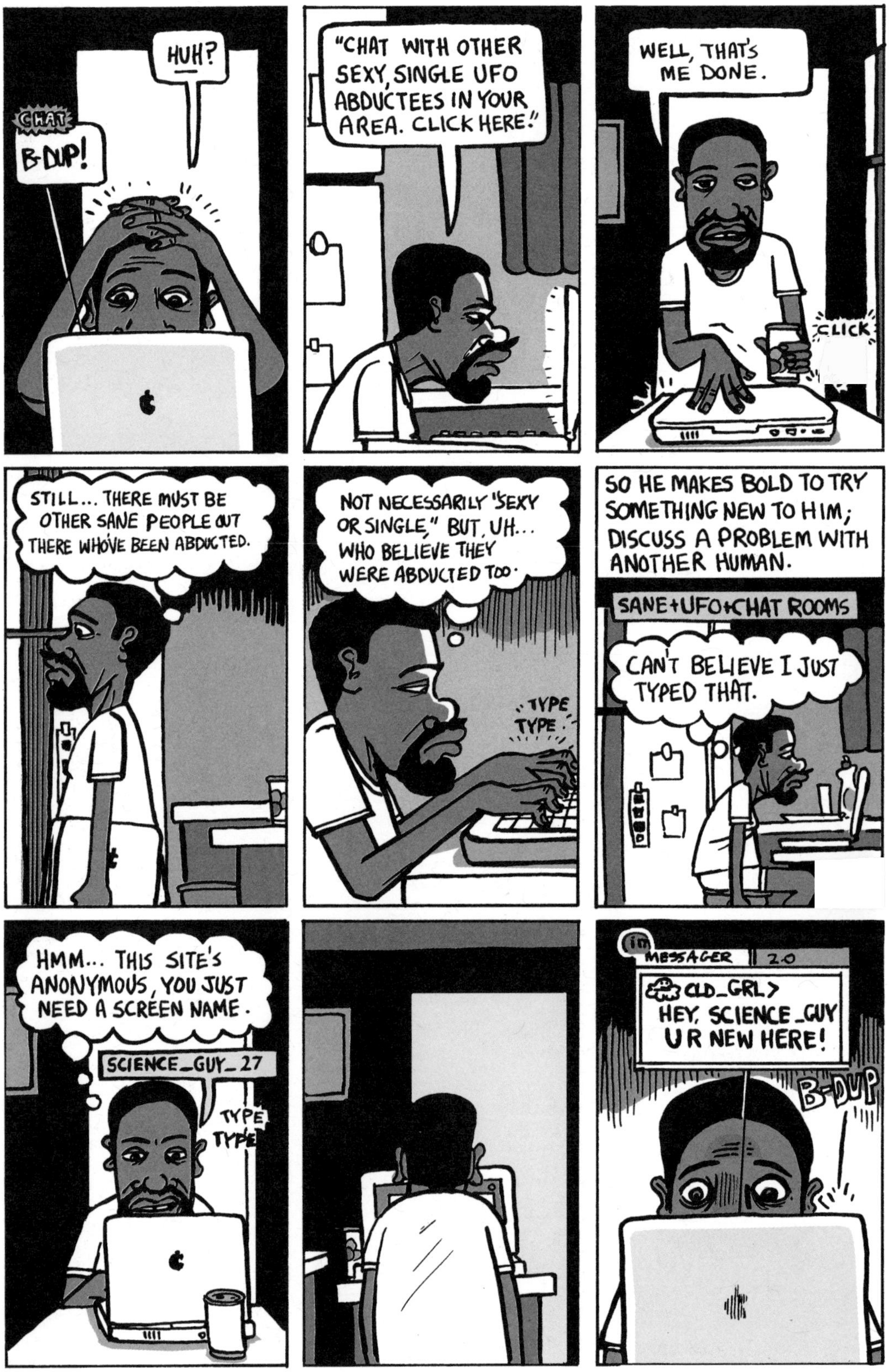
HUH?
CHAT
B-DUP!
"CHAT WITH OTHER SEXY, SINGLE UFO ABDUCTEES IN YOUR AREA. CLICK HERE."
WELL, THAT'S ME DONE.
CLICK
STILL... THERE MUST BE OTHER SANE PEOPLE OUT THERE WHO'VE BEEN ABDUCTED.
NOT NECESSARILY "SEXY OR SINGLE," BUT, UH... WHO BELIEVE THEY WERE ABDUCTED TOO.
TYPE TYPE
SO HE MAKES BOLD TO TRY SOMETHING NEW TO HIM; DISCUSS A PROBLEM WITH ANOTHER HUMAN.
SANE+UFO+CHAT ROOMS
CAN'T BELIEVE I JUST TYPED THAT.
HMM... THIS SITE'S ANONYMOUS, YOU JUST NEED A SCREEN NAME.
SCIENCE_GUY_27
TYPE TYPE
MESSAGER 2.0
CLD_GRL>
HEY, SCIENCE_GUY U R NEW HERE!
B-DUP

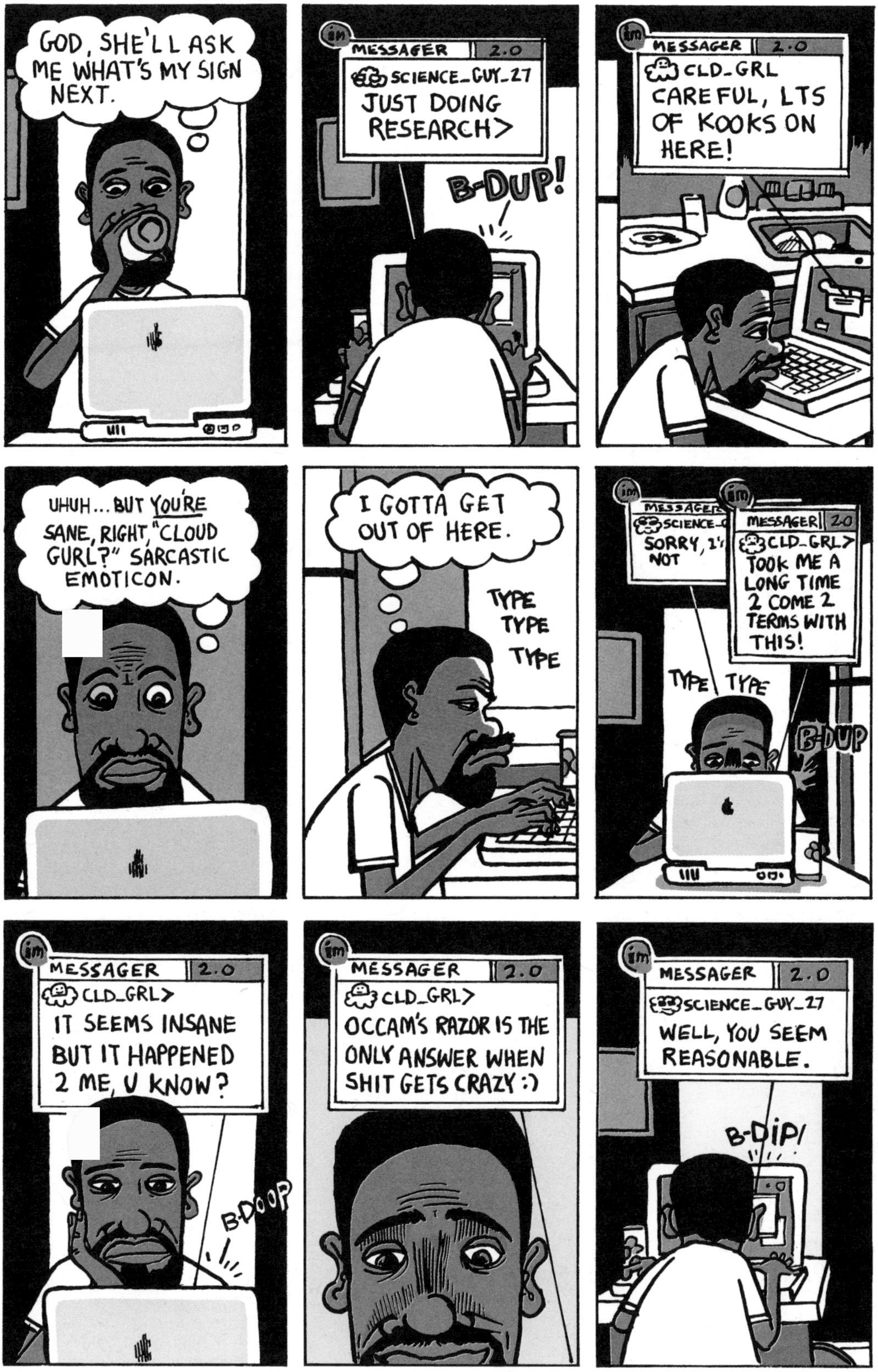
GOD, SHE'LL ASK ME WHAT'S MY SIGN NEXT.
MESSAGER 2.0
SCIENCE_GUY_27
JUST DOING RESEARCH>
B-DUP!
MESSAGER 2.0
CLD_GRL
CAREFUL, LTS OF KOOKS ON HERE!
UHUH... BUT YOU'RE SANE, RIGHT, "CLOUD GURL?" SARCASTIC EMOTICON.
I GOTTA GET OUT OF HERE.
TYPE TYPE TYPE
MESSAGER
SCIENCE_
SORRY, I'
NOT
MESSAGER 2.0
CLD_GRL>
TOOK ME A LONG TIME 2 COME 2 TERMS WITH THIS!
TYPE TYPE
B-DUP
MESSAGER 2.0
CLD_GRL>
IT SEEMS INSANE BUT IT HAPPENED 2 ME, U KNOW?
B-DOOP
MESSAGER 2.0
CLD_GRL>
OCCAM'S RAZOR IS THE ONLY ANSWER WHEN SHIT GETS CRAZY :)
MESSAGER 2.0
SCIENCE_GUY_27
WELL, YOU SEEM REASONABLE.
B-DIP!

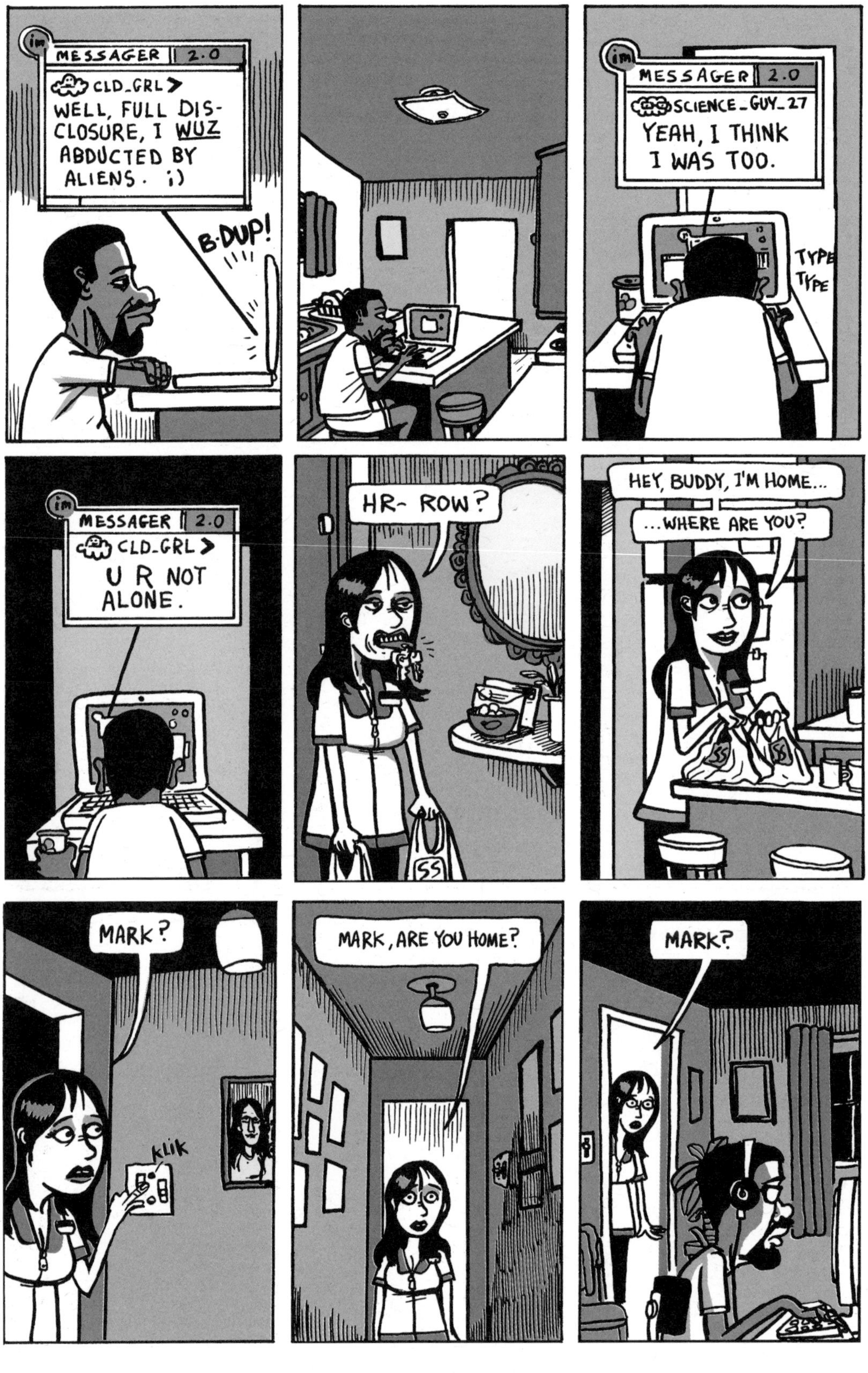
MESSAGER 2.0
CLD_GRL >
WELL, FULL DISCLOSURE, I WUZ ABDUCTED BY ALIENS. ;)
B-DUP!
MESSAGER 2.0
SCIENCE_GUY_27
YEAH, I THINK I WAS TOO.
TYPE TYPE
MESSAGER 2.0
CLD_GRL >
U R NOT ALONE.
HR- ROW?
HEY, BUDDY, I'M HOME...
...WHERE ARE YOU?
MARK?
KLIK
MARK, ARE YOU HOME?
MARK?

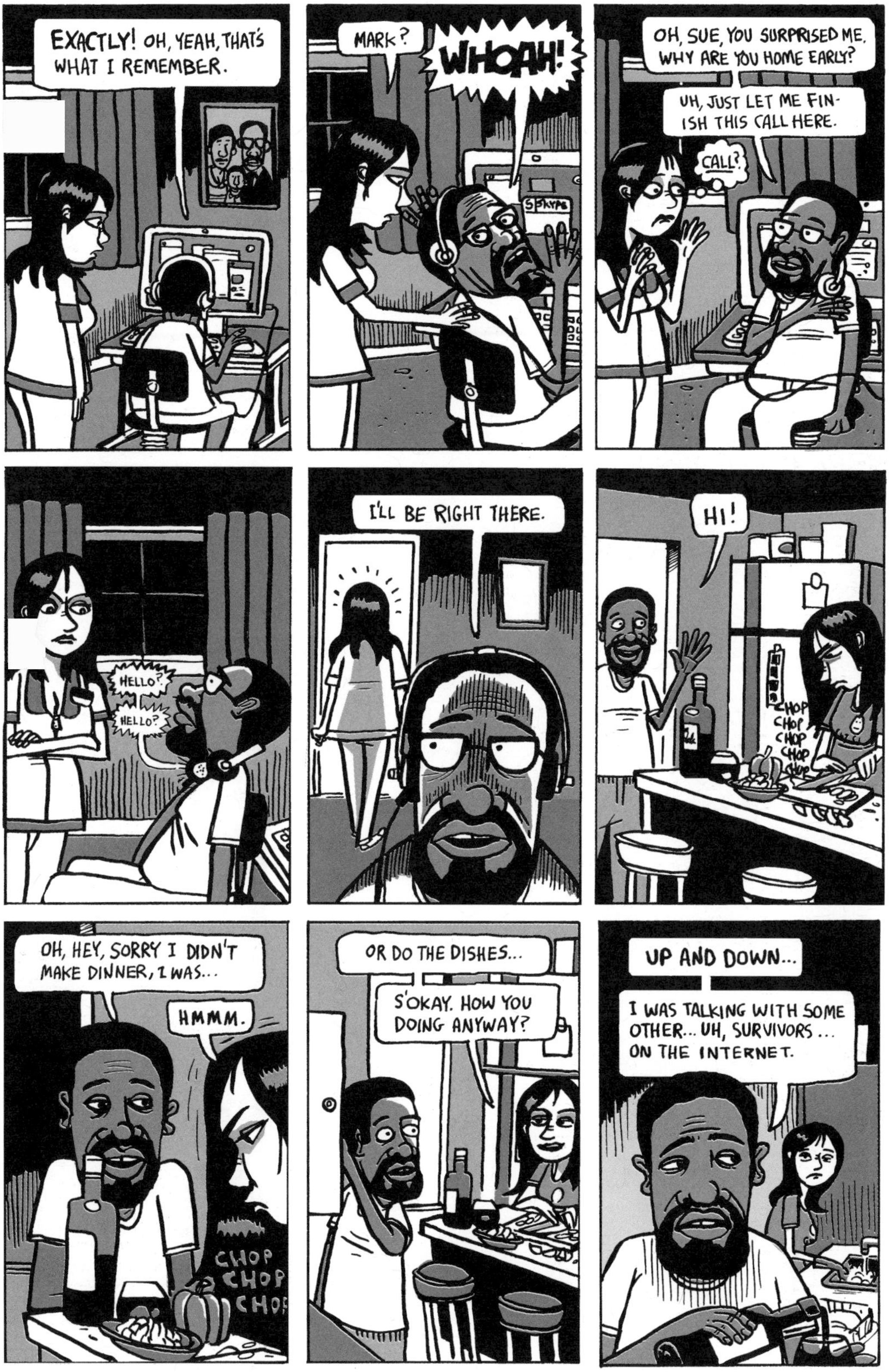
EXACTLY! OH, YEAH, THAT'S WHAT I REMEMBER.
MARK?
WHOAH!
SKYPE
OH, SUE, YOU SURPRISED ME. WHY ARE YOU HOME EARLY?
UH, JUST LET ME FIN-ISH THIS CALL HERE.
CALL?
HELLO?
HELLO?
I'LL BE RIGHT THERE.
HI!
CHOP CHOP CHOP CHOP CHOP
OH, HEY, SORRY I DIDN'T MAKE DINNER, I WAS...
HMMM.
CHOP CHOP CHOP
OR DO THE DISHES...
S'OKAY. HOW YOU DOING ANYWAY?
UP AND DOWN...
I WAS TALKING WITH SOME OTHER... UH, SURVIVORS... ON THE INTERNET.

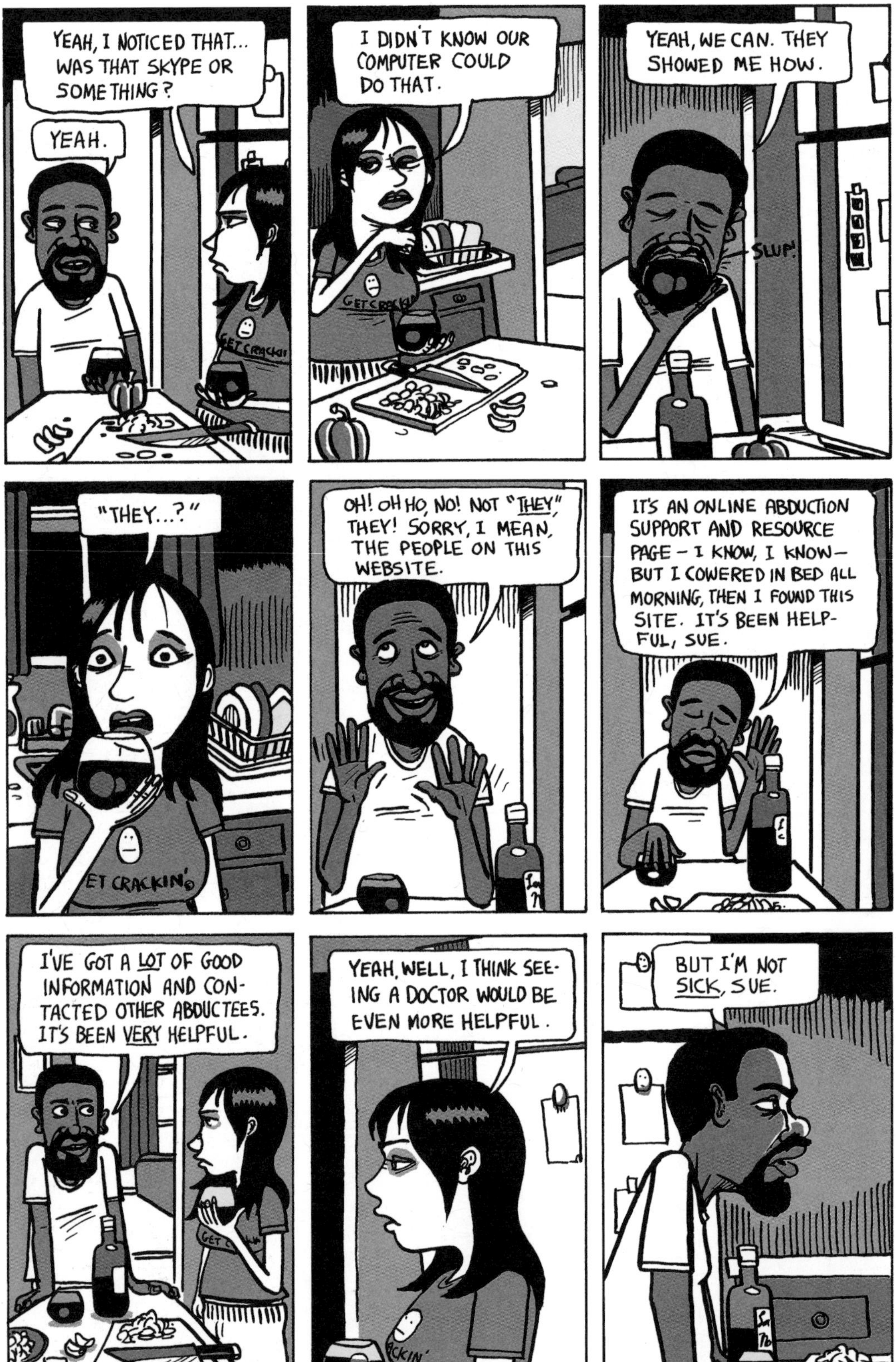
YEAH, I NOTICED THAT... WAS THAT SKYPE OR SOMETHING?
YEAH.
I DIDN'T KNOW OUR COMPUTER COULD DO THAT.
YEAH, WE CAN. THEY SHOWED ME HOW.
SLUP!
"THEY...?"
OH! OH HO, NO! NOT "THEY," THEY! SORRY, I MEAN, THE PEOPLE ON THIS WEBSITE.
IT'S AN ONLINE ABDUCTION SUPPORT AND RESOURCE PAGE – I KNOW, I KNOW– BUT I COWERED IN BED ALL MORNING, THEN I FOUND THIS SITE. IT'S BEEN HELPFUL, SUE.
I'VE GOT A LOT OF GOOD INFORMATION AND CONTACTED OTHER ABDUCTEES. IT'S BEEN VERY HELPFUL.
YEAH, WELL, I THINK SEEING A DOCTOR WOULD BE EVEN MORE HELPFUL.
BUT I'M NOT SICK, SUE.

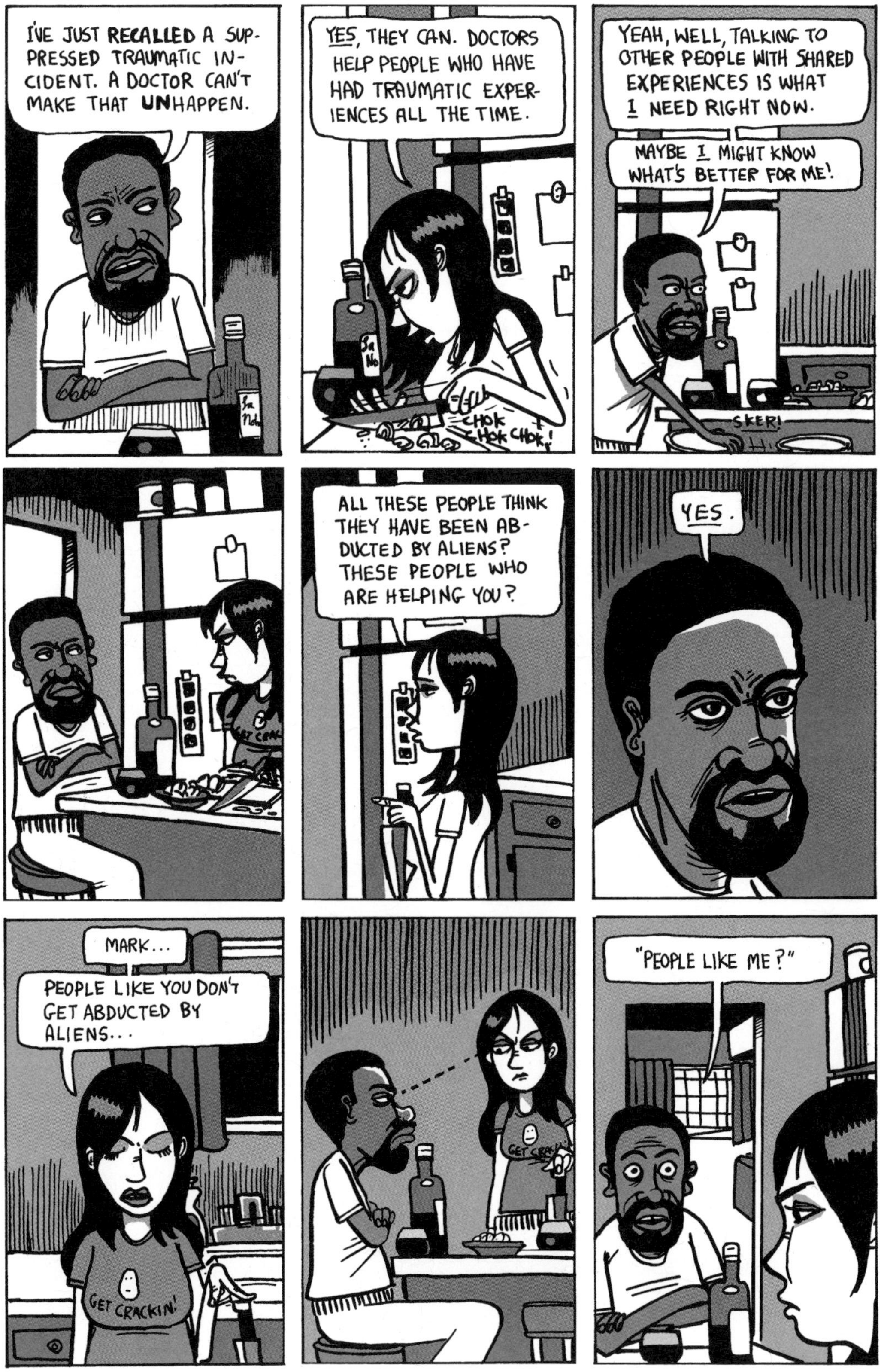
I'VE JUST RECALLED A SUPPRESSED TRAUMATIC INCIDENT. A DOCTOR CAN'T MAKE THAT UNHAPPEN.
YES, THEY CAN. DOCTORS HELP PEOPLE WHO HAVE HAD TRAUMATIC EXPERIENCES ALL THE TIME.
CHOK CHOK CHOK!
YEAH, WELL, TALKING TO OTHER PEOPLE WITH SHARED EXPERIENCES IS WHAT I NEED RIGHT NOW.
MAYBE I MIGHT KNOW WHAT'S BETTER FOR ME!
SKER!
ALL THESE PEOPLE THINK THEY HAVE BEEN ABDUCTED BY ALIENS? THESE PEOPLE WHO ARE HELPING YOU?
YES.
MARK...
PEOPLE LIKE YOU DON'T GET ABDUCTED BY ALIENS...
GET CRACKIN'
"PEOPLE LIKE ME?"

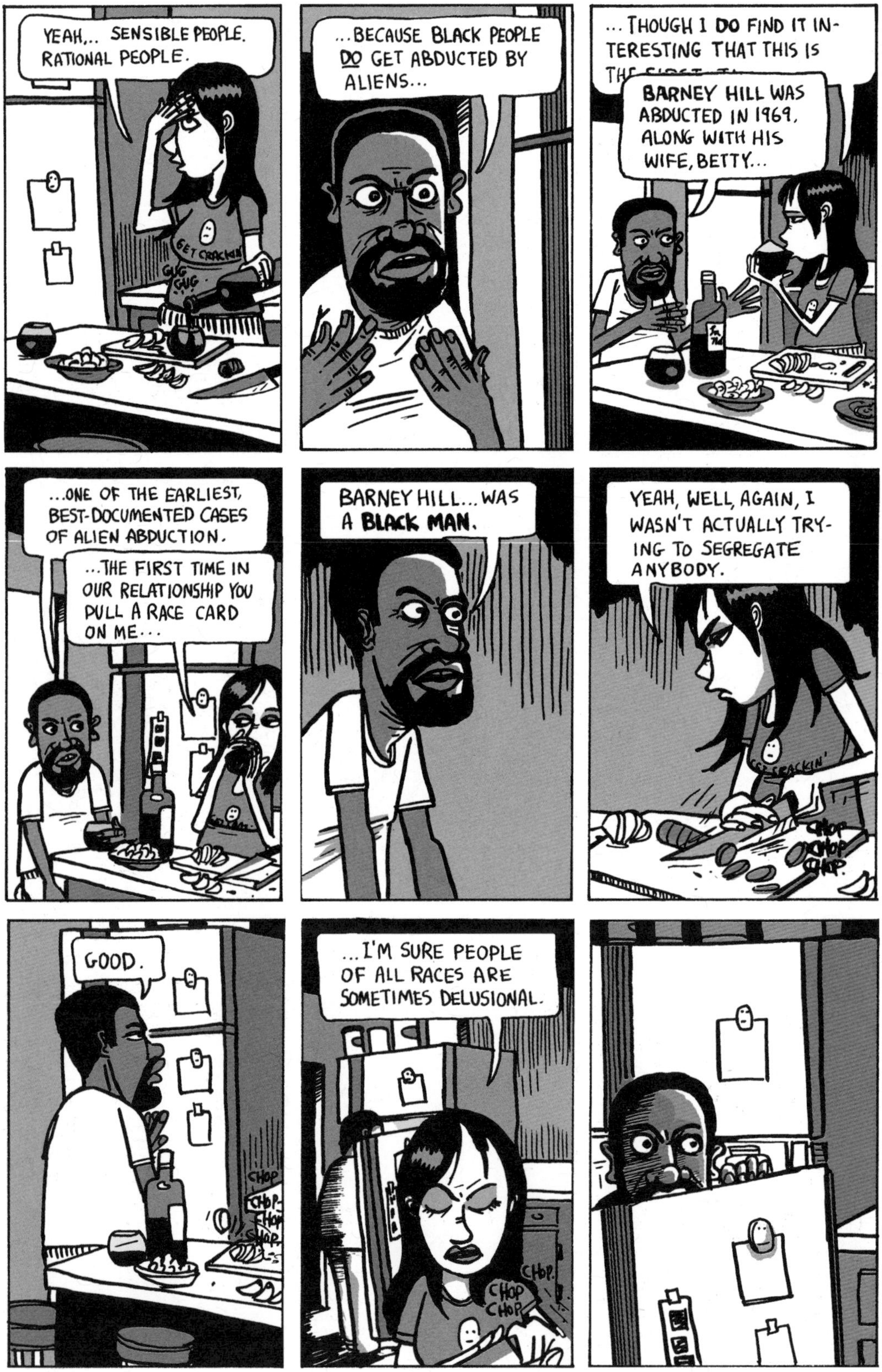

YEAH,.. SENSIBLE PEOPLE. RATIONAL PEOPLE.
GET CRACKIN'
GUG GUG
...BECAUSE BLACK PEOPLE DO GET ABDUCTED BY ALIENS...
... THOUGH I DO FIND IT IN-TERESTING THAT THIS IS
BARNEY HILL WAS ABDUCTED IN 1969, ALONG WITH HIS WIFE, BETTY...
...ONE OF THE EARLIEST, BEST-DOCUMENTED CASES OF ALIEN ABDUCTION.
...THE FIRST TIME IN OUR RELATIONSHIP YOU PULL A RACE CARD ON ME...
BARNEY HILL...WAS A BLACK MAN.
YEAH, WELL, AGAIN, I WASN'T ACTUALLY TRY-ING TO SEGREGATE ANYBODY.
CHOP CHOP CHOP
GOOD.
CHOP CHOP CHOP
...I'M SURE PEOPLE OF ALL RACES ARE SOMETIMES DELUSIONAL.
CHOP CHOP CHOP

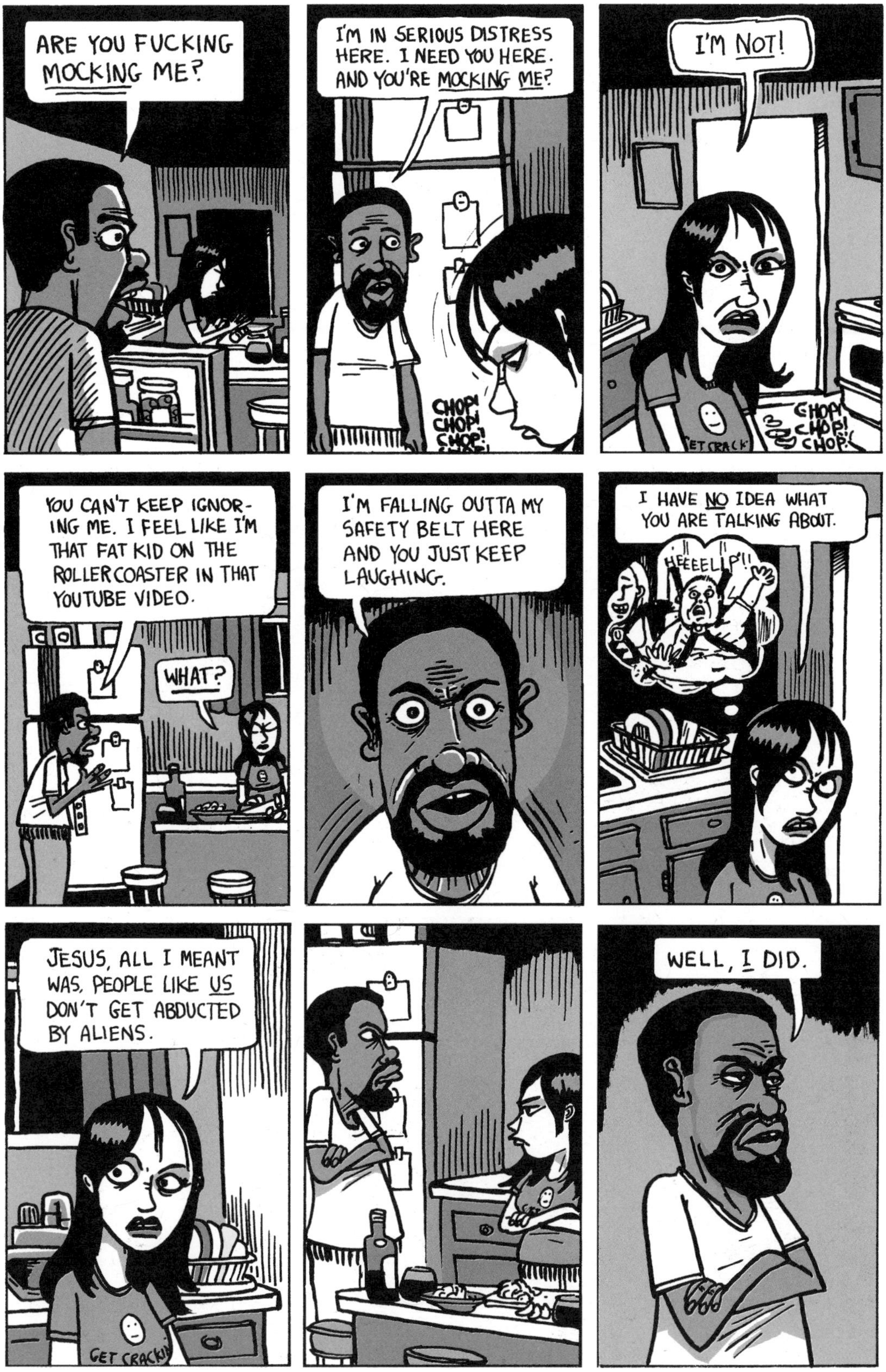
ARE YOU FUCKING MOCKING ME?
I'M IN SERIOUS DISTRESS HERE. I NEED YOU HERE. AND YOU'RE MOCKING ME?
CHOP! CHOP! CHOP!
I'M NOT!
CHOP! CHOP! CHOP!
YOU CAN'T KEEP IGNORING ME. I FEEL LIKE I'M THAT FAT KID ON THE ROLLERCOASTER IN THAT YOUTUBE VIDEO.
WHAT?
I'M FALLING OUTTA MY SAFETY BELT HERE AND YOU JUST KEEP LAUGHING.
I HAVE NO IDEA WHAT YOU ARE TALKING ABOUT.
HEEEELLP!!
JESUS, ALL I MEANT WAS, PEOPLE LIKE US DON'T GET ABDUCTED BY ALIENS.
WELL, I DID.

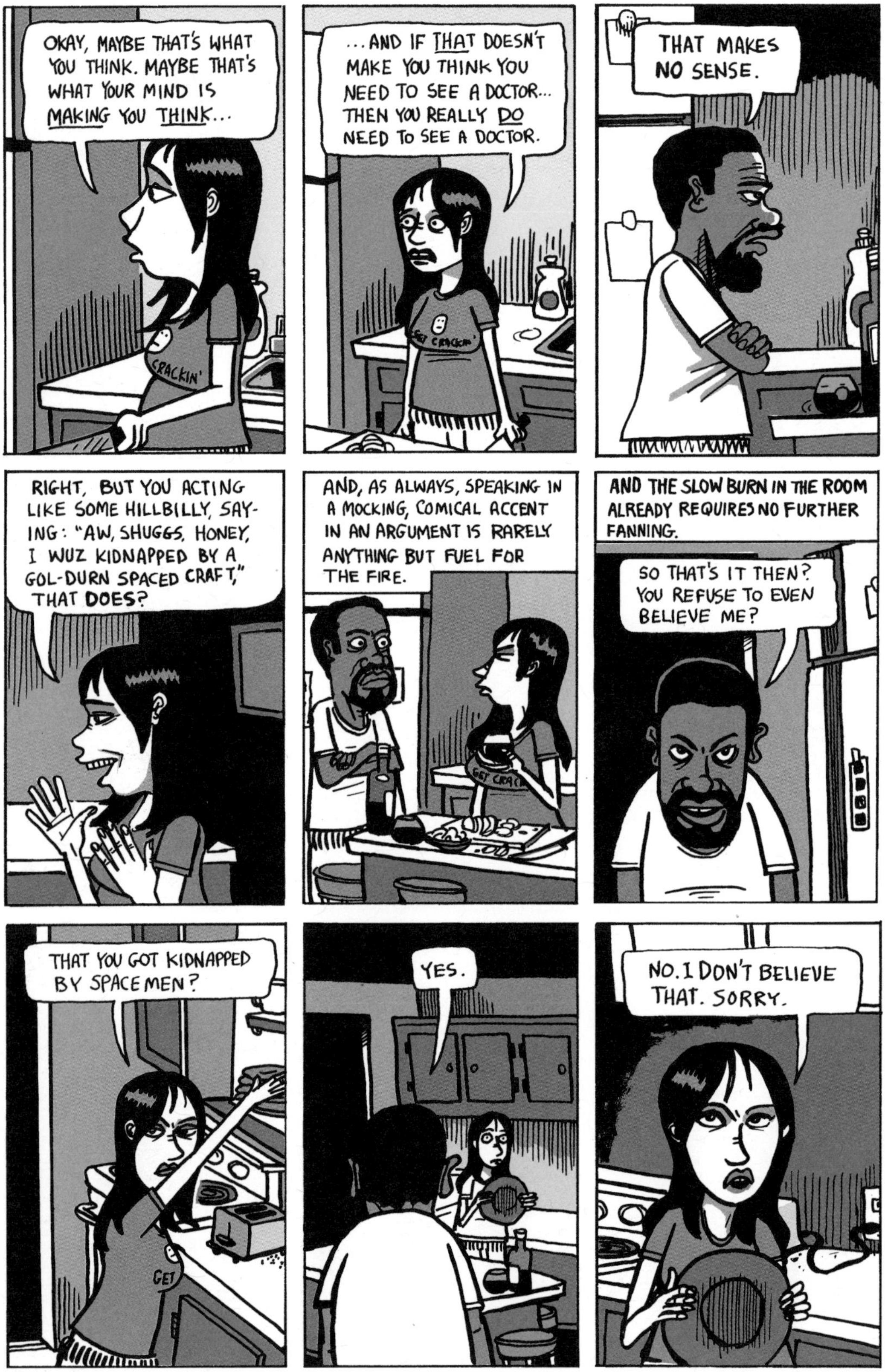
OKAY, MAYBE THAT'S WHAT YOU THINK. MAYBE THAT'S WHAT YOUR MIND IS MAKING YOU THINK...
...AND IF THAT DOESN'T MAKE YOU THINK YOU NEED TO SEE A DOCTOR... THEN YOU REALLY DO NEED TO SEE A DOCTOR.
THAT MAKES NO SENSE.
RIGHT, BUT YOU ACTING LIKE SOME HILLBILLY, SAYING: "AW, SHUGGS, HONEY, I WUZ KIDNAPPED BY A GOL-DURN SPACED CRAFT," THAT DOES?
AND, AS ALWAYS, SPEAKING IN A MOCKING, COMICAL ACCENT IN AN ARGUMENT IS RARELY ANYTHING BUT FUEL FOR THE FIRE.
AND THE SLOW BURN IN THE ROOM ALREADY REQUIRES NO FURTHER FANNING.
SO THAT'S IT THEN? YOU REFUSE TO EVEN BELIEVE ME?
THAT YOU GOT KIDNAPPED BY SPACEMEN?
YES.
NO. I DON'T BELIEVE THAT. SORRY.

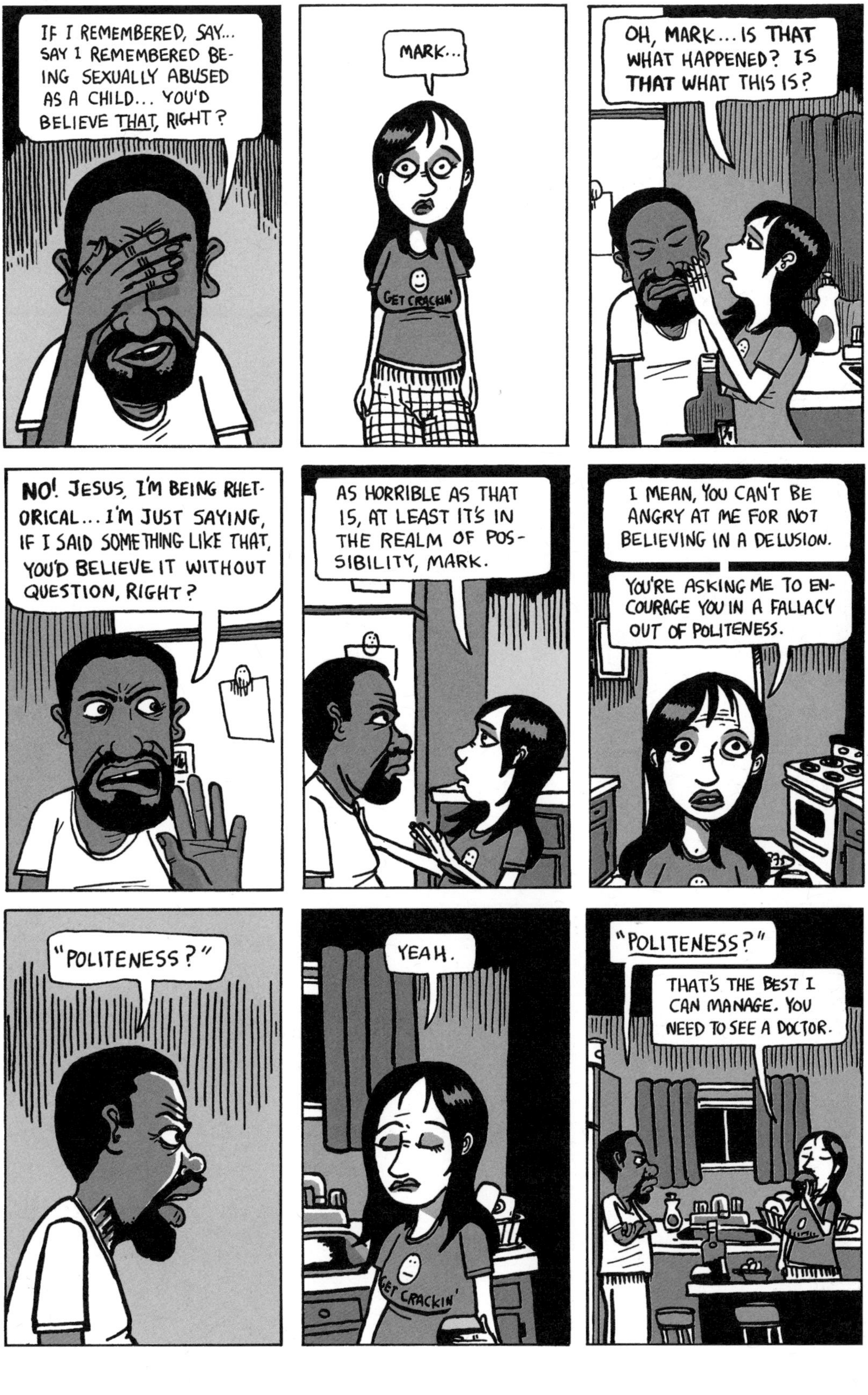
IF I REMEMBERED, SAY... SAY I REMEMBERED BE-ING SEXUALLY ABUSED AS A CHILD... YOU'D BELIEVE THAT, RIGHT?
MARK...
GET CRACKIN'
OH, MARK... IS THAT WHAT HAPPENED? IS THAT WHAT THIS IS?
NO! JESUS, I'M BEING RHET-ORICAL... I'M JUST SAYING, IF I SAID SOMETHING LIKE THAT, YOU'D BELIEVE IT WITHOUT QUESTION, RIGHT?
AS HORRIBLE AS THAT IS, AT LEAST IT'S IN THE REALM OF POS-SIBILITY, MARK.
I MEAN, YOU CAN'T BE ANGRY AT ME FOR NOT BELIEVING IN A DELUSION.
YOU'RE ASKING ME TO EN-COURAGE YOU IN A FALLACY OUT OF POLITENESS.
"POLITENESS?"
YEAH.
GET CRACKIN'
"POLITENESS?"
THAT'S THE BEST I CAN MANAGE. YOU NEED TO SEE A DOCTOR.

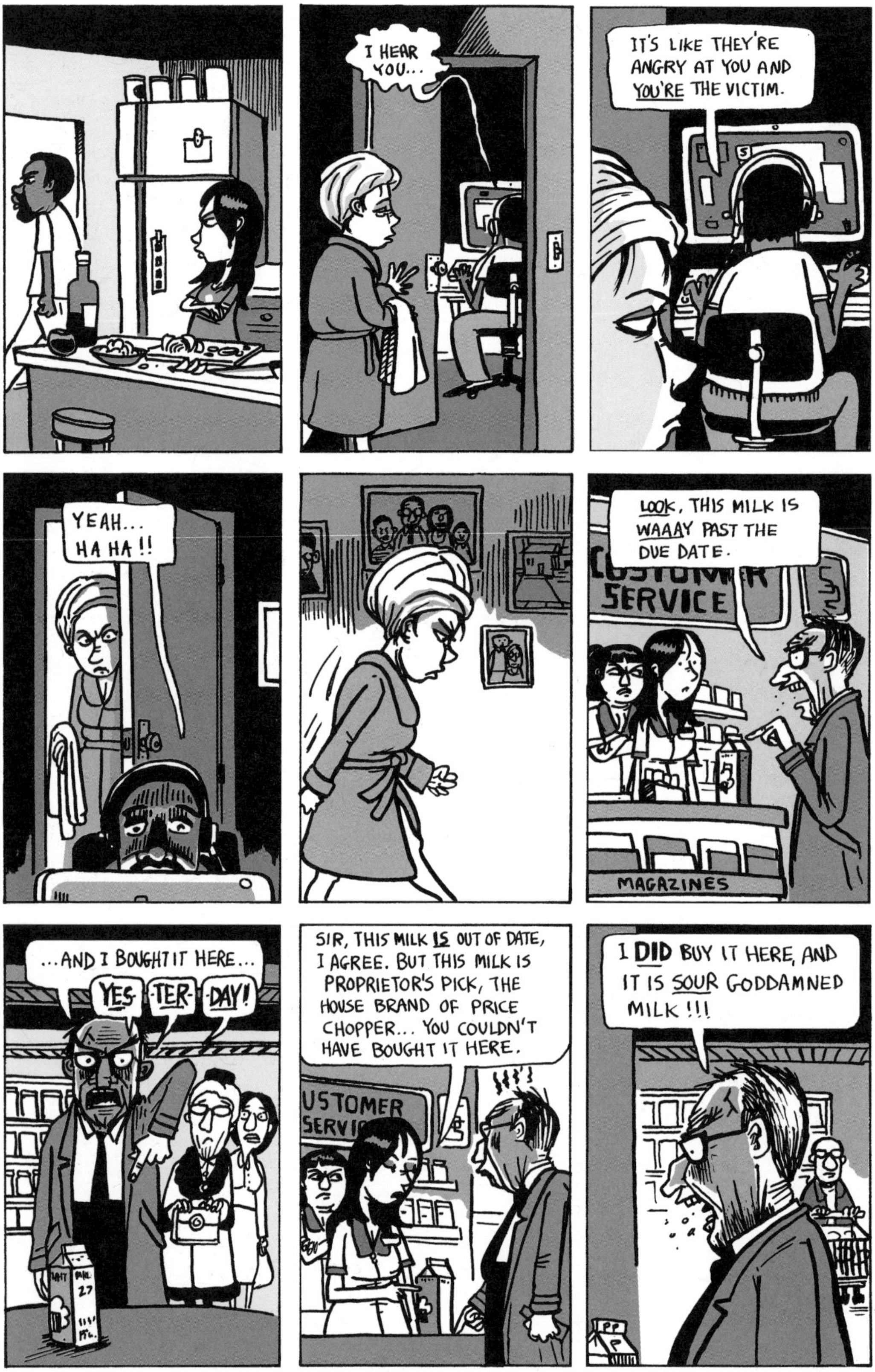
I HEAR YOU...
IT'S LIKE THEY'RE ANGRY AT YOU AND YOU'RE THE VICTIM.
YEAH... HA HA!!
LOOK, THIS MILK IS WAAAY PAST THE DUE DATE.
CUSTOMER SERVICE
MAGAZINES
...AND I BOUGHT IT HERE...
YES-
TER-
DAY!
SIR, THIS MILK IS OUT OF DATE, I AGREE. BUT THIS MILK IS PROPRIETOR'S PICK, THE HOUSE BRAND OF PRICE CHOPPER... YOU COULDN'T HAVE BOUGHT IT HERE.
I DID BUY IT HERE, AND IT IS SOUR GODDAMNED MILK!!!

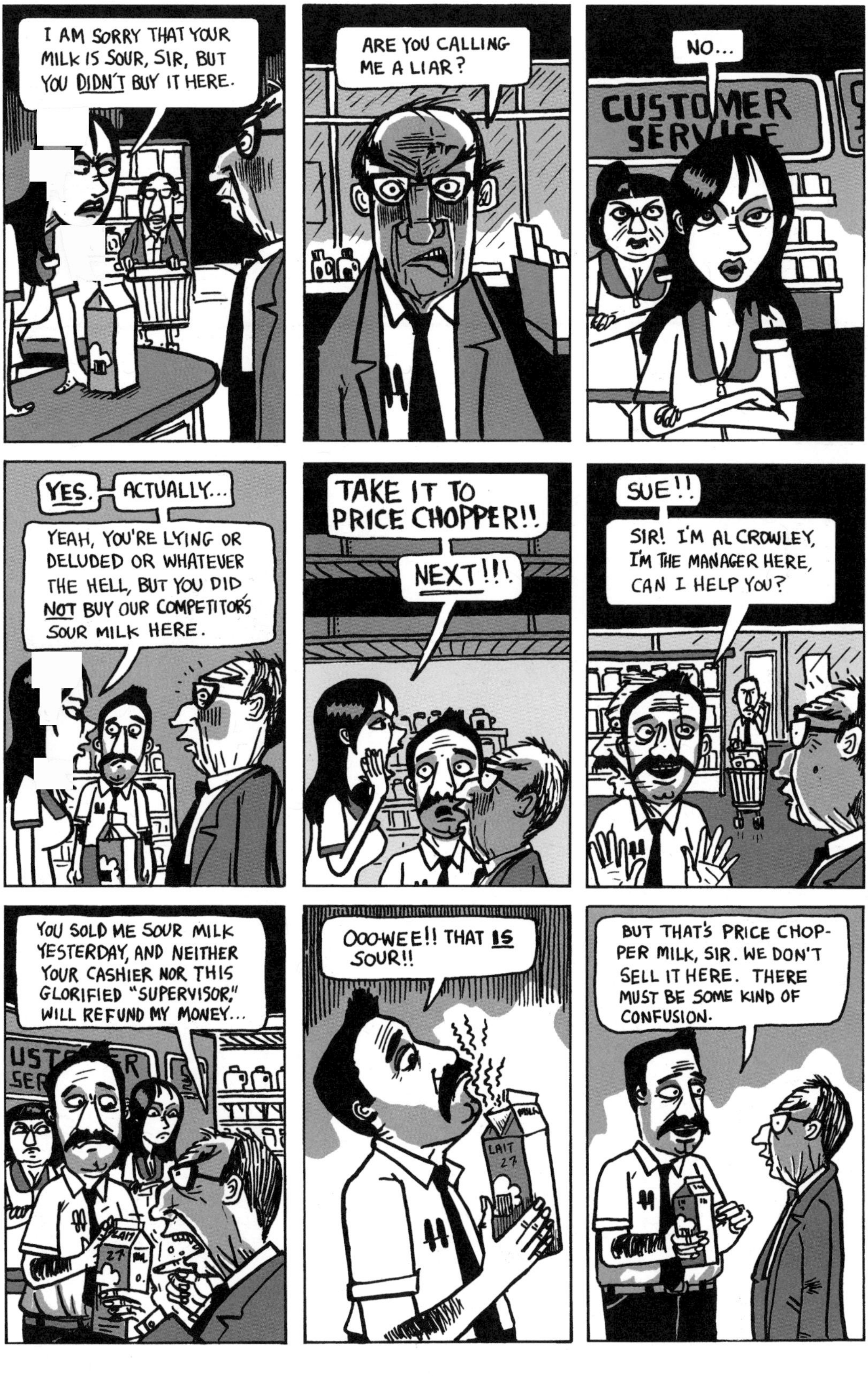
I AM SORRY THAT YOUR MILK IS SOUR, SIR, BUT YOU DIDN'T BUY IT HERE.
ARE YOU CALLING ME A LIAR?
NO...
CUSTOMER
YES.
ACTUALLY...
YEAH, YOU'RE LYING OR DELUDED OR WHATEVER THE HELL, BUT YOU DID NOT BUY OUR COMPETITOR'S SOUR MILK HERE.
TAKE IT TO PRICE CHOPPER!!
NEXT!!!
SUE!!
SIR! I'M AL CROWLEY, I'M THE MANAGER HERE, CAN I HELP YOU?
YOU SOLD ME SOUR MILK YESTERDAY, AND NEITHER YOUR CASHIER NOR THIS GLORIFIED "SUPERVISOR," WILL REFUND MY MONEY...
OOO-WEE!! THAT IS SOUR!!
BUT THAT'S PRICE CHOPPER MILK, SIR. WE DON'T SELL IT HERE. THERE MUST BE SOME KIND OF CONFUSION.

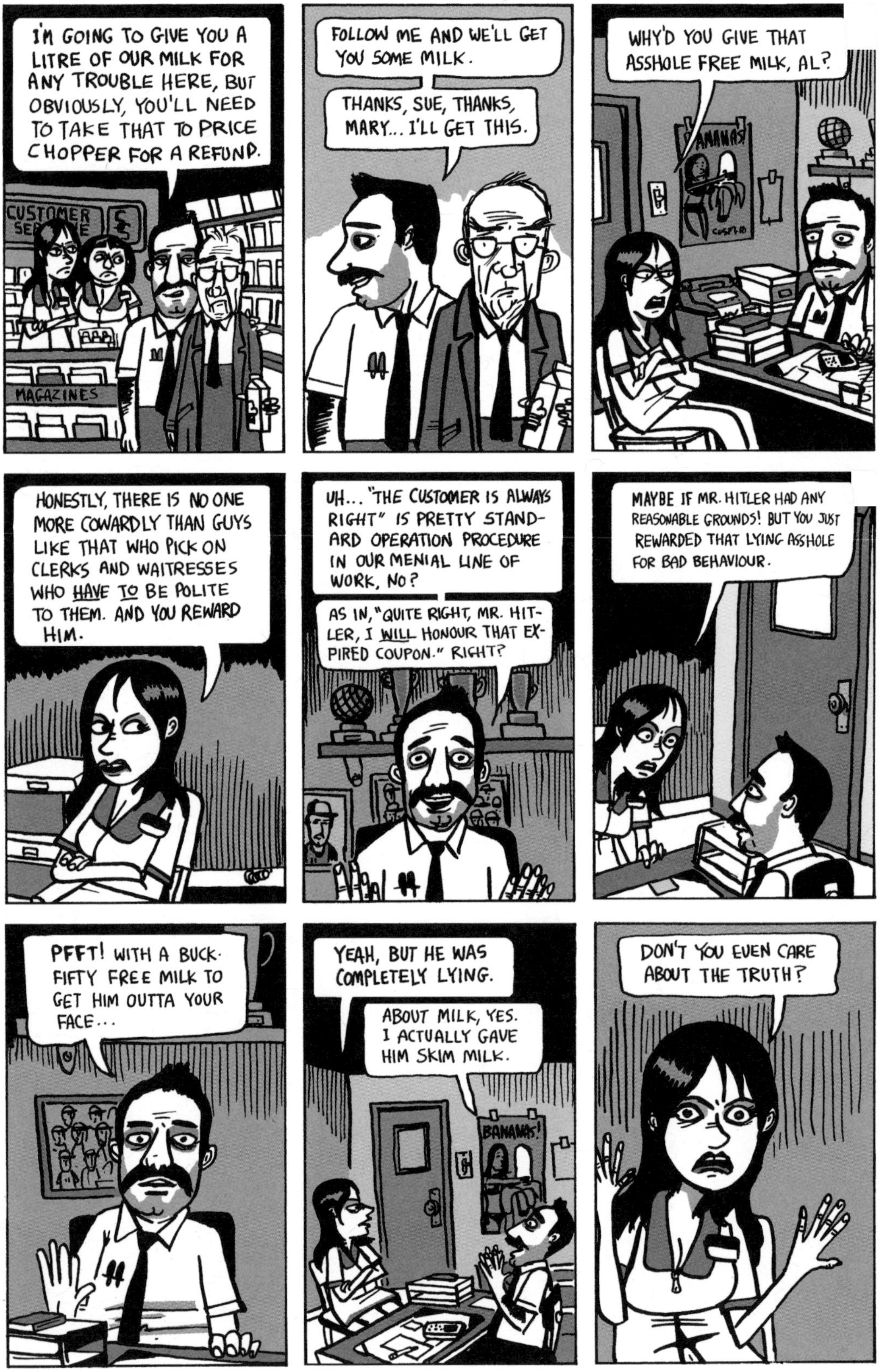

I'M GOING TO GIVE YOU A LITRE OF OUR MILK FOR ANY TROUBLE HERE, BUT OBVIOUSLY, YOU'LL NEED TO TAKE THAT TO PRICE CHOPPER FOR A REFUND.
CUSTOMER SERVICE
MAGAZINES
FOLLOW ME AND WE'LL GET YOU SOME MILK.
THANKS, SUE, THANKS, MARY... I'LL GET THIS.
WHY'D YOU GIVE THAT ASSHOLE FREE MILK, AL?
BANANAS!
HONESTLY, THERE IS NO ONE MORE COWARDLY THAN GUYS LIKE THAT WHO PICK ON CLERKS AND WAITRESSES WHO HAVE TO BE POLITE TO THEM. AND YOU REWARD HIM.
UH... "THE CUSTOMER IS ALWAYS RIGHT" IS PRETTY STANDARD OPERATION PROCEDURE IN OUR MENIAL LINE OF WORK, NO?
AS IN, "QUITE RIGHT, MR. HITLER, I WILL HONOUR THAT EXPIRED COUPON." RIGHT?
MAYBE IF MR. HITLER HAD ANY REASONABLE GROUNDS! BUT YOU JUST REWARDED THAT LYING ASSHOLE FOR BAD BEHAVIOUR.
PFFT! WITH A BUCK-FIFTY FREE MILK TO GET HIM OUTTA YOUR FACE...
YEAH, BUT HE WAS COMPLETELY LYING.
ABOUT MILK, YES. I ACTUALLY GAVE HIM SKIM MILK.
BANANAS!
DON'T YOU EVEN CARE ABOUT THE TRUTH?

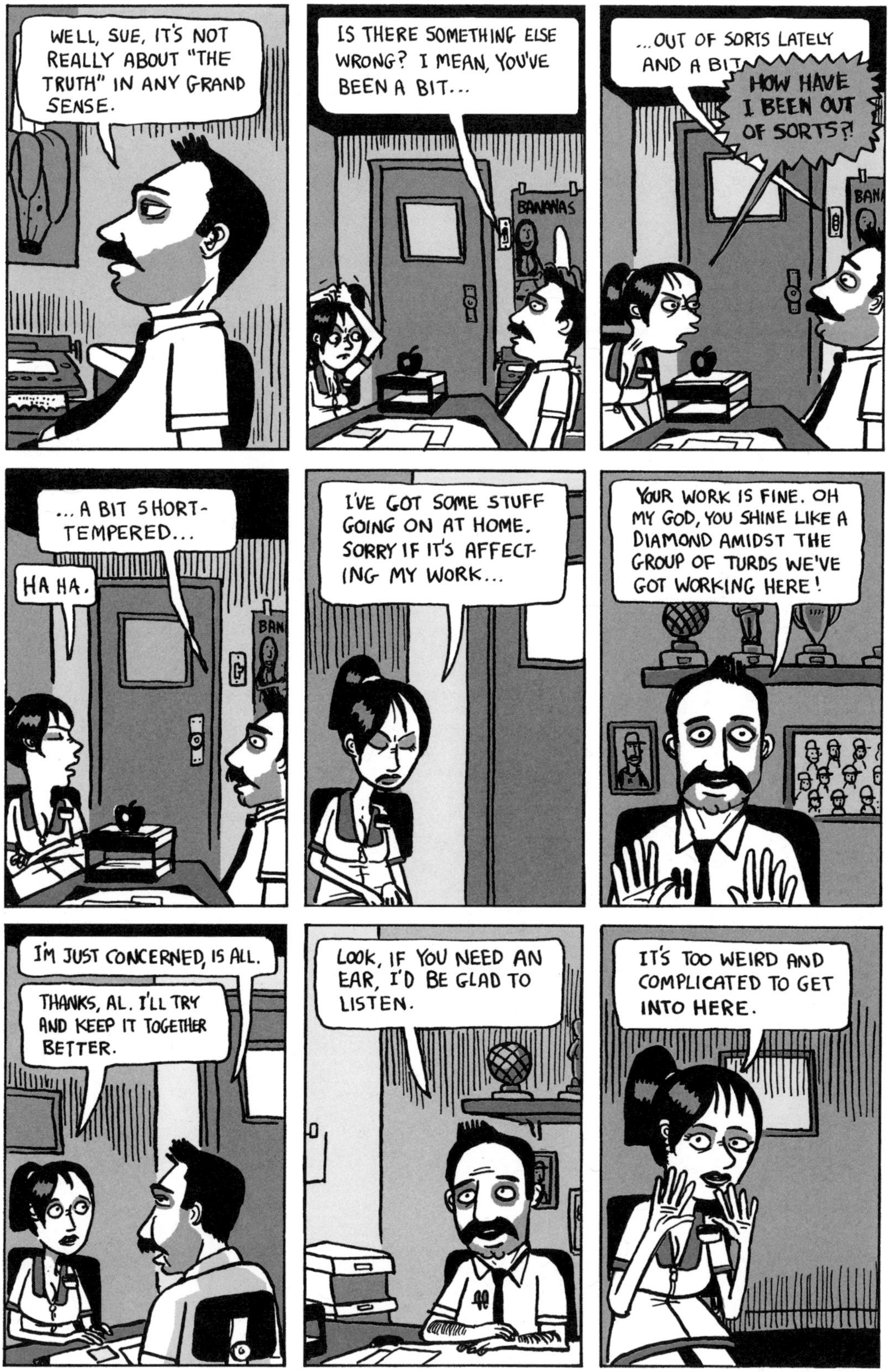
WELL, SUE, IT'S NOT REALLY ABOUT "THE TRUTH" IN ANY GRAND SENSE.
IS THERE SOMETHING ELSE WRONG? I MEAN, YOU'VE BEEN A BIT...
BANANAS
...OUT OF SORTS LATELY AND A BIT
HOW HAVE I BEEN OUT OF SORTS?!
...A BIT SHORT-TEMPERED...
HA HA.
I'VE GOT SOME STUFF GOING ON AT HOME. SORRY IF IT'S AFFECTING MY WORK...
YOUR WORK IS FINE. OH MY GOD, YOU SHINE LIKE A DIAMOND AMIDST THE GROUP OF TURDS WE'VE GOT WORKING HERE!
I'M JUST CONCERNED, IS ALL.
THANKS, AL. I'LL TRY AND KEEP IT TOGETHER BETTER.
LOOK, IF YOU NEED AN EAR, I'D BE GLAD TO LISTEN.
IT'S TOO WEIRD AND COMPLICATED TO GET INTO HERE.

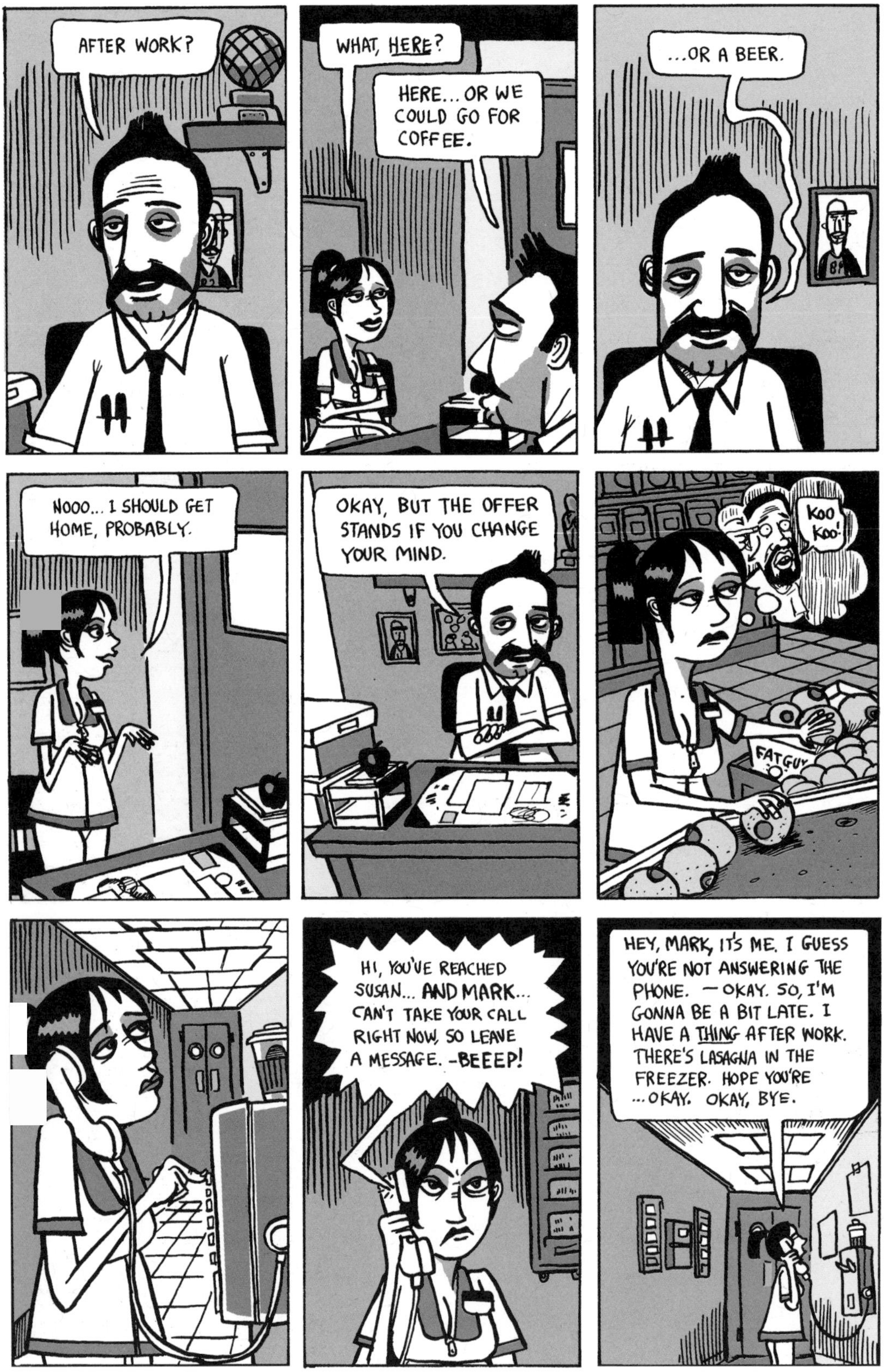
AFTER WORK?
WHAT, HERE?
HERE... OR WE COULD GO FOR COFFEE.
...OR A BEER.
NOOO... I SHOULD GET HOME, PROBABLY.
OKAY, BUT THE OFFER STANDS IF YOU CHANGE YOUR MIND.
KOO KOO!
FAT GUY
HI, YOU'VE REACHED SUSAN... AND MARK... CAN'T TAKE YOUR CALL RIGHT NOW, SO LEAVE A MESSAGE. -BEEEP!
HEY, MARK, IT'S ME. I GUESS YOU'RE NOT ANSWERING THE PHONE. —OKAY. SO, I'M GONNA BE A BIT LATE. I HAVE A THING AFTER WORK. THERE'S LASAGNA IN THE FREEZER. HOPE YOU'RE ...OKAY. OKAY, BYE.

SHE JUST WANTS TO RUN THE STORY PAST SOMEONE ELSE AND SEE IF SHE'S BEING UNREASONABLE IS ALL, SHE TELLS HERSELF...

TOC TOC

AL, CAN I TAKE YOU UP ON YOUR OFFER AFTER ALL?

WHAT?

OH, NO, SORRY, THEY GOT ME HANDING OUT FREE MILK AT THAT ASSHOLE CONVENTION TONIGHT.

SURE.

AND CAN'T A GOOD LISTENER INCIDENTALLY BE GOOD-LOOKING IN A DORKY, POST-MODERN TOM SELLECK KIND OF WAY?

HEY, I'M HOME...

CLINK!

HEY!

SPACE

THE GREAT

OH, HEY, YOU'RE HOME...

SPACE NUT

YEAH, THERE WAS A STAFF MEETING THING.

SMOOCH.

POOH!

A STAFF DRINK-MEETING IS MORE LIKE IT.

JESUS, MARK! WE HAD BEERS IN THE LOCKER ROOM WHILE WE GOT YELLED AT FOR NOT ROTATING THE BREAD PROPERLY. BUT, YEAH,

MY EXOTIC LIFESTYLE, YEAH, I WAS AT A FANCY COCKTAIL PARTY...

MY WORK IS SUFFERING FROM ALL OF YOUR...

FROM ALL OF THIS **SHIT** THAT'S BEEN GOING ON... AND YOU... I GOT IN SHIT FOR YELLING AT A CUSTOMER ABOUT MILK TODAY, MARK.

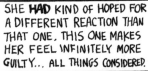

HEY, HEY, HEY...

YOU SMELLED LIKE BEER AND I WANTED ONE TOO, THAT'S ALL. I'M SORRY.

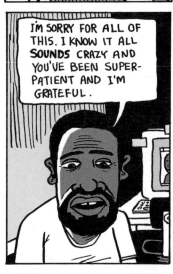

I'M SORRY FOR ALL OF THIS. I KNOW IT ALL **SOUNDS** CRAZY AND YOU'VE BEEN SUPER-PATIENT AND I'M GRATEFUL.

SHE **HAD** KIND OF HOPED FOR A DIFFERENT REACTION THAN THAT ONE, THIS ONE MAKES HER FEEL INFINITELY MORE GUILTY... ALL THINGS CONSIDERED.

...COMPLETELY OFF HIS NUT, REALLY, AND HE REFUSES TO SEE A DOCTOR...

ALIENS!

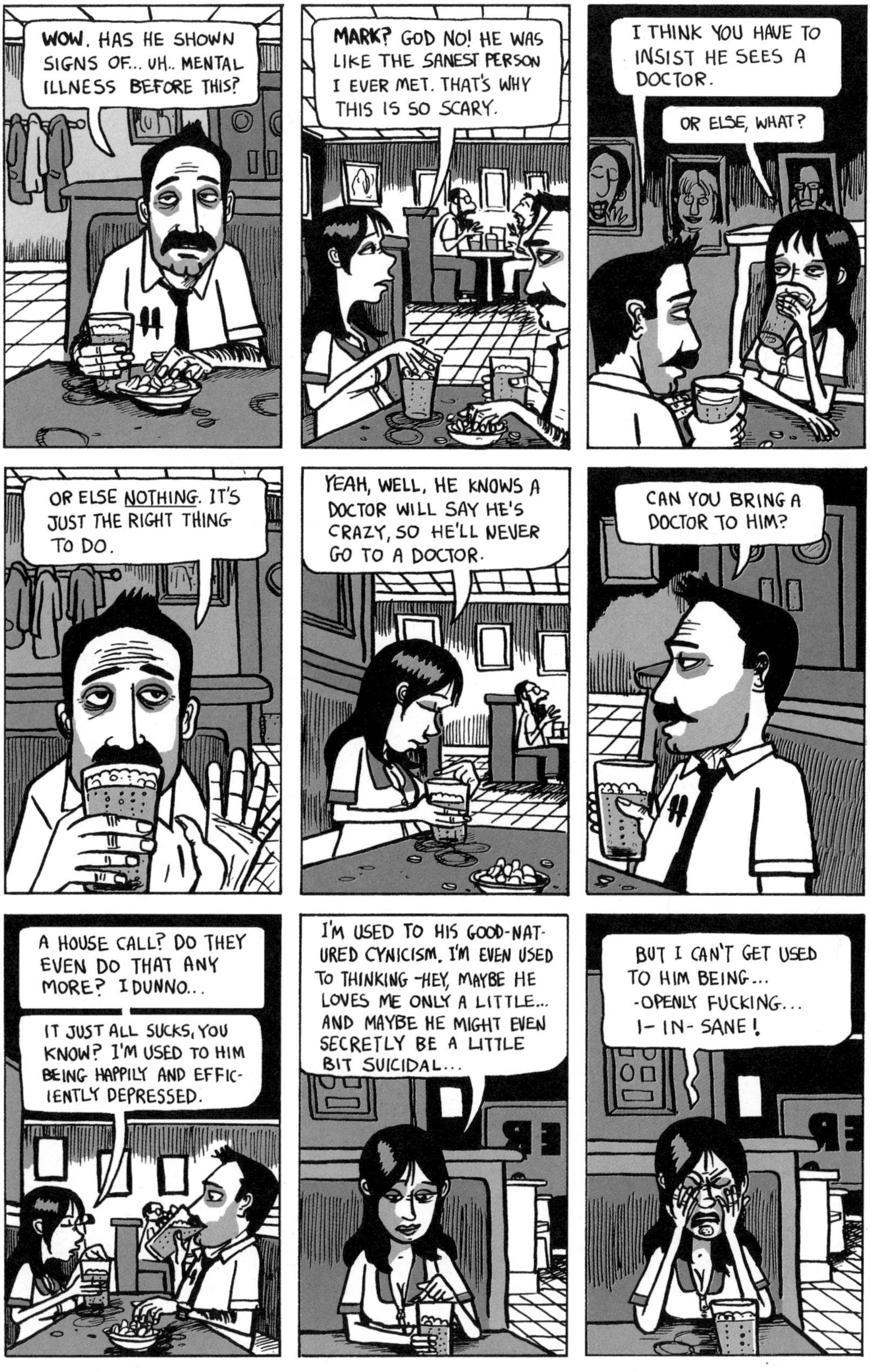
WOW. HAS HE SHOWN SIGNS OF... UH.. MENTAL ILLNESS BEFORE THIS?
MARK? GOD NO! HE WAS LIKE THE SANEST PERSON I EVER MET. THAT'S WHY THIS IS SO SCARY.
I THINK YOU HAVE TO INSIST HE SEES A DOCTOR.
OR ELSE, WHAT?
OR ELSE NOTHING. IT'S JUST THE RIGHT THING TO DO.
YEAH, WELL, HE KNOWS A DOCTOR WILL SAY HE'S CRAZY, SO HE'LL NEVER GO TO A DOCTOR.
CAN YOU BRING A DOCTOR TO HIM?
A HOUSE CALL? DO THEY EVEN DO THAT ANY MORE? I DUNNO...
IT JUST ALL SUCKS, YOU KNOW? I'M USED TO HIM BEING HAPPILY AND EFFICIENTLY DEPRESSED.
I'M USED TO HIS GOOD-NATURED CYNICISM. I'M EVEN USED TO THINKING -HEY, MAYBE HE LOVES ME ONLY A LITTLE... AND MAYBE HE MIGHT EVEN SECRETLY BE A LITTLE BIT SUICIDAL...
BUT I CAN'T GET USED TO HIM BEING... -OPENLY FUCKING... I- IN- SANE!

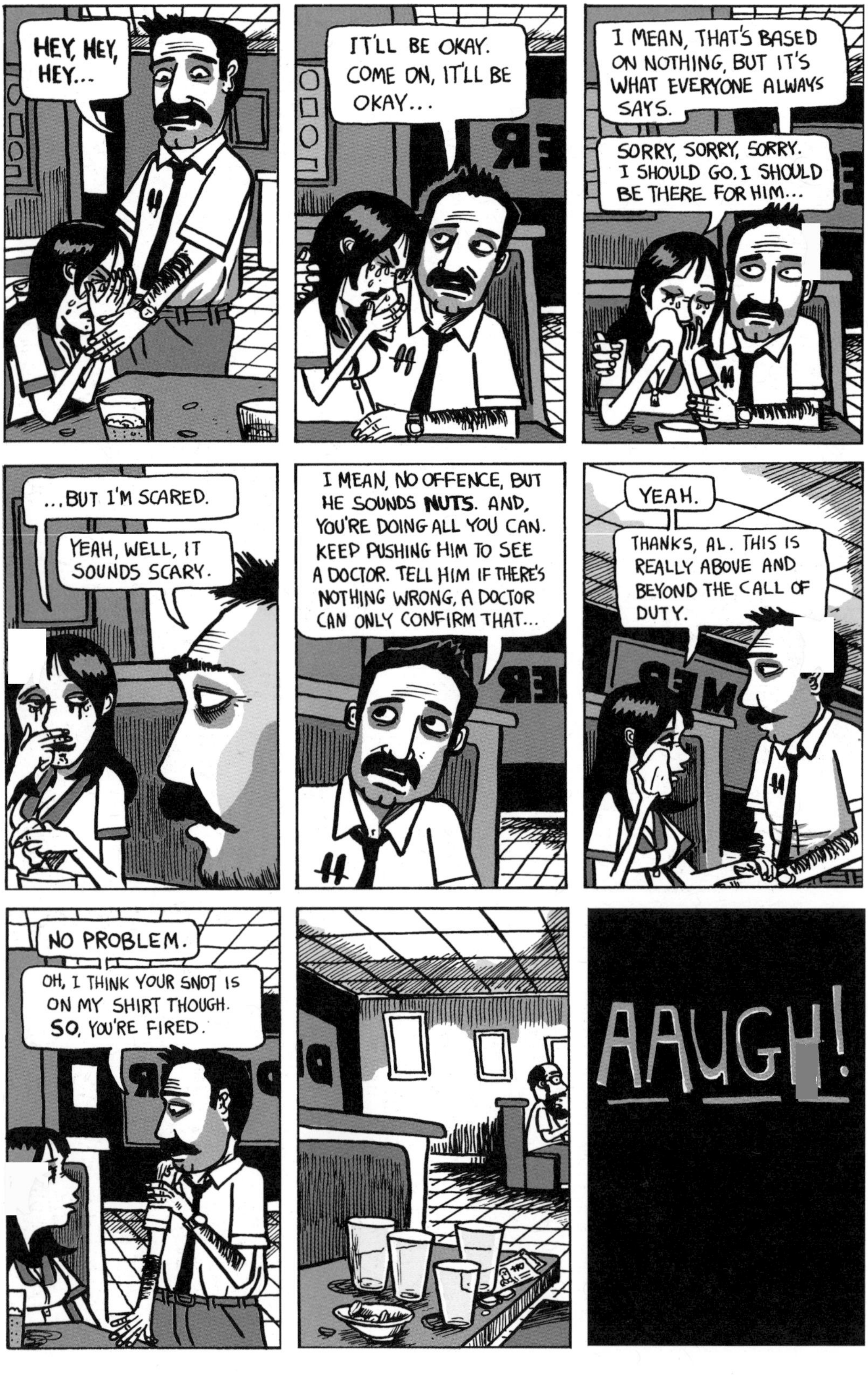

HEY, HEY, HEY...
IT'LL BE OKAY. COME ON, IT'LL BE OKAY...
I MEAN, THAT'S BASED ON NOTHING, BUT IT'S WHAT EVERYONE ALWAYS SAYS.
SORRY, SORRY, SORRY. I SHOULD GO. I SHOULD BE THERE FOR HIM...
...BUT I'M SCARED.
YEAH, WELL, IT SOUNDS SCARY.
I MEAN, NO OFFENCE, BUT HE SOUNDS **NUTS**. AND, YOU'RE DOING ALL YOU CAN. KEEP PUSHING HIM TO SEE A DOCTOR. TELL HIM IF THERE'S NOTHING WRONG, A DOCTOR CAN ONLY CONFIRM THAT...
YEAH.
THANKS, AL. THIS IS REALLY ABOVE AND BEYOND THE CALL OF DUTY.
NO PROBLEM.
OH, I THINK YOUR SNOT IS ON MY SHIRT THOUGH. SO, YOU'RE FIRED.
AAUGH!

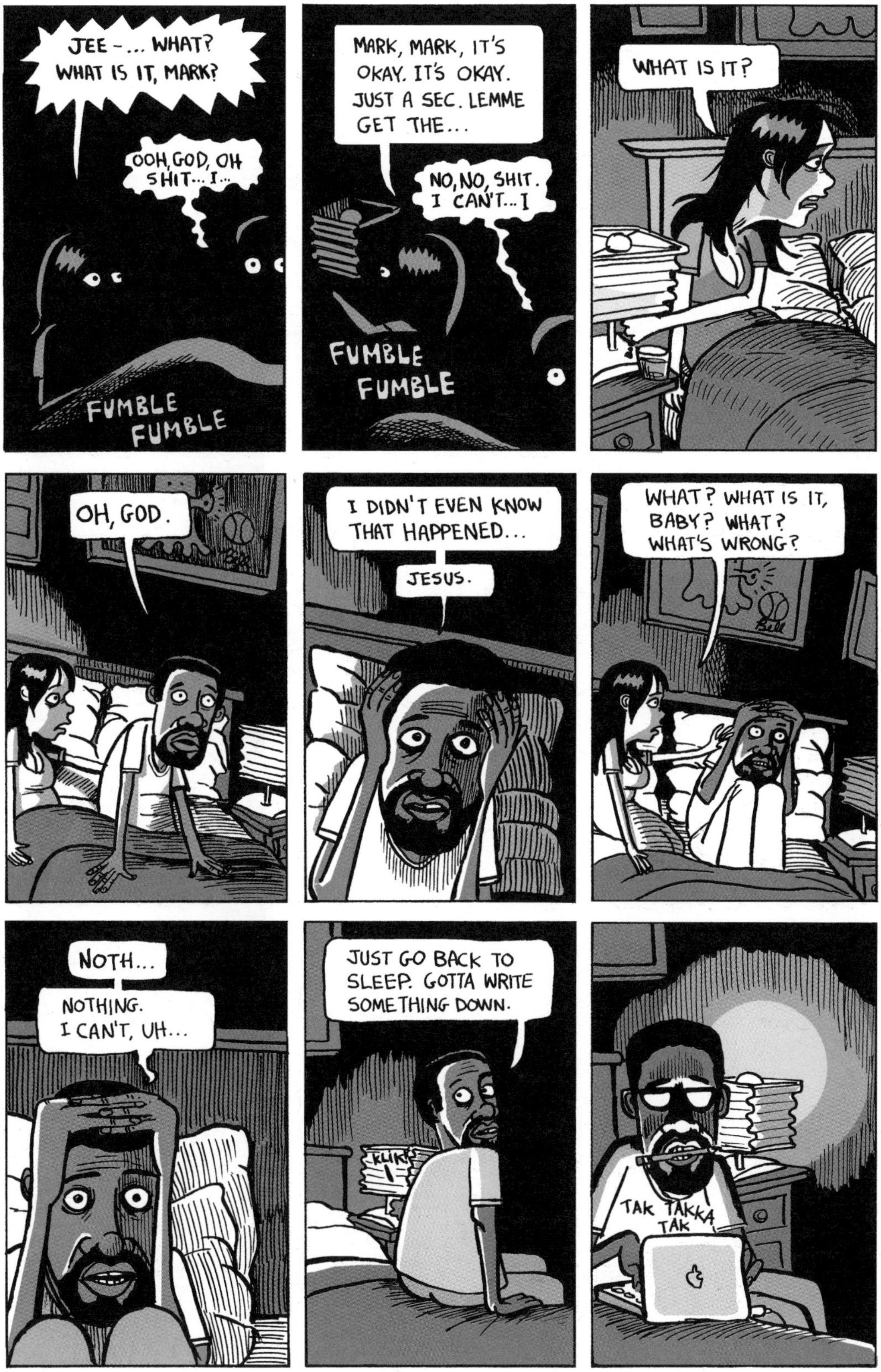
JEE-... WHAT? WHAT IS IT, MARK?
OOH, GOD, OH SHIT... I...
FUMBLE FUMBLE
MARK, MARK, IT'S OKAY. IT'S OKAY. JUST A SEC. LEMME GET THE...
NO, NO, SHIT. I CAN'T... I
FUMBLE FUMBLE
WHAT IS IT?
OH, GOD.
I DIDN'T EVEN KNOW THAT HAPPENED...
JESUS.
WHAT? WHAT IS IT, BABY? WHAT? WHAT'S WRONG?
NOTH...
NOTHING. I CAN'T, UH...
JUST GO BACK TO SLEEP. GOTTA WRITE SOMETHING DOWN.
KLIK
TAK TAKKA TAK

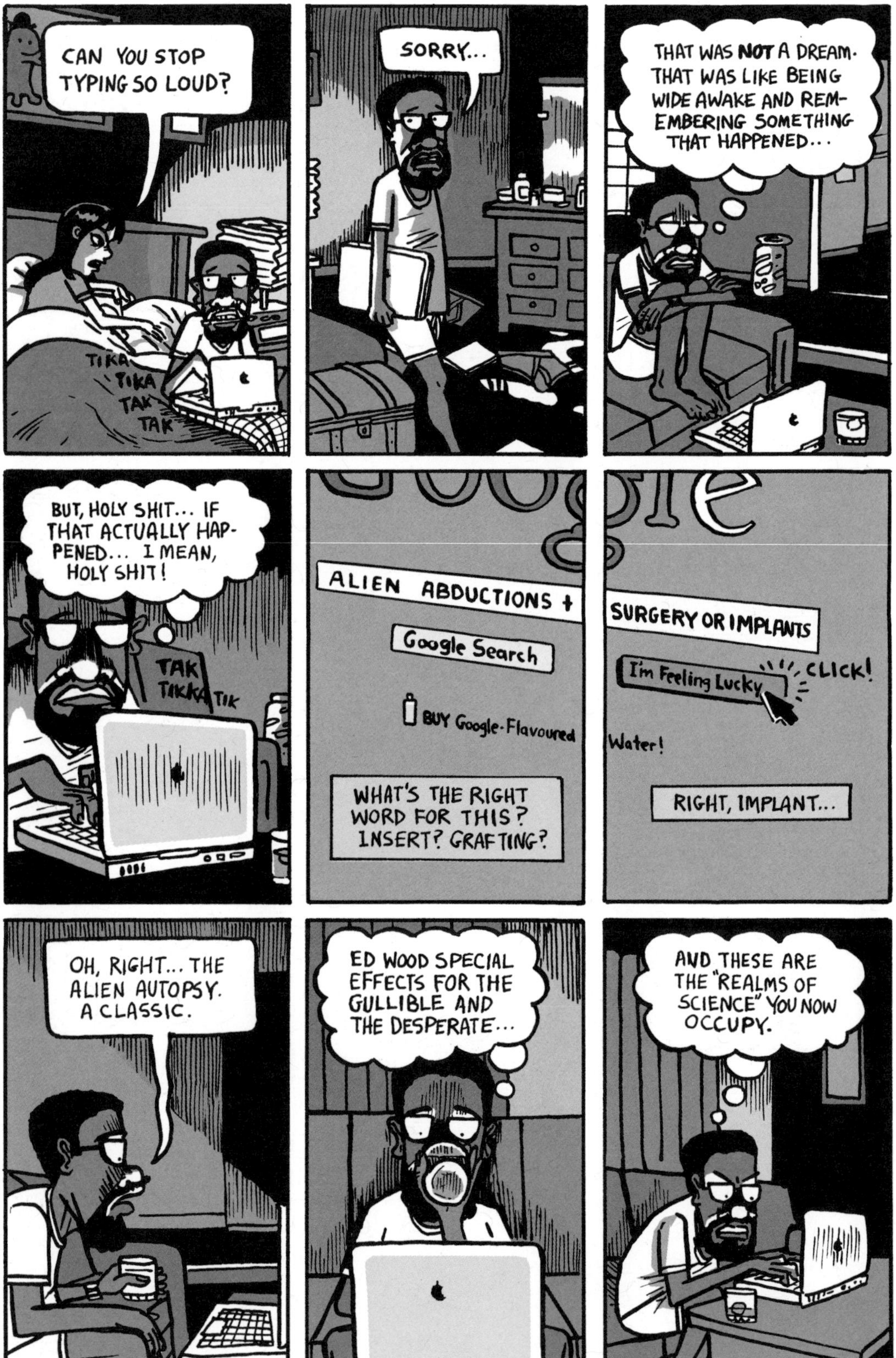
CAN YOU STOP TYPING SO LOUD?
TIKA TIKA TAK TAK
SORRY...
THAT WAS NOT A DREAM. THAT WAS LIKE BEING WIDE AWAKE AND REMEMBERING SOMETHING THAT HAPPENED...
BUT, HOLY SHIT... IF THAT ACTUALLY HAPPENED... I MEAN, HOLY SHIT!
TAK TIKKA TIK
ALIEN ABDUCTIONS + SURGERY OR IMPLANTS
Google Search
I'm Feeling Lucky
CLICK!
BUY Google-Flavoured Water!
WHAT'S THE RIGHT WORD FOR THIS? INSERT? GRAFTING?
RIGHT, IMPLANT...
OH, RIGHT... THE ALIEN AUTOPSY. A CLASSIC.
ED WOOD SPECIAL EFFECTS FOR THE GULLIBLE AND THE DESPERATE...
AND THESE ARE THE "REALMS OF SCIENCE" YOU NOW OCCUPY.

STILL, FOR THE FIRST TIME IN HIS LIFE, HE HAS NO DOUBT, NO SCIENTIFIC QUESTIONING, NO CYNICISM. ONLY CERTAINTY.

AND WHAT IS THAT THEN, HE WONDERS? FAITH?

BUT WHAT ARE THE FACTS MARK? WHAT DO YOU BELIEVE?

SOMETHING... OR SOMEONE... TOOK ME INTO THE WOODS...

THEY RESTRAINED MY LIMBS... AND MAY HAVE PERFORMED SOME KIND OF SURGERY.

AND POSSIBLY PUT SOMETHING METAL INTO AN INCISION.

SIGH...

I BELIEVE THAT ALL OF THAT HAPPENED.

SIGH...

MARK?

SSSKKK

MARK! YOU'RE ASLEEP.

MARK! COME TO BED!

HUH?

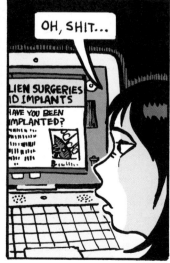

OH, SHIT...

LIEN SURGERIES
D IMPLANTS

AVE YOU BEEN
MPLANTED?

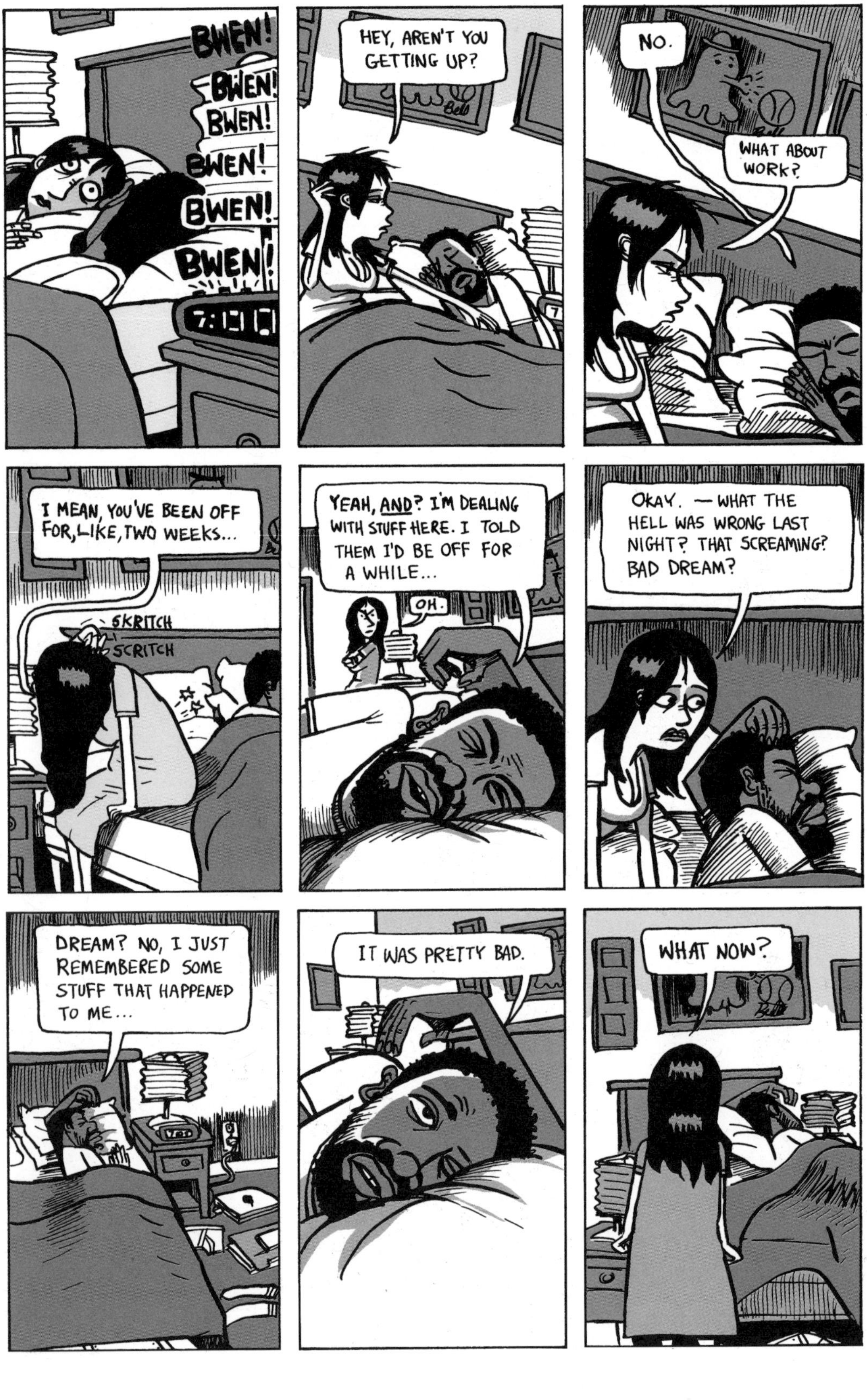
BWEN! BWEN! BWEN! BWEN! BWEN! BWEN!
HEY, AREN'T YOU GETTING UP?
NO.
WHAT ABOUT WORK?
I MEAN, YOU'VE BEEN OFF FOR, LIKE, TWO WEEKS...
SKRITCH SCRITCH
YEAH, AND? I'M DEALING WITH STUFF HERE. I TOLD THEM I'D BE OFF FOR A WHILE...
OH.
OKAY. —WHAT THE HELL WAS WRONG LAST NIGHT? THAT SCREAMING? BAD DREAM?
DREAM? NO, I JUST REMEMBERED SOME STUFF THAT HAPPENED TO ME...
IT WAS PRETTY BAD.
WHAT NOW?

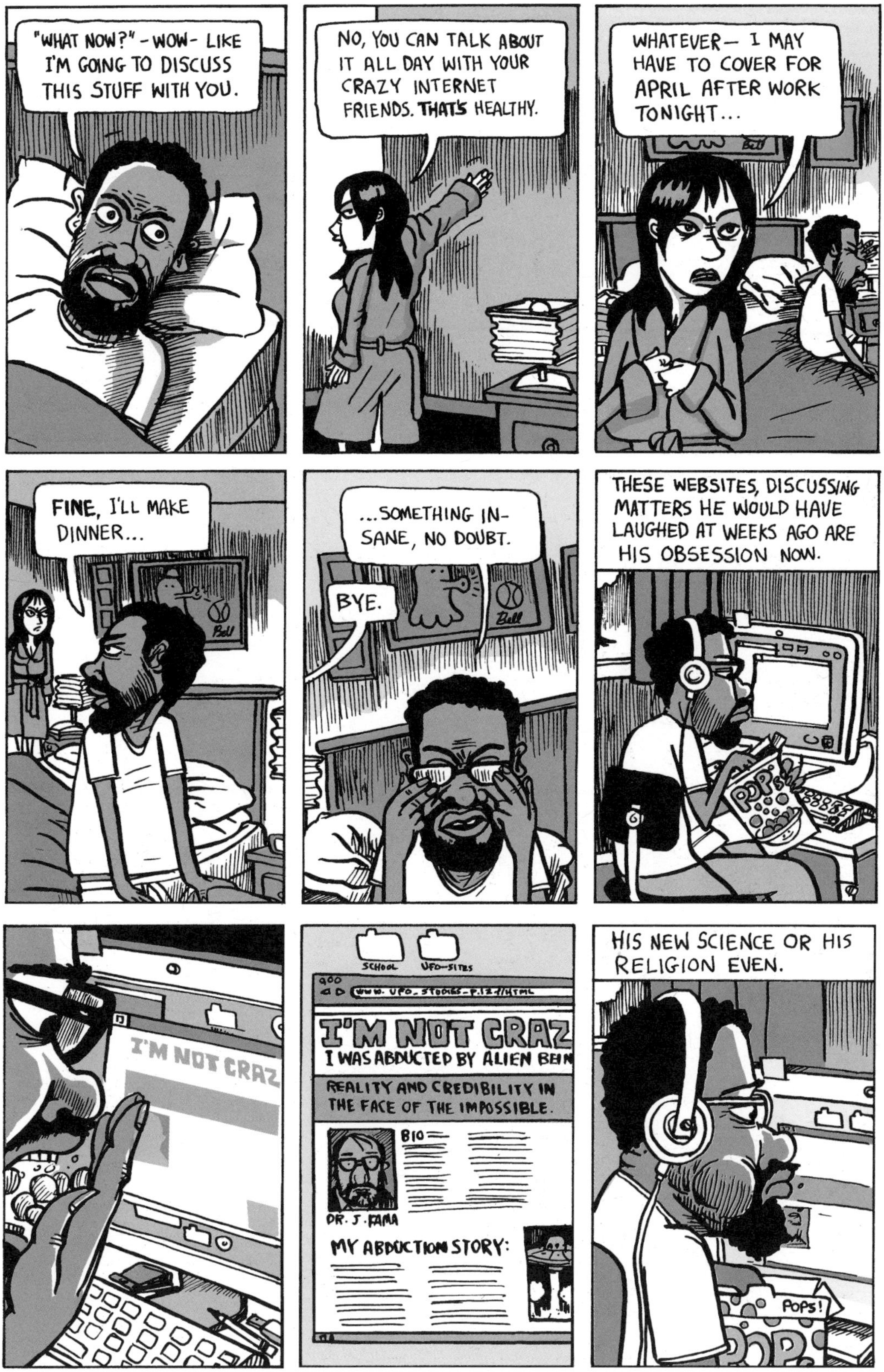

"WHAT NOW?" - WOW - LIKE I'M GOING TO DISCUSS THIS STUFF WITH YOU.
NO, YOU CAN TALK ABOUT IT ALL DAY WITH YOUR CRAZY INTERNET FRIENDS. THAT'S HEALTHY.
WHATEVER— I MAY HAVE TO COVER FOR APRIL AFTER WORK TONIGHT...
FINE, I'LL MAKE DINNER...
...SOMETHING IN-SANE, NO DOUBT.
BYE.
THESE WEBSITES, DISCUSSING MATTERS HE WOULD HAVE LAUGHED AT WEEKS AGO ARE HIS OBSESSION NOW.
POPS
I'M NOT CRAZ
SCHOOL
UFO-SITES
I'M NOT CRAZ
I WAS ABDUCTED BY ALIEN BEIN
REALITY AND CREDIBILITY IN THE FACE OF THE IMPOSSIBLE.
BIO
DR. J. FAMA
MY ABDUCTION STORY:
HIS NEW SCIENCE OR HIS RELIGION EVEN.
POPS!

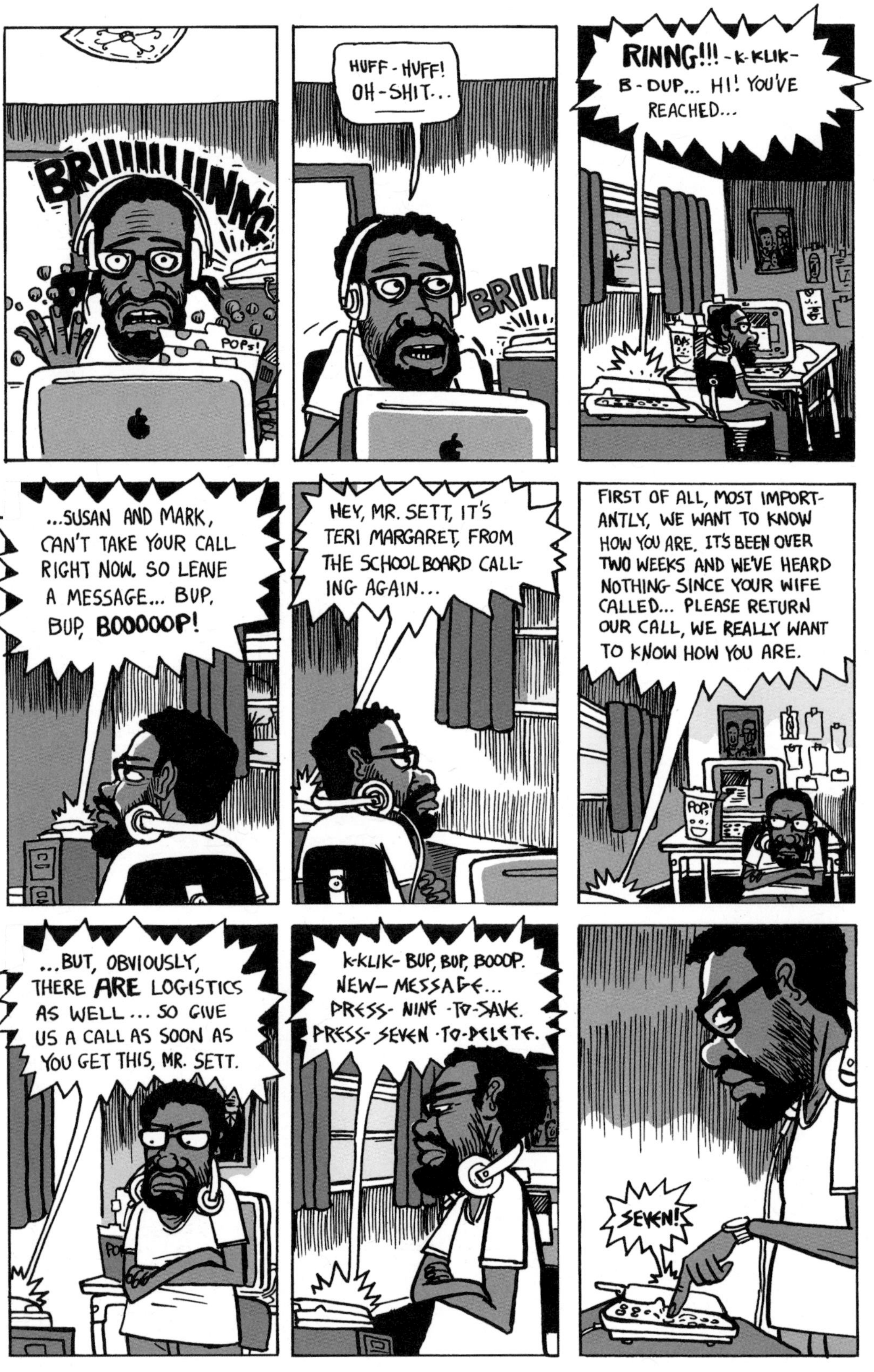
BRIIIIIIINNG
POPs!
HUFF-HUFF! OH-SHIT...
BRIIII
RINNG!!! -K-KLIK- B-DUP... HI! YOU'VE REACHED...
...SUSAN AND MARK, CAN'T TAKE YOUR CALL RIGHT NOW. SO LEAVE A MESSAGE... BUP, BUP, BOOOOOP!
HEY, MR. SETT, IT'S TERI MARGARET, FROM THE SCHOOLBOARD CALLING AGAIN...
FIRST OF ALL, MOST IMPORTANTLY, WE WANT TO KNOW HOW YOU ARE. IT'S BEEN OVER TWO WEEKS AND WE'VE HEARD NOTHING SINCE YOUR WIFE CALLED... PLEASE RETURN OUR CALL, WE REALLY WANT TO KNOW HOW YOU ARE.
...BUT, OBVIOUSLY, THERE ARE LOGISTICS AS WELL... SO GIVE US A CALL AS SOON AS YOU GET THIS, MR. SETT.
K-KLIK- BUP, BUP, BOOOP. NEW-MESSAGE... PRESS-NINE-TO-SAVE. PRESS-SEVEN-TO-DELETE.
SEVEN!

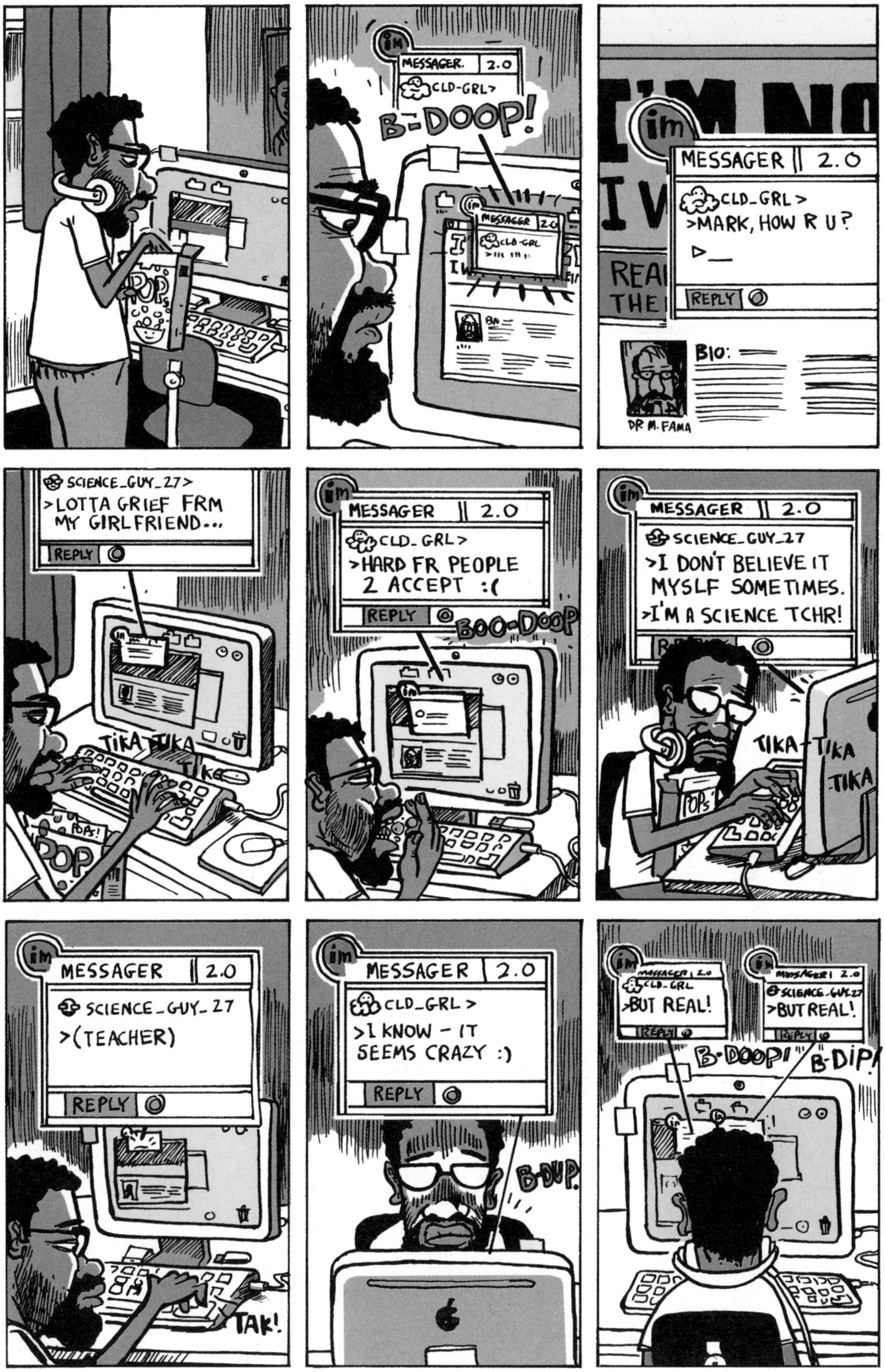
POPs
MESSAGER 2.0
CLD-GRL>
B-DOOP!
MESSAGER 2.0
CLD-GRL>
>MARK, HOW R U?
REPLY
BIO:
DR M. FAMA
SCIENCE_GUY_27>
>LOTTA GRIEF FRM MY GIRLFRIEND...
REPLY
TIKA TIKA TIKA
POPs!
MESSAGER 2.0
CLD_GRL>
>HARD FR PEOPLE 2 ACCEPT :(
REPLY
BOO-DOOP
MESSAGER 2.0
SCIENCE_GUY_27
>I DON'T BELIEVE IT MYSLF SOMETIMES.
>I'M A SCIENCE TCHR!
TIKA TIKA TIKA
POPs
MESSAGER 2.0
SCIENCE_GUY_27
>(TEACHER)
REPLY
TAK!
MESSAGER 2.0
CLD_GRL>
>I KNOW - IT SEEMS CRAZY :)
REPLY
B-DUP.
MESSAGER 2.0
CLD-GRL
>BUT REAL!
MESSAGER 2.0
SCIENCE-GUY27
>BUT REAL!
B-DOOP!
B-DIP!

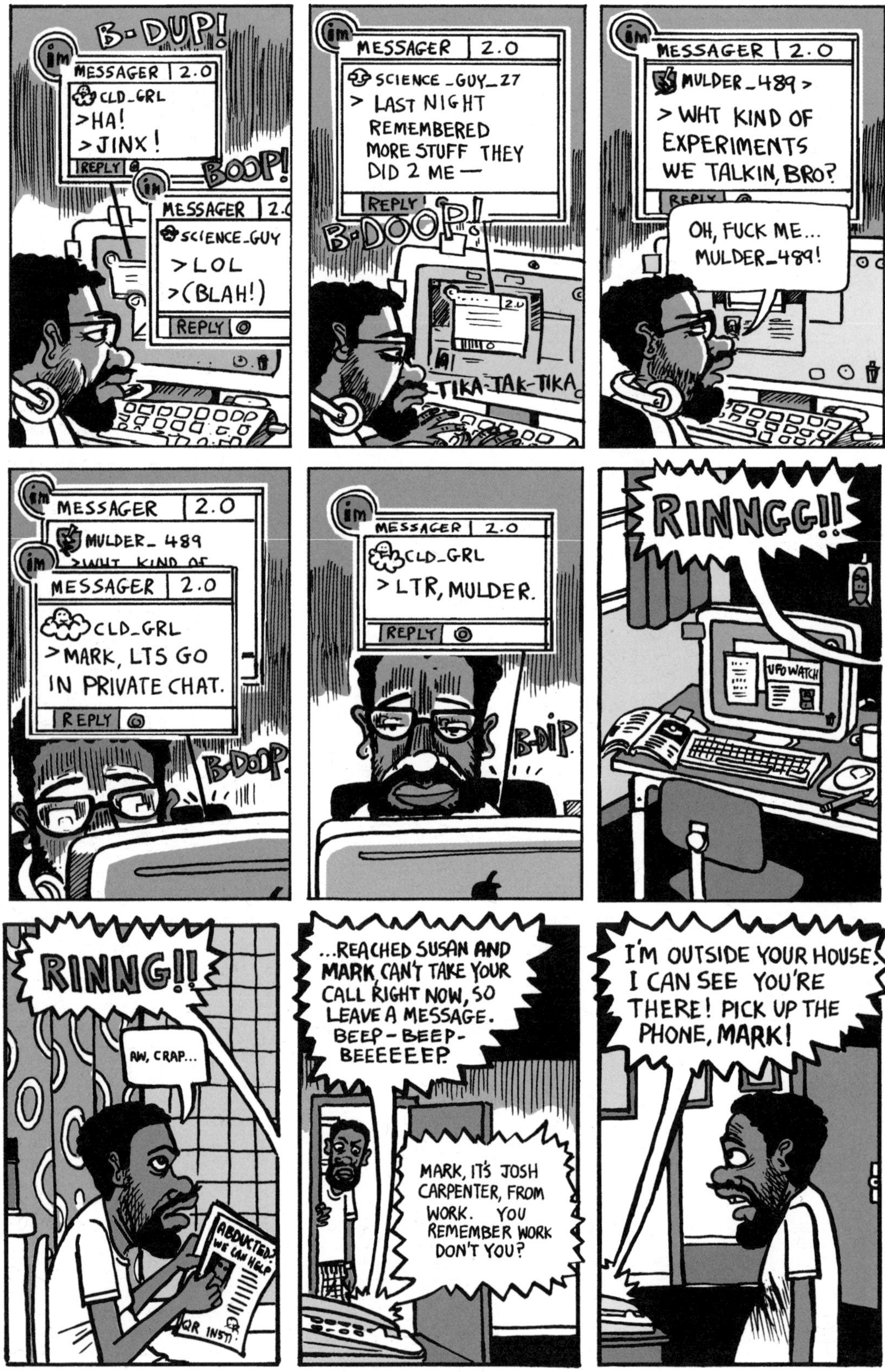
B-DUP!
MESSAGER 2.0
CLD_GRL
>HA!
>JINX!
REPLY
BOOP!
MESSAGER 2.0
SCIENCE_GUY
>LOL
>(BLAH!)
REPLY
MESSAGER 2.0
SCIENCE_GUY_27
> LAST NIGHT REMEMBERED MORE STUFF THEY DID 2 ME—
REPLY
B-DOOP!
TIKA-TAK-TIKA
MESSAGER 2.0
MULDER_489 >
> WHT KIND OF EXPERIMENTS WE TALKIN, BRO?
OH, FUCK ME... MULDER_489!
MESSAGER 2.0
MULDER_489
MESSAGER 2.0
CLD_GRL
>MARK, LTS GO IN PRIVATE CHAT.
REPLY
B-DOOP.
MESSAGER 2.0
CLD_GRL
>LTR, MULDER.
REPLY
B-DIP.
RINNGG!!
UFO WATCH
RINNG!!
AW, CRAP...
ABDUCTED? WE CAN HELP
QR INST.
...REACHED SUSAN AND MARK, CAN'T TAKE YOUR CALL RIGHT NOW, SO LEAVE A MESSAGE. BEEP-BEEP-BEEEEEEP.
MARK, IT'S JOSH CARPENTER, FROM WORK. YOU REMEMBER WORK DON'T YOU?
I'M OUTSIDE YOUR HOUSE. I CAN SEE YOU'RE THERE! PICK UP THE PHONE, MARK!

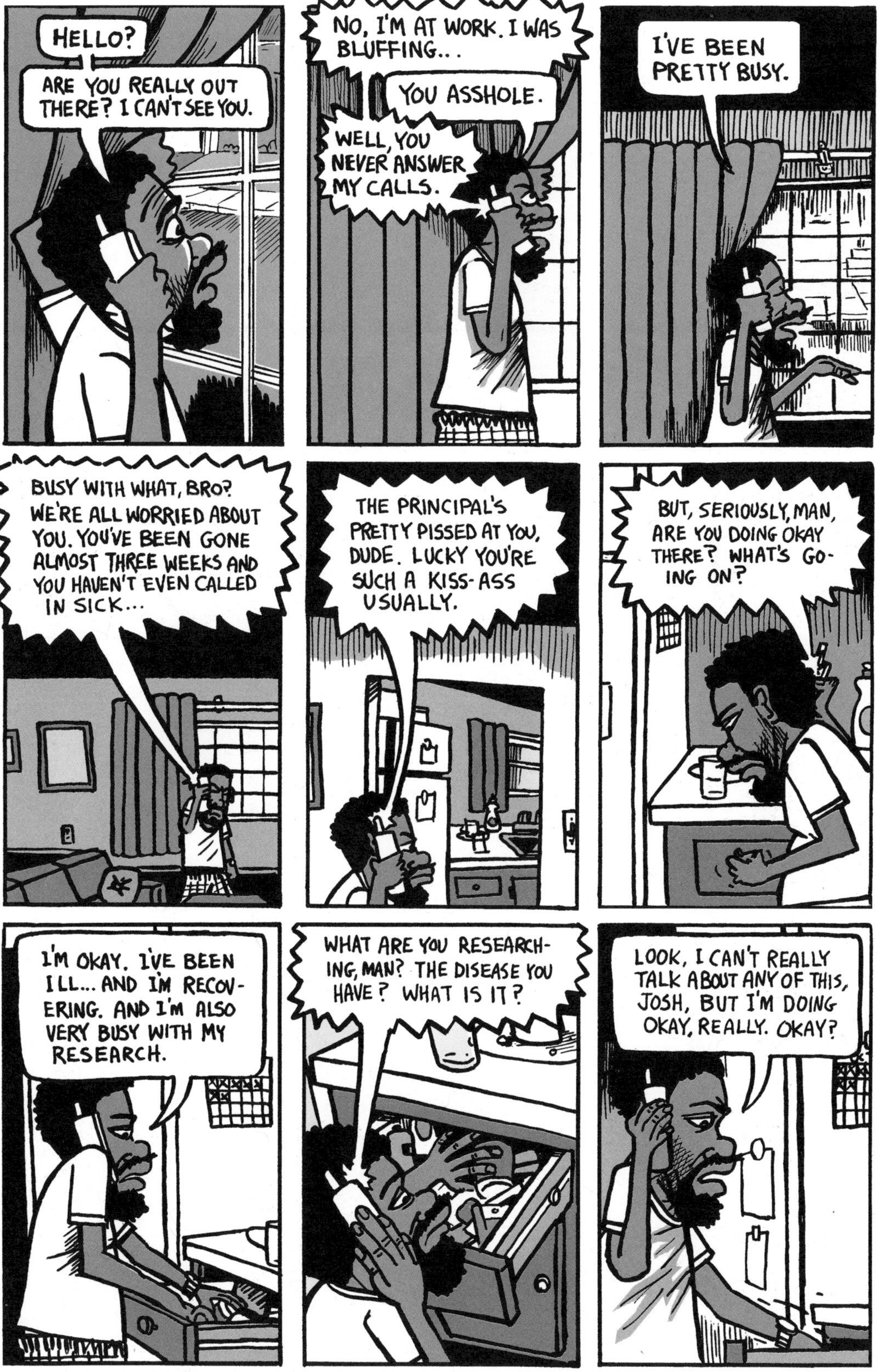
HELLO?
ARE YOU REALLY OUT THERE? I CAN'T SEE YOU.
NO, I'M AT WORK. I WAS BLUFFING...
YOU ASSHOLE.
WELL, YOU NEVER ANSWER MY CALLS.
I'VE BEEN PRETTY BUSY.
BUSY WITH WHAT, BRO? WE'RE ALL WORRIED ABOUT YOU. YOU'VE BEEN GONE ALMOST THREE WEEKS AND YOU HAVEN'T EVEN CALLED IN SICK...
THE PRINCIPAL'S PRETTY PISSED AT YOU, DUDE. LUCKY YOU'RE SUCH A KISS-ASS USUALLY.
BUT, SERIOUSLY, MAN, ARE YOU DOING OKAY THERE? WHAT'S GO-ING ON?
I'M OKAY. I'VE BEEN ILL... AND I'M RECOV-ERING. AND I'M ALSO VERY BUSY WITH MY RESEARCH.
WHAT ARE YOU RESEARCH-ING, MAN? THE DISEASE YOU HAVE? WHAT IS IT?
LOOK, I CAN'T REALLY TALK ABOUT ANY OF THIS, JOSH, BUT I'M DOING OKAY, REALLY. OKAY?

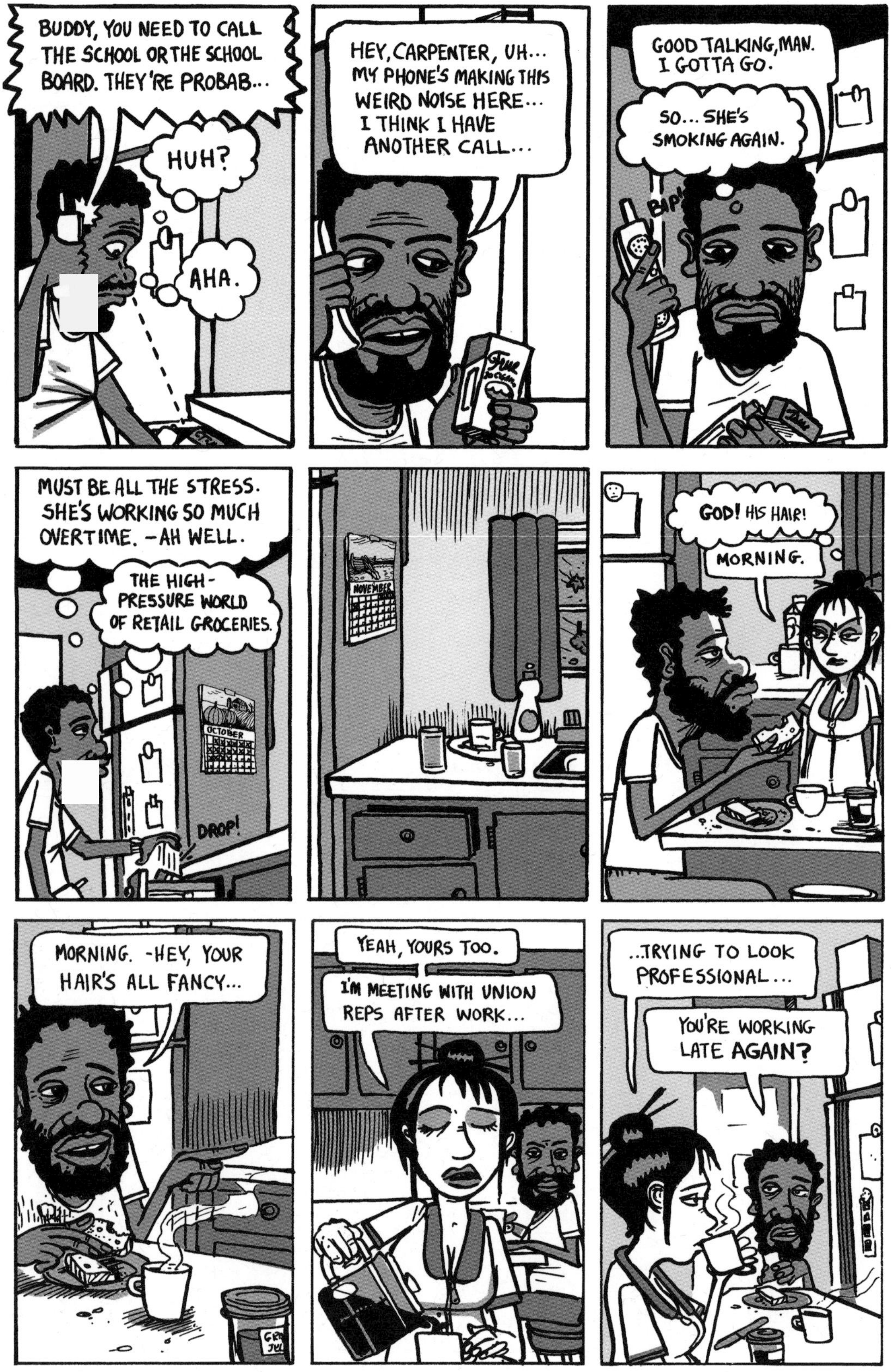

BUDDY, YOU NEED TO CALL THE SCHOOL OR THE SCHOOL BOARD. THEY'RE PROBAB...
HUH?
AHA.
HEY, CARPENTER, UH... MY PHONE'S MAKING THIS WEIRD NOISE HERE... I THINK I HAVE ANOTHER CALL...
GOOD TALKING, MAN. I GOTTA GO.
SO... SHE'S SMOKING AGAIN.
MUST BE ALL THE STRESS. SHE'S WORKING SO MUCH OVERTIME. -AH WELL.
THE HIGH-PRESSURE WORLD OF RETAIL GROCERIES.
OCTOBER
DROP!
NOVEMBER
GOD! HIS HAIR!
MORNING.
MORNING. -HEY, YOUR HAIR'S ALL FANCY...
YEAH, YOURS TOO.
I'M MEETING WITH UNION REPS AFTER WORK...
...TRYING TO LOOK PROFESSIONAL...
YOU'RE WORKING LATE AGAIN?

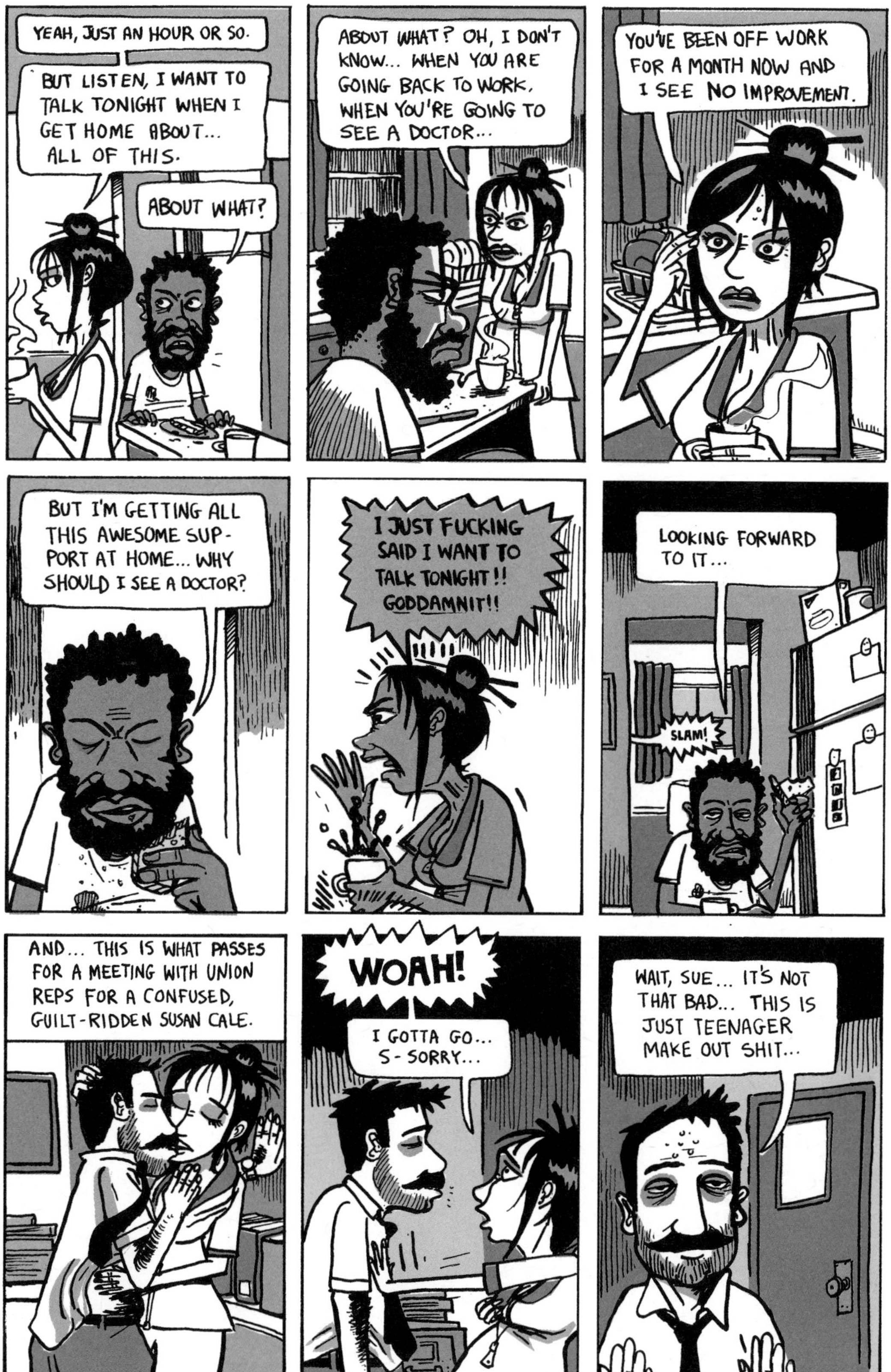
YEAH, JUST AN HOUR OR SO.
BUT LISTEN, I WANT TO TALK TONIGHT WHEN I GET HOME ABOUT... ALL OF THIS.
ABOUT WHAT?
ABOUT WHAT? OH, I DON'T KNOW... WHEN YOU ARE GOING BACK TO WORK, WHEN YOU'RE GOING TO SEE A DOCTOR...
YOU'VE BEEN OFF WORK FOR A MONTH NOW AND I SEE NO IMPROVEMENT.
BUT I'M GETTING ALL THIS AWESOME SUP-PORT AT HOME... WHY SHOULD I SEE A DOCTOR?
I JUST FUCKING SAID I WANT TO TALK TONIGHT!! GODDAMNIT!!
LOOKING FORWARD TO IT...
SLAM!
AND... THIS IS WHAT PASSES FOR A MEETING WITH UNION REPS FOR A CONFUSED, GUILT-RIDDEN SUSAN CALE.
WOAH!
I GOTTA GO... S-SORRY...
WAIT, SUE... IT'S NOT THAT BAD... THIS IS JUST TEENAGER MAKE OUT SHIT...

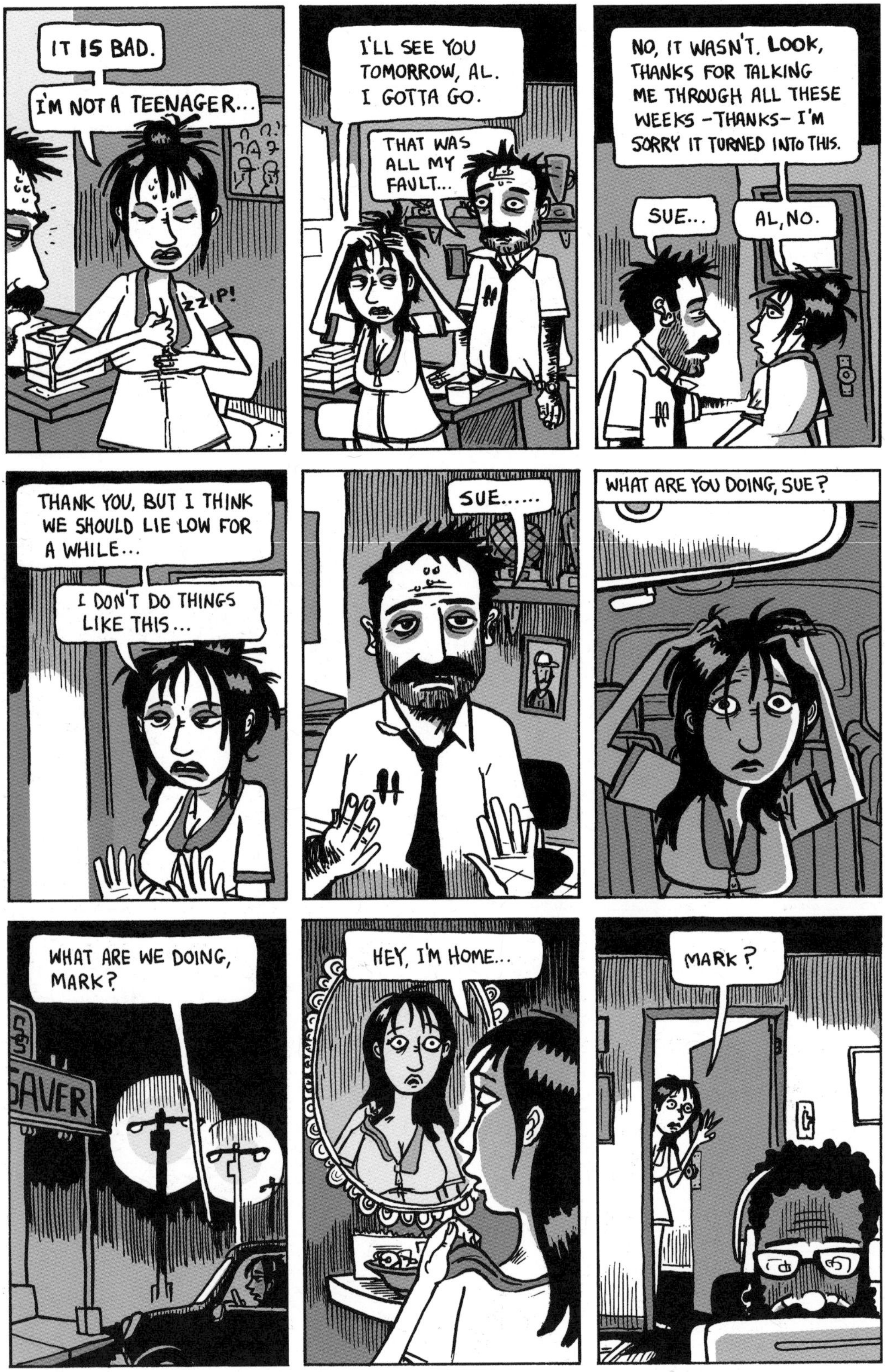
IT IS BAD.
I'M NOT A TEENAGER...
ZZIP!
I'LL SEE YOU TOMORROW, AL. I GOTTA GO.
THAT WAS ALL MY FAULT...
NO, IT WASN'T. LOOK, THANKS FOR TALKING ME THROUGH ALL THESE WEEKS -THANKS- I'M SORRY IT TURNED INTO THIS.
SUE..
AL, NO.
THANK YOU, BUT I THINK WE SHOULD LIE LOW FOR A WHILE...
I DON'T DO THINGS LIKE THIS...
SUE......
WHAT ARE YOU DOING, SUE?
WHAT ARE WE DOING, MARK?
SAVER
HEY, I'M HOME...
MARK?

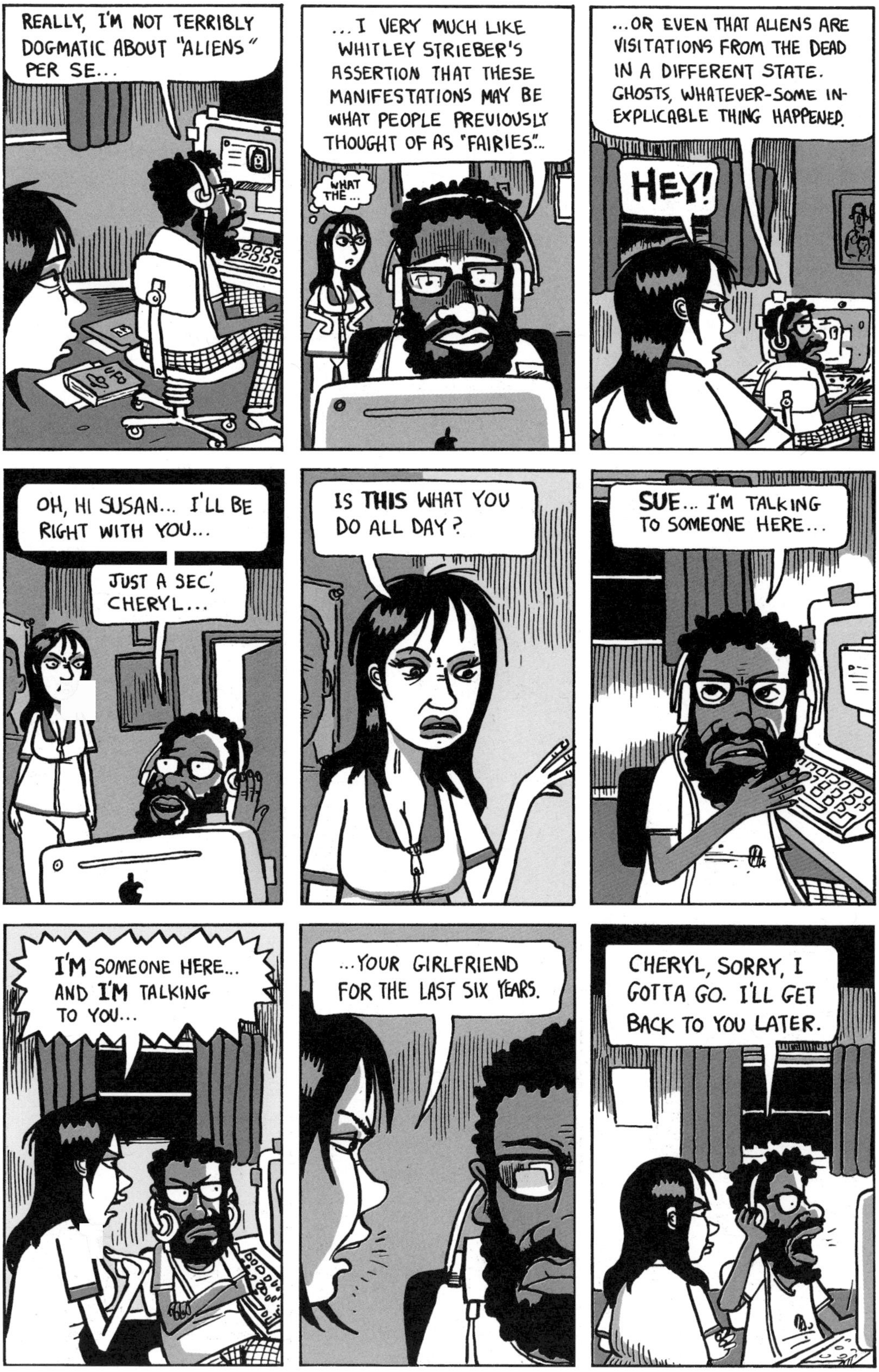
REALLY, I'M NOT TERRIBLY DOGMATIC ABOUT "ALIENS" PER SE...
...I VERY MUCH LIKE WHITLEY STRIEBER'S ASSERTION THAT THESE MANIFESTATIONS MAY BE WHAT PEOPLE PREVIOUSLY THOUGHT OF AS "FAIRIES"...
WHAT THE...
...OR EVEN THAT ALIENS ARE VISITATIONS FROM THE DEAD IN A DIFFERENT STATE. GHOSTS, WHATEVER-SOME INEXPLICABLE THING HAPPENED.
HEY!
OH, HI SUSAN... I'LL BE RIGHT WITH YOU...
JUST A SEC', CHERYL...
IS THIS WHAT YOU DO ALL DAY?
SUE... I'M TALKING TO SOMEONE HERE...
I'M SOMEONE HERE... AND I'M TALKING TO YOU...
...YOUR GIRLFRIEND FOR THE LAST SIX YEARS.
CHERYL, SORRY, I GOTTA GO. I'LL GET BACK TO YOU LATER.

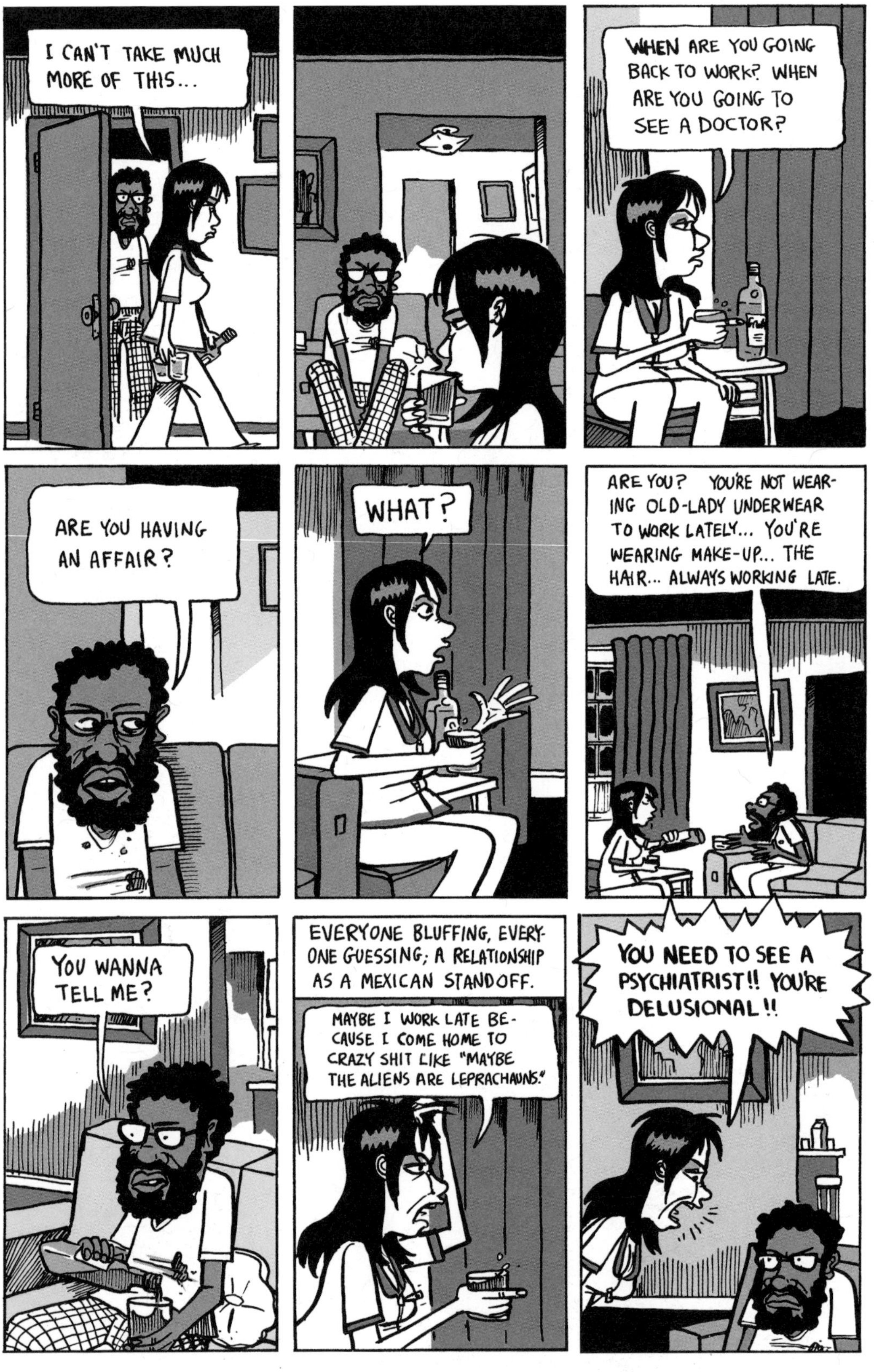
I CAN'T TAKE MUCH MORE OF THIS...
WHEN ARE YOU GOING BACK TO WORK? WHEN ARE YOU GOING TO SEE A DOCTOR?
ARE YOU HAVING AN AFFAIR?
WHAT?
ARE YOU? YOU'RE NOT WEARING OLD-LADY UNDERWEAR TO WORK LATELY... YOU'RE WEARING MAKE-UP... THE HAIR... ALWAYS WORKING LATE.
YOU WANNA TELL ME?
EVERYONE BLUFFING, EVERYONE GUESSING; A RELATIONSHIP AS A MEXICAN STANDOFF.
MAYBE I WORK LATE BECAUSE I COME HOME TO CRAZY SHIT LIKE "MAYBE THE ALIENS ARE LEPRACHAUNS."
YOU NEED TO SEE A PSYCHIATRIST!! YOU'RE DELUSIONAL!!

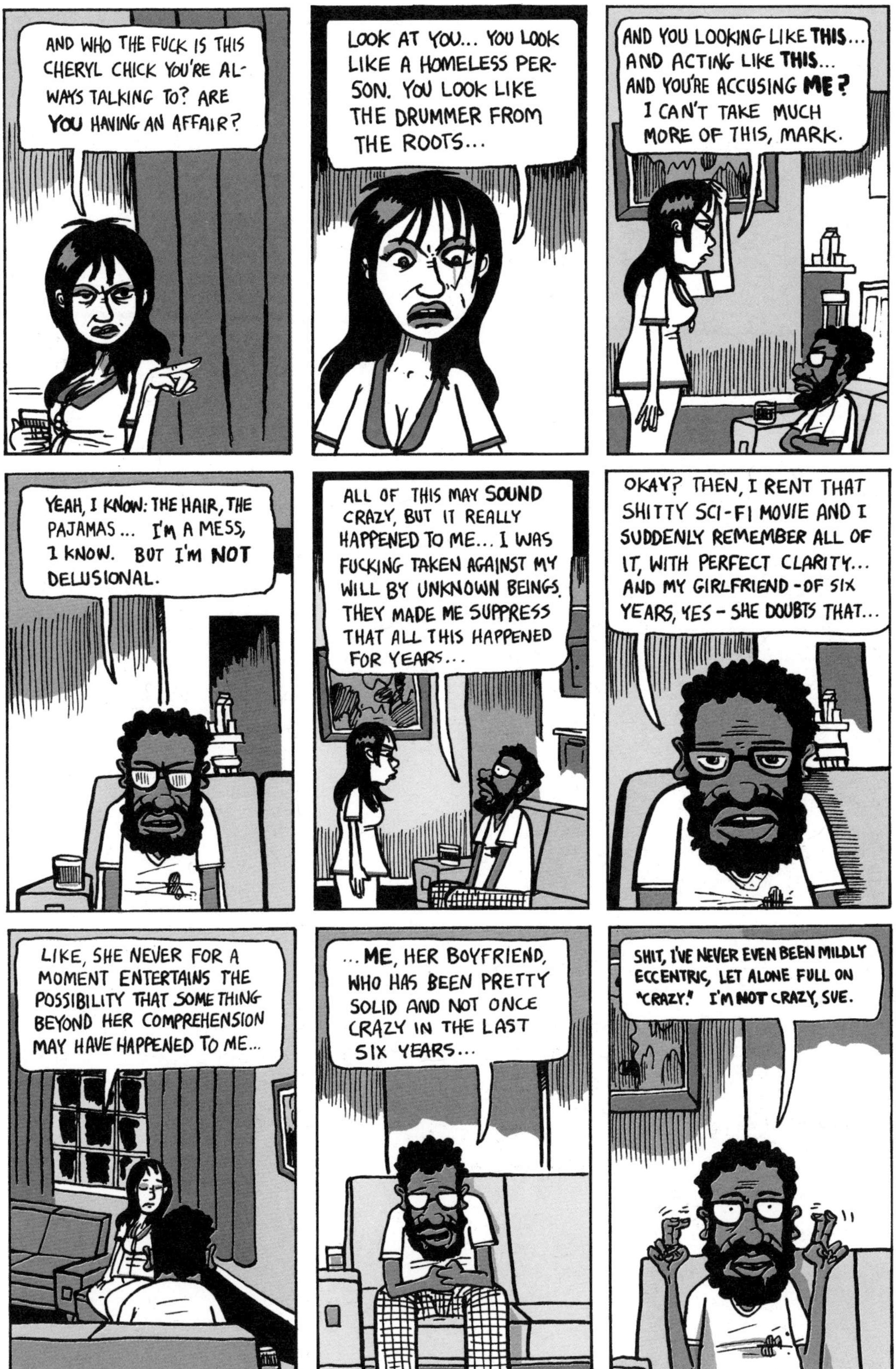
AND WHO THE FUCK IS THIS CHERYL CHICK YOU'RE AL-WAYS TALKING TO? ARE YOU HAVING AN AFFAIR?
LOOK AT YOU... YOU LOOK LIKE A HOMELESS PER-SON. YOU LOOK LIKE THE DRUMMER FROM THE ROOTS...
AND YOU LOOKING LIKE THIS... AND ACTING LIKE THIS... AND YOU'RE ACCUSING ME? I CAN'T TAKE MUCH MORE OF THIS, MARK.
YEAH, I KNOW: THE HAIR, THE PAJAMAS... I'M A MESS, I KNOW. BUT I'M NOT DELUSIONAL.
ALL OF THIS MAY SOUND CRAZY, BUT IT REALLY HAPPENED TO ME... I WAS FUCKING TAKEN AGAINST MY WILL BY UNKNOWN BEINGS. THEY MADE ME SUPPRESS THAT ALL THIS HAPPENED FOR YEARS...
OKAY? THEN, I RENT THAT SHITTY SCI-FI MOVIE AND I SUDDENLY REMEMBER ALL OF IT, WITH PERFECT CLARITY... AND MY GIRLFRIEND - OF SIX YEARS, YES - SHE DOUBTS THAT...
LIKE, SHE NEVER FOR A MOMENT ENTERTAINS THE POSSIBILITY THAT SOMETHING BEYOND HER COMPREHENSION MAY HAVE HAPPENED TO ME...
...ME, HER BOYFRIEND, WHO HAS BEEN PRETTY SOLID AND NOT ONCE CRAZY IN THE LAST SIX YEARS...
SHIT, I'VE NEVER EVEN BEEN MILDLY ECCENTRIC, LET ALONE FULL ON "CRAZY." I'M NOT CRAZY, SUE.

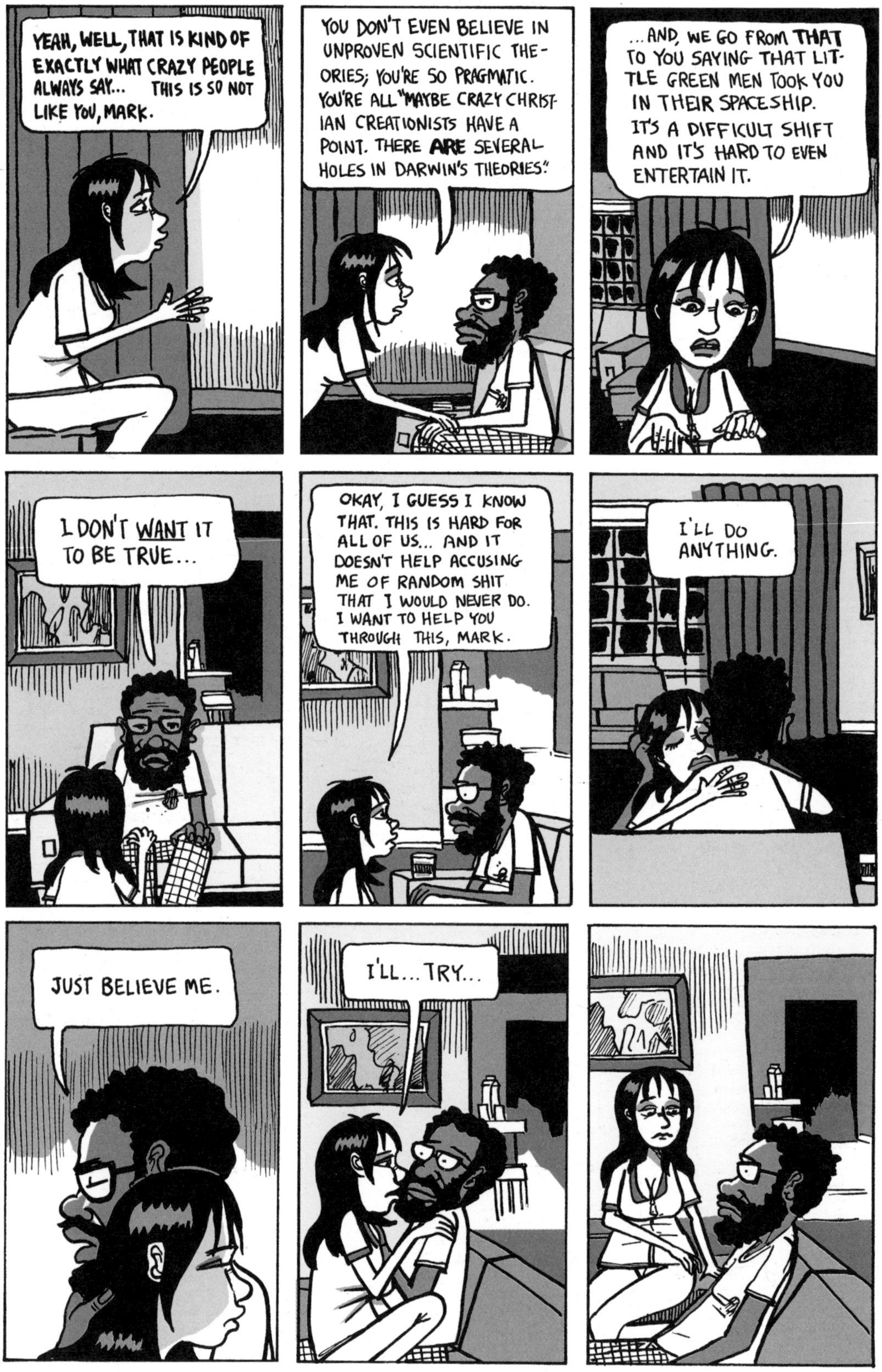
YEAH, WELL, THAT IS KIND OF EXACTLY WHAT CRAZY PEOPLE ALWAYS SAY... THIS IS SO NOT LIKE YOU, MARK.
YOU DON'T EVEN BELIEVE IN UNPROVEN SCIENTIFIC THEORIES; YOU'RE SO PRAGMATIC. YOU'RE ALL "MAYBE CRAZY CHRISTIAN CREATIONISTS HAVE A POINT. THERE ARE SEVERAL HOLES IN DARWIN'S THEORIES."
...AND, WE GO FROM THAT TO YOU SAYING THAT LITTLE GREEN MEN TOOK YOU IN THEIR SPACESHIP. IT'S A DIFFICULT SHIFT AND IT'S HARD TO EVEN ENTERTAIN IT.
I DON'T WANT IT TO BE TRUE...
OKAY, I GUESS I KNOW THAT. THIS IS HARD FOR ALL OF US... AND IT DOESN'T HELP ACCUSING ME OF RANDOM SHIT THAT I WOULD NEVER DO. I WANT TO HELP YOU THROUGH THIS, MARK.
I'LL DO ANYTHING.
JUST BELIEVE ME.
I'LL... TRY...

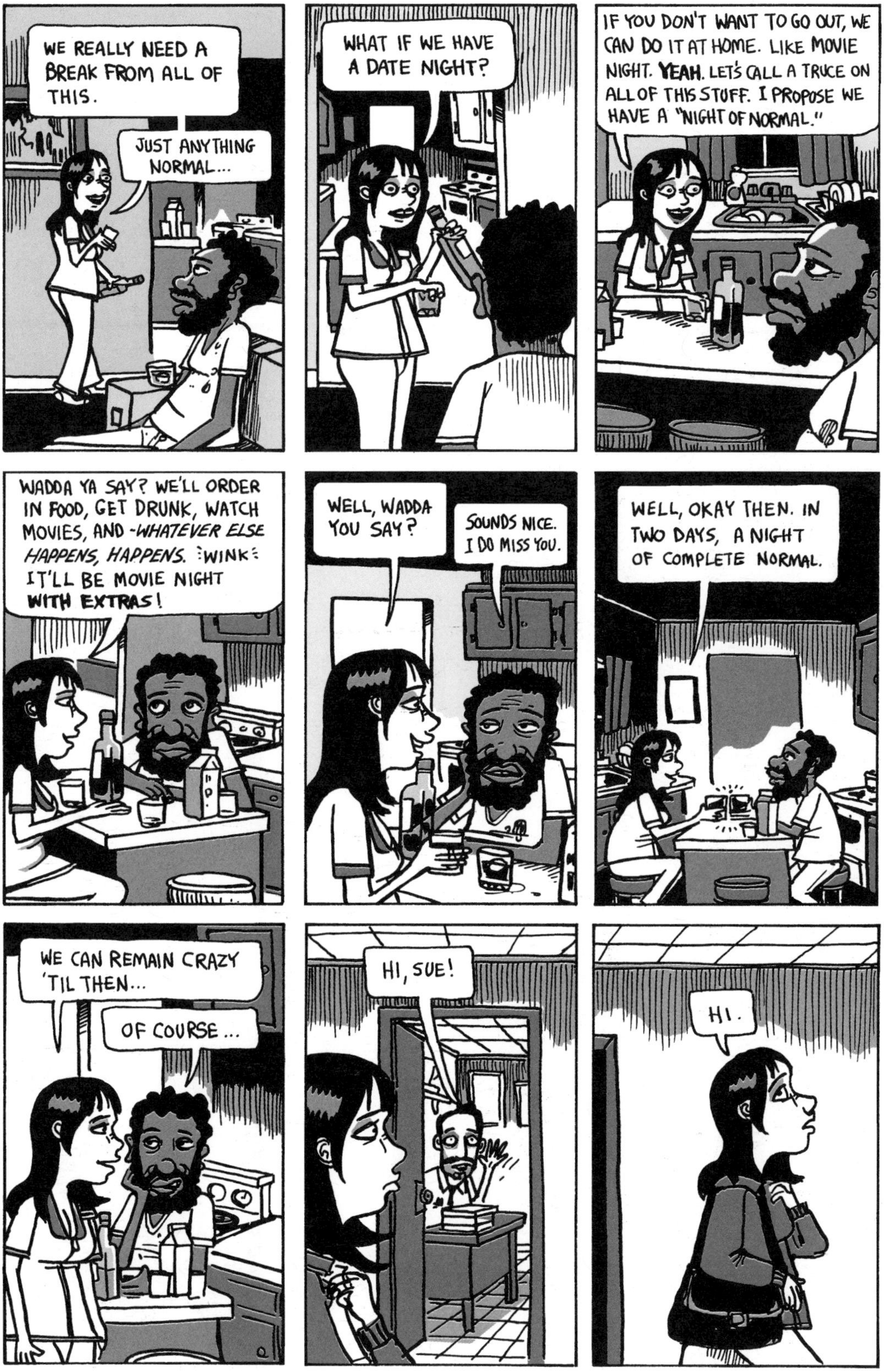
WE REALLY NEED A BREAK FROM ALL OF THIS.
JUST ANYTHING NORMAL...
WHAT IF WE HAVE A DATE NIGHT?
IF YOU DON'T WANT TO GO OUT, WE CAN DO IT AT HOME. LIKE MOVIE NIGHT. YEAH. LET'S CALL A TRUCE ON ALL OF THIS STUFF. I PROPOSE WE HAVE A "NIGHT OF NORMAL."
WADDA YA SAY? WE'LL ORDER IN FOOD, GET DRUNK, WATCH MOVIES, AND -WHATEVER ELSE HAPPENS, HAPPENS. WINK IT'LL BE MOVIE NIGHT WITH EXTRAS!
WELL, WADDA YOU SAY?
SOUNDS NICE. I DO MISS YOU.
WELL, OKAY THEN. IN TWO DAYS, A NIGHT OF COMPLETE NORMAL.
WE CAN REMAIN CRAZY 'TIL THEN...
OF COURSE...
HI, SUE!
HI.

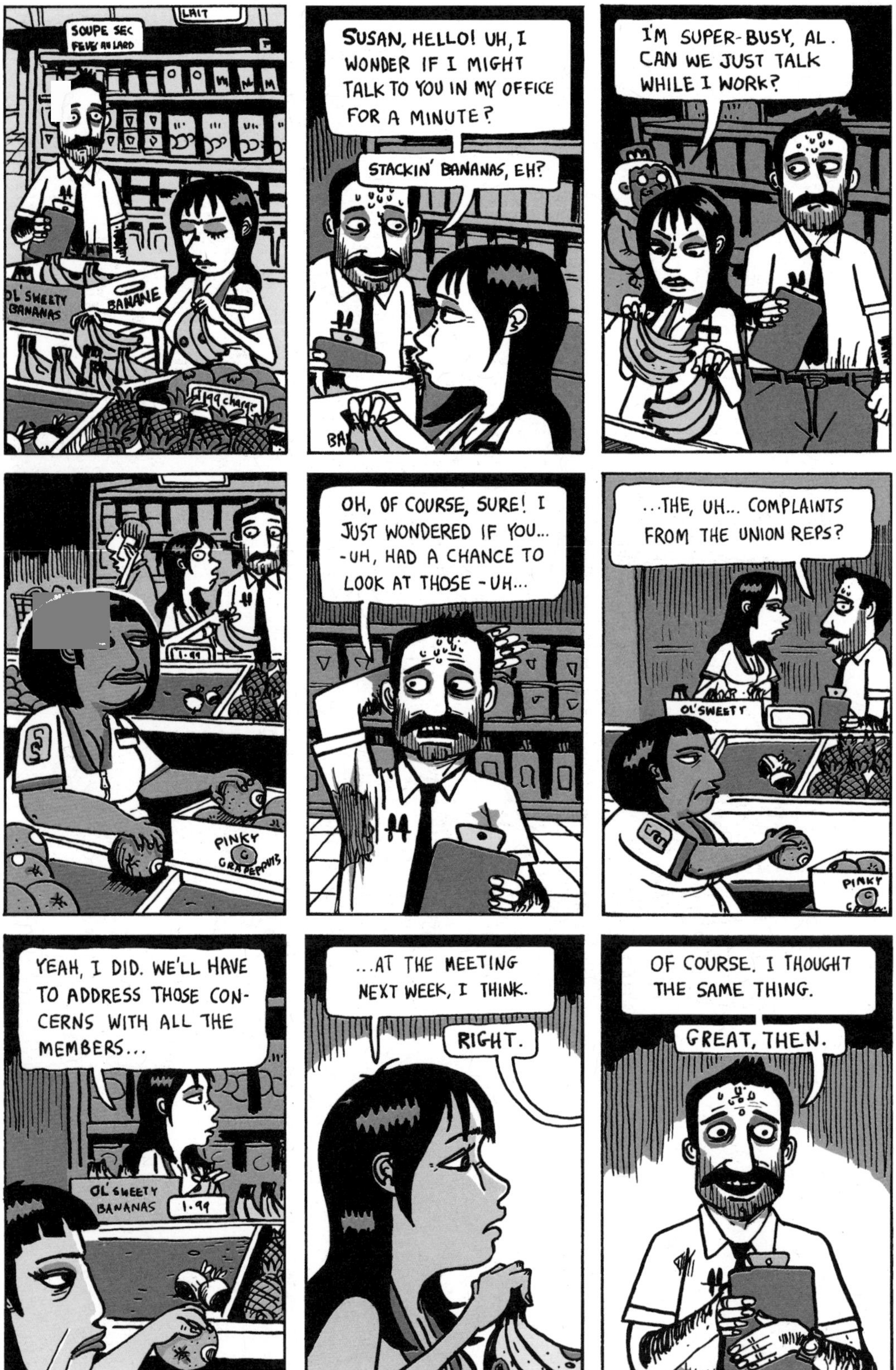
LAIT
SOUPE SEC
OL' SWEETY BANANAS
BANANE
SUSAN, HELLO! UH, I WONDER IF I MIGHT TALK TO YOU IN MY OFFICE FOR A MINUTE?
STACKIN' BANANAS, EH?
I'M SUPER-BUSY, AL. CAN WE JUST TALK WHILE I WORK?
PINKY GRAPEFRUITS
OH, OF COURSE, SURE! I JUST WONDERED IF YOU... -UH, HAD A CHANCE TO LOOK AT THOSE -UH...
...THE, UH... COMPLAINTS FROM THE UNION REPS?
OL' SWEETY
PINKY
YEAH, I DID. WE'LL HAVE TO ADDRESS THOSE CON-CERNS WITH ALL THE MEMBERS...
OL' SWEETY BANANAS
1.99
...AT THE MEETING NEXT WEEK, I THINK.
RIGHT.
OF COURSE. I THOUGHT THE SAME THING.
GREAT, THEN.

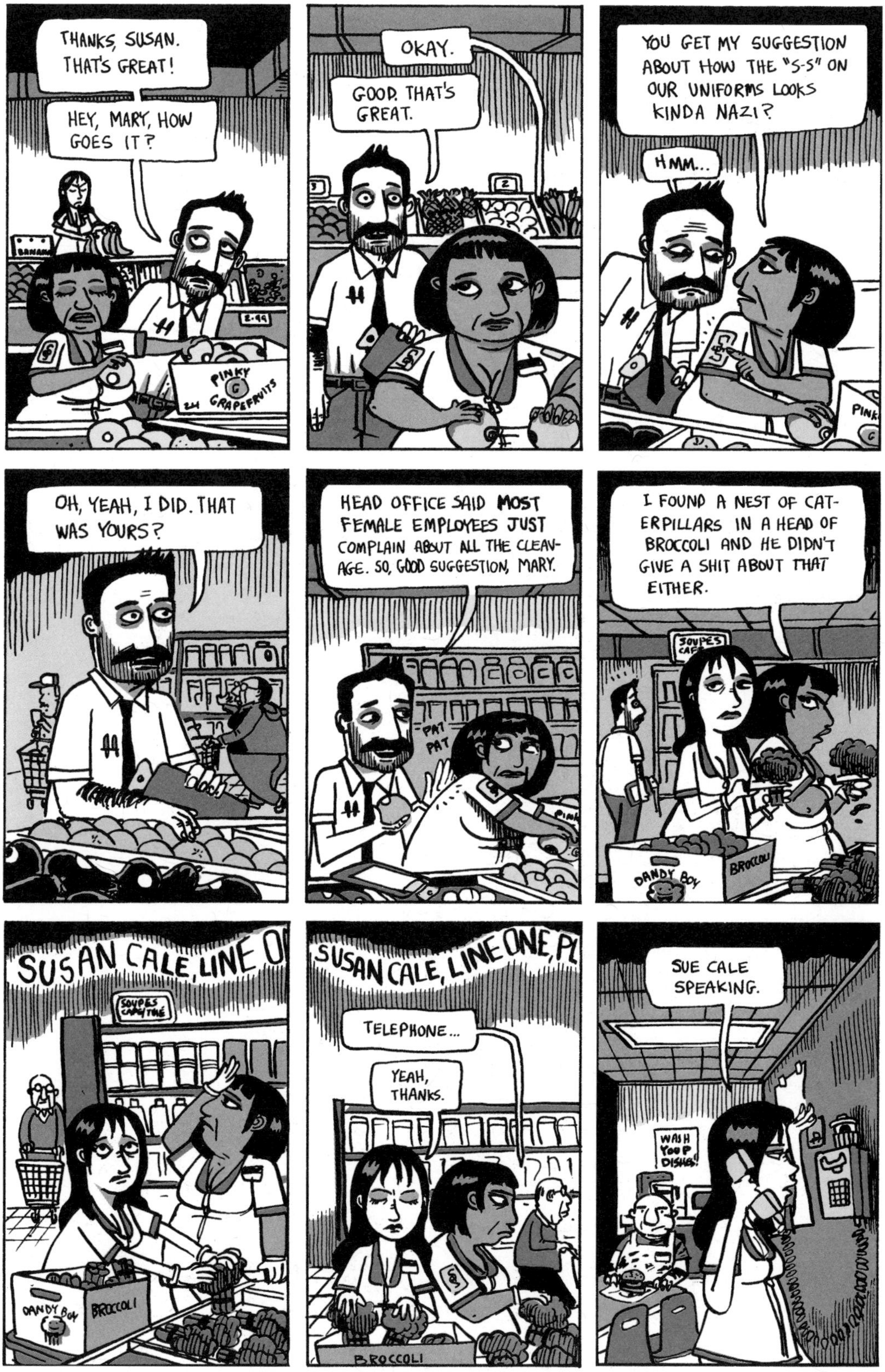
THANKS, SUSAN. THAT'S GREAT!
HEY, MARY, HOW GOES IT?
PINKY GRAPEFRUITS
2.99
OKAY.
GOOD. THAT'S GREAT.
YOU GET MY SUGGESTION ABOUT HOW THE "S-S" ON OUR UNIFORMS LOOKS KINDA NAZI?
HMM...
OH, YEAH, I DID. THAT WAS YOURS?
HEAD OFFICE SAID MOST FEMALE EMPLOYEES JUST COMPLAIN ABOUT ALL THE CLEAVAGE. SO, GOOD SUGGESTION, MARY.
PAT PAT
I FOUND A NEST OF CATERPILLARS IN A HEAD OF BROCCOLI AND HE DIDN'T GIVE A SHIT ABOUT THAT EITHER.
DANDY BOY
BROCCOLI
SUSAN CALE, LINE O
SUSAN CALE, LINE ONE, PL
TELEPHONE...
YEAH, THANKS.
BROCCOLI
SUE CALE SPEAKING.
WASH YOUR DISHES!

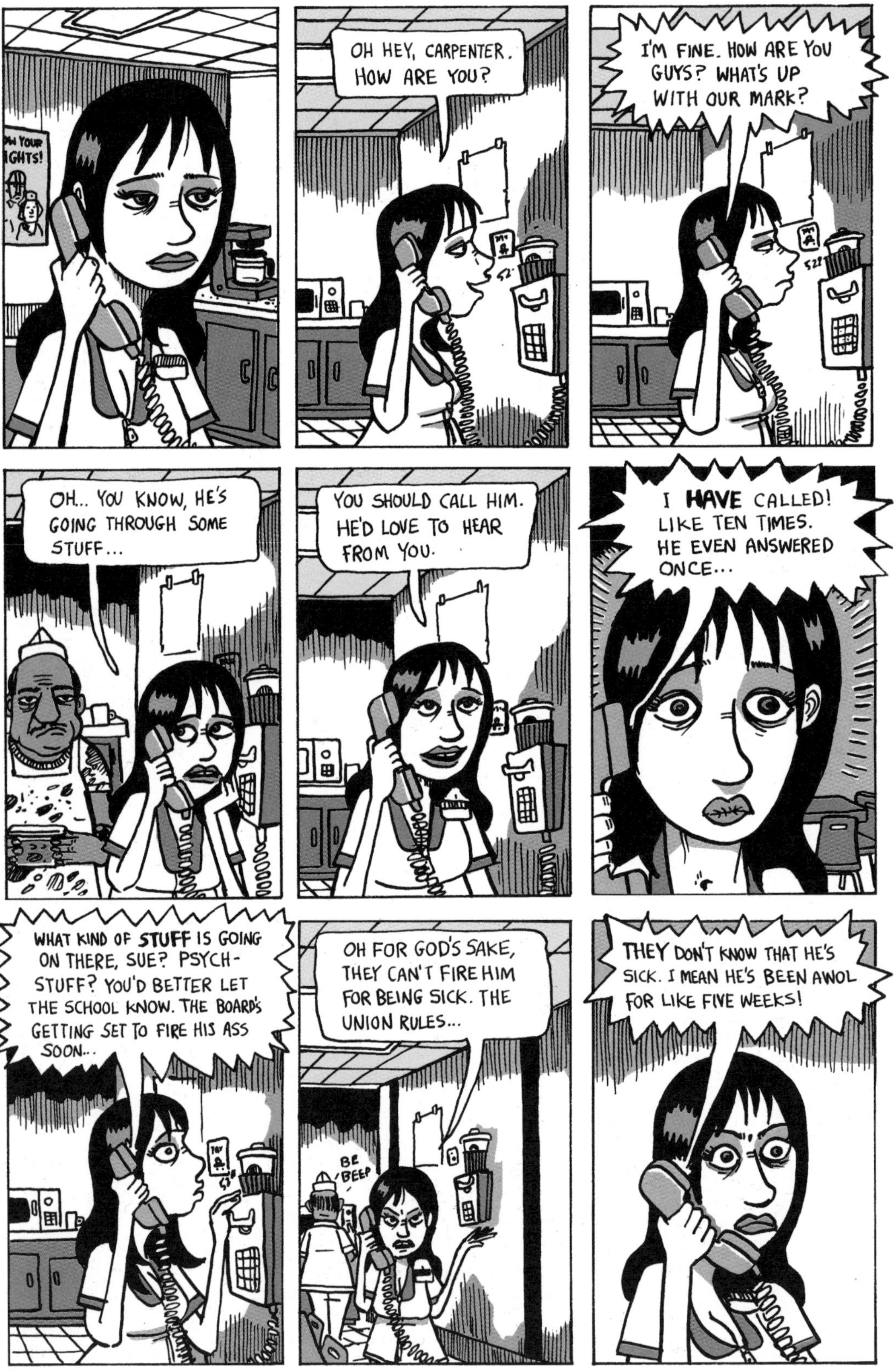

OW YOUR
IGHTS!
OH HEY, CARPENTER. HOW ARE YOU?
I'M FINE. HOW ARE YOU GUYS? WHAT'S UP WITH OUR MARK?
OH... YOU KNOW, HE'S GOING THROUGH SOME STUFF...
YOU SHOULD CALL HIM. HE'D LOVE TO HEAR FROM YOU.
I **HAVE** CALLED! LIKE TEN TIMES. HE EVEN ANSWERED ONCE...
WHAT KIND OF **STUFF** IS GOING ON THERE, SUE? PSYCH-STUFF? YOU'D BETTER LET THE SCHOOL KNOW. THE BOARD'S GETTING SET TO FIRE HIS ASS SOON...
OH FOR GOD'S SAKE, THEY CAN'T FIRE HIM FOR BEING SICK. THE UNION RULES...
BE BEEP
THEY DON'T KNOW THAT HE'S SICK. I MEAN HE'S BEEN AWOL FOR LIKE FIVE WEEKS!

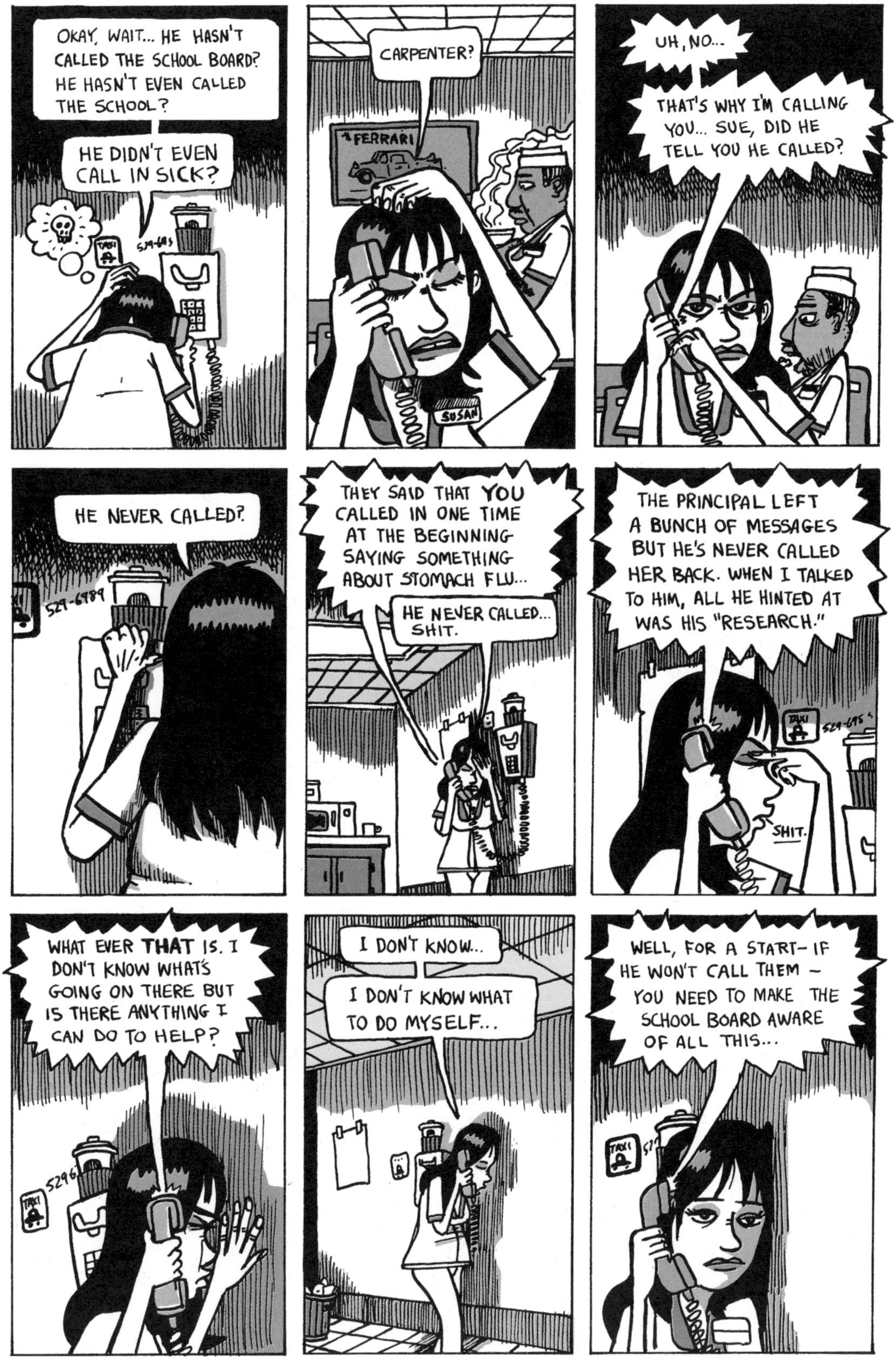

OKAY, WAIT... HE HASN'T CALLED THE SCHOOL BOARD? HE HASN'T EVEN CALLED THE SCHOOL?
HE DIDN'T EVEN CALL IN SICK?
TAXI
CARPENTER?
FERRARI
SUSAN
UH, NO...
THAT'S WHY I'M CALLING YOU... SUE, DID HE TELL YOU HE CALLED?
HE NEVER CALLED?
529-6789
THEY SAID THAT YOU CALLED IN ONE TIME AT THE BEGINNING SAYING SOMETHING ABOUT STOMACH FLU...
HE NEVER CALLED... SHIT.
THE PRINCIPAL LEFT A BUNCH OF MESSAGES BUT HE'S NEVER CALLED HER BACK. WHEN I TALKED TO HIM, ALL HE HINTED AT WAS HIS "RESEARCH."
TAXI
SHIT.
WHAT EVER THAT IS. I DON'T KNOW WHAT'S GOING ON THERE BUT IS THERE ANYTHING I CAN DO TO HELP?
TAXI
I DON'T KNOW...
I DON'T KNOW WHAT TO DO MYSELF...
WELL, FOR A START- IF HE WON'T CALL THEM - YOU NEED TO MAKE THE SCHOOL BOARD AWARE OF ALL THIS...
TAXI

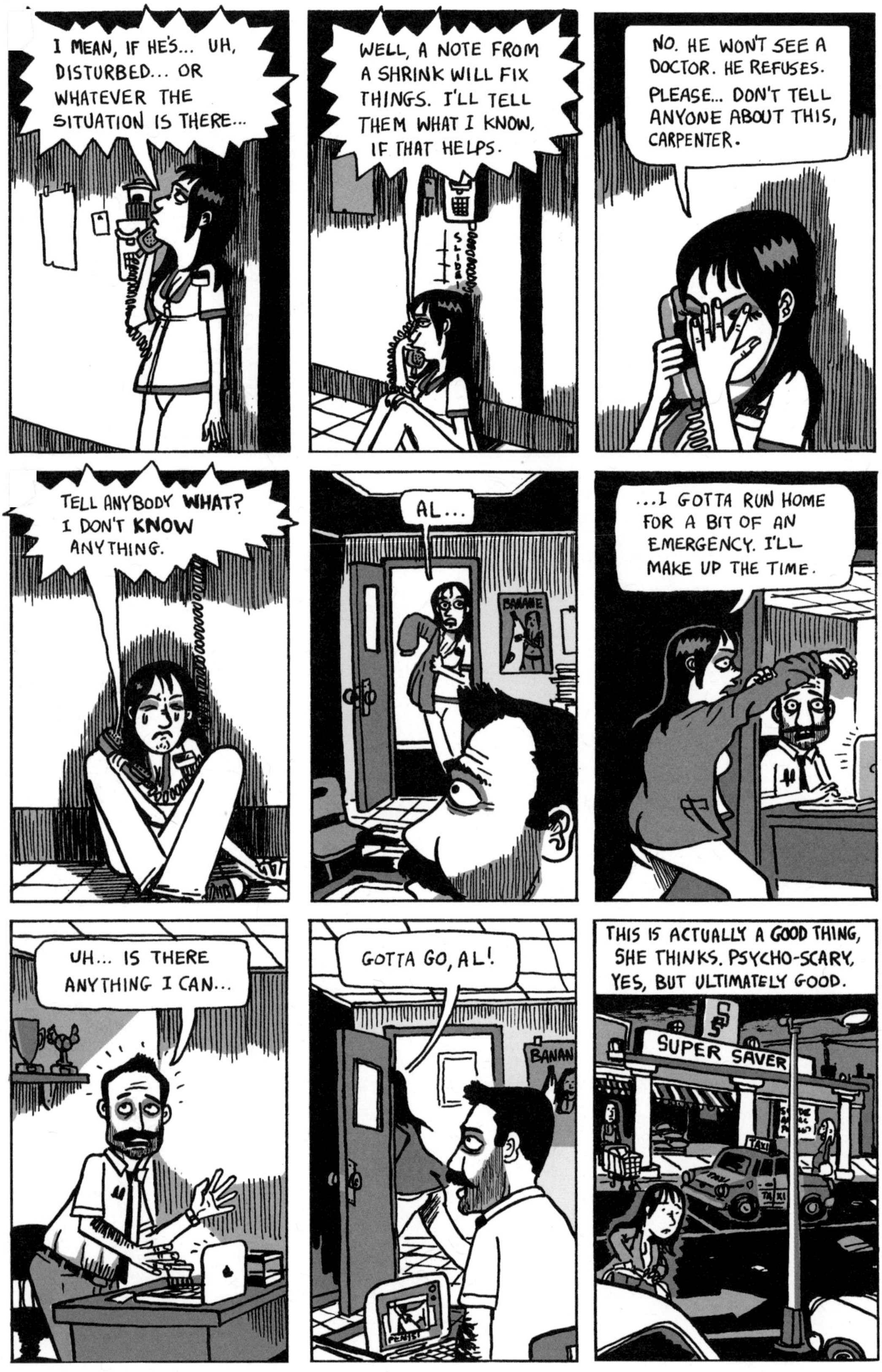
I MEAN, IF HE'S... UH, DISTURBED... OR WHATEVER THE SITUATION IS THERE...
WELL, A NOTE FROM A SHRINK WILL FIX THINGS. I'LL TELL THEM WHAT I KNOW, IF THAT HELPS.
SLIDE
NO. HE WON'T SEE A DOCTOR. HE REFUSES.
PLEASE... DON'T TELL ANYONE ABOUT THIS, CARPENTER.
TELL ANYBODY **WHAT**? I DON'T **KNOW** ANYTHING.
AL...
BANANE
...I GOTTA RUN HOME FOR A BIT OF AN EMERGENCY. I'LL MAKE UP THE TIME.
UH... IS THERE ANYTHING I CAN...
GOTTA GO, AL!
BANAN
THIS IS ACTUALLY A **GOOD** THING, SHE THINKS. PSYCHO-SCARY, YES, BUT ULTIMATELY GOOD.
SUPER SAVER
TAXI

...MARK?

-KLIMT!

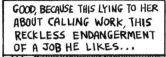

GOOD, BECAUSE THIS LYING TO HER ABOUT CALLING WORK, THIS RECKLESS ENDANGERMENT OF A JOB HE LIKES...

IT'S ALL BEHAVIOUR THAT IS PRETTY MUCH UNDENIABLY, CATEGORICALLY THE BEHAVIOUR OF SOMEONE IN NEED OF PSYCHOLOGICAL EVALUATION.

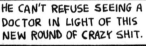

HE CAN'T REFUSE SEEING A DOCTOR IN LIGHT OF THIS NEW ROUND OF CRAZY SHIT.

MARK!

OH, JESUS, IS THIS SOME MORE SPACE MAN BULL-SHIT, MARK?

'CAUSE I'M GETTING SICK TO DEATH OF THIS.

SUE! Y-YOU'RE... WHY ARE YOU HOME EARLY?

YOU NEVER CALLED IN TO YOUR WORK... DID YOU?

NO.

KLAK

AND YOU TRY TO ACCUSE **ME** OF LYING AND CHEATING.

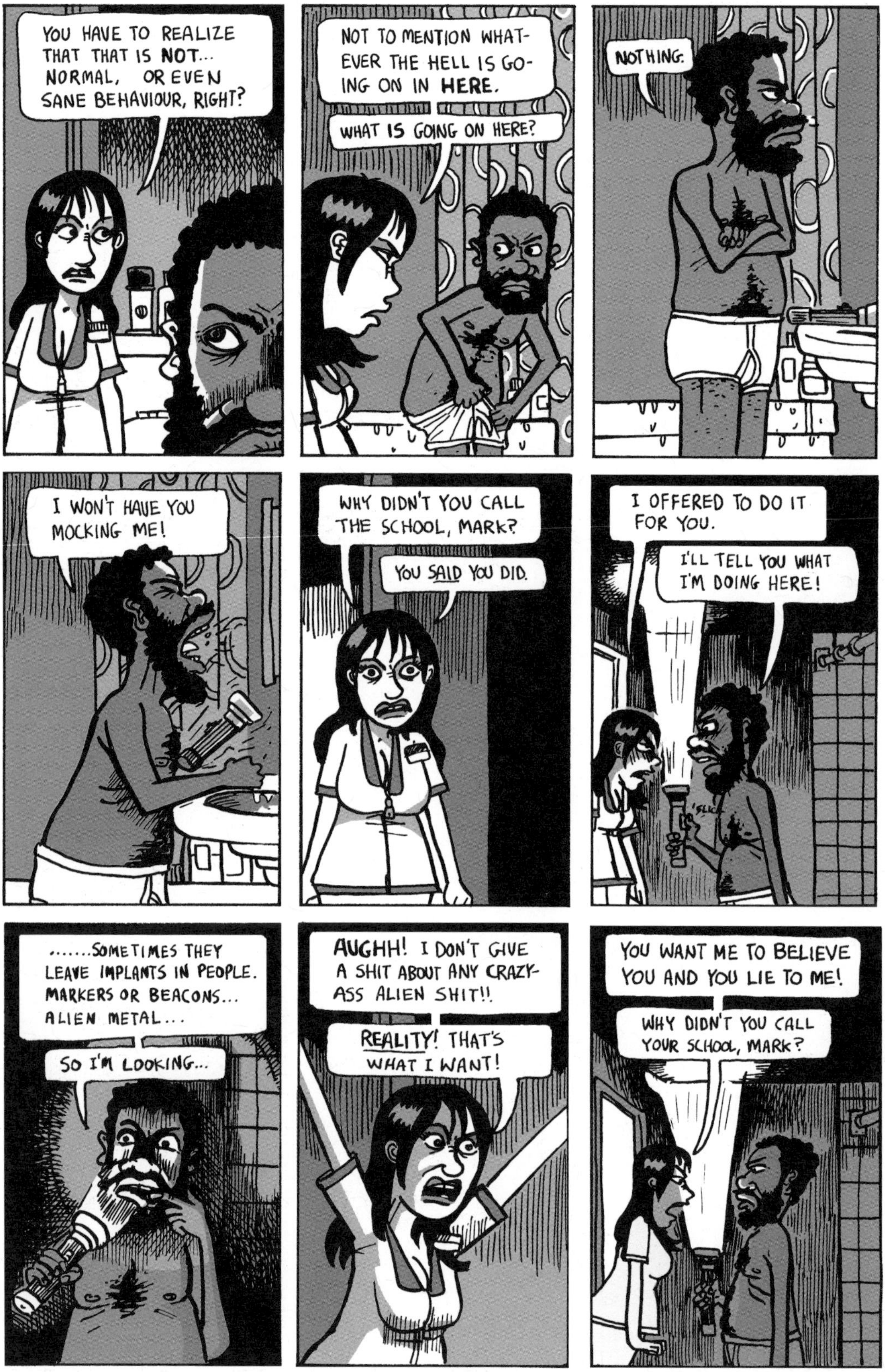
YOU HAVE TO REALIZE THAT THAT IS NOT... NORMAL, OR EVEN SANE BEHAVIOUR, RIGHT?
NOT TO MENTION WHATEVER THE HELL IS GOING ON IN HERE.
WHAT IS GOING ON HERE?
NOTHING.
I WON'T HAVE YOU MOCKING ME!
WHY DIDN'T YOU CALL THE SCHOOL, MARK?
YOU SAID YOU DID.
I OFFERED TO DO IT FOR YOU.
I'LL TELL YOU WHAT I'M DOING HERE!
CLICK
.......SOMETIMES THEY LEAVE IMPLANTS IN PEOPLE. MARKERS OR BEACONS... ALIEN METAL...
SO I'M LOOKING...
AUGHH! I DON'T GIVE A SHIT ABOUT ANY CRAZY-ASS ALIEN SHIT!!
REALITY! THAT'S WHAT I WANT!
YOU WANT ME TO BELIEVE YOU AND YOU LIE TO ME!
WHY DIDN'T YOU CALL YOUR SCHOOL, MARK?

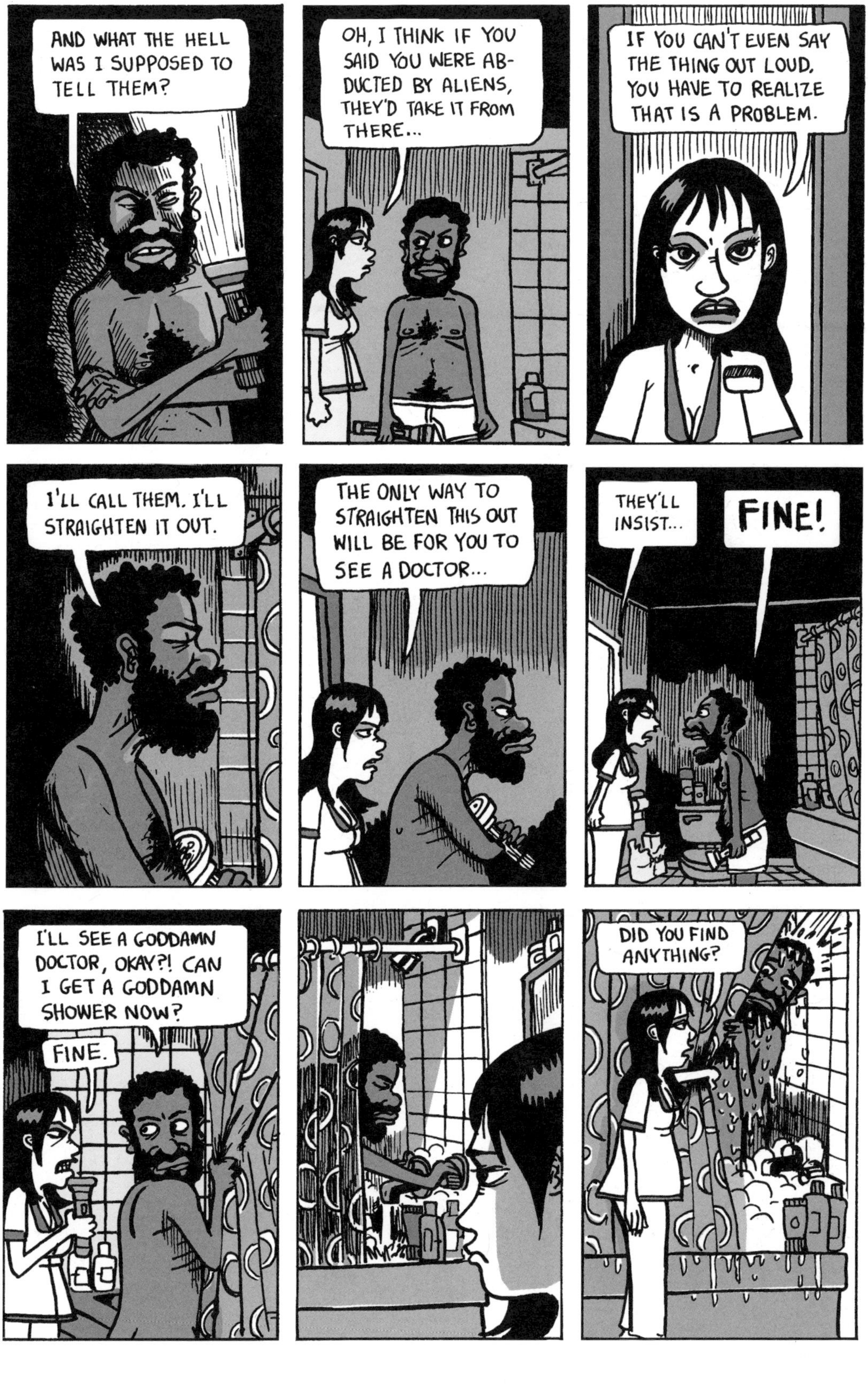
AND WHAT THE HELL WAS I SUPPOSED TO TELL THEM?
OH, I THINK IF YOU SAID YOU WERE ABDUCTED BY ALIENS, THEY'D TAKE IT FROM THERE...
IF YOU CAN'T EVEN SAY THE THING OUT LOUD, YOU HAVE TO REALIZE THAT IS A PROBLEM.
I'LL CALL THEM. I'LL STRAIGHTEN IT OUT.
THE ONLY WAY TO STRAIGHTEN THIS OUT WILL BE FOR YOU TO SEE A DOCTOR...
THEY'LL INSIST...
FINE!
I'LL SEE A GODDAMN DOCTOR, OKAY?! CAN I GET A GODDAMN SHOWER NOW?
FINE.
DID YOU FIND ANYTHING?

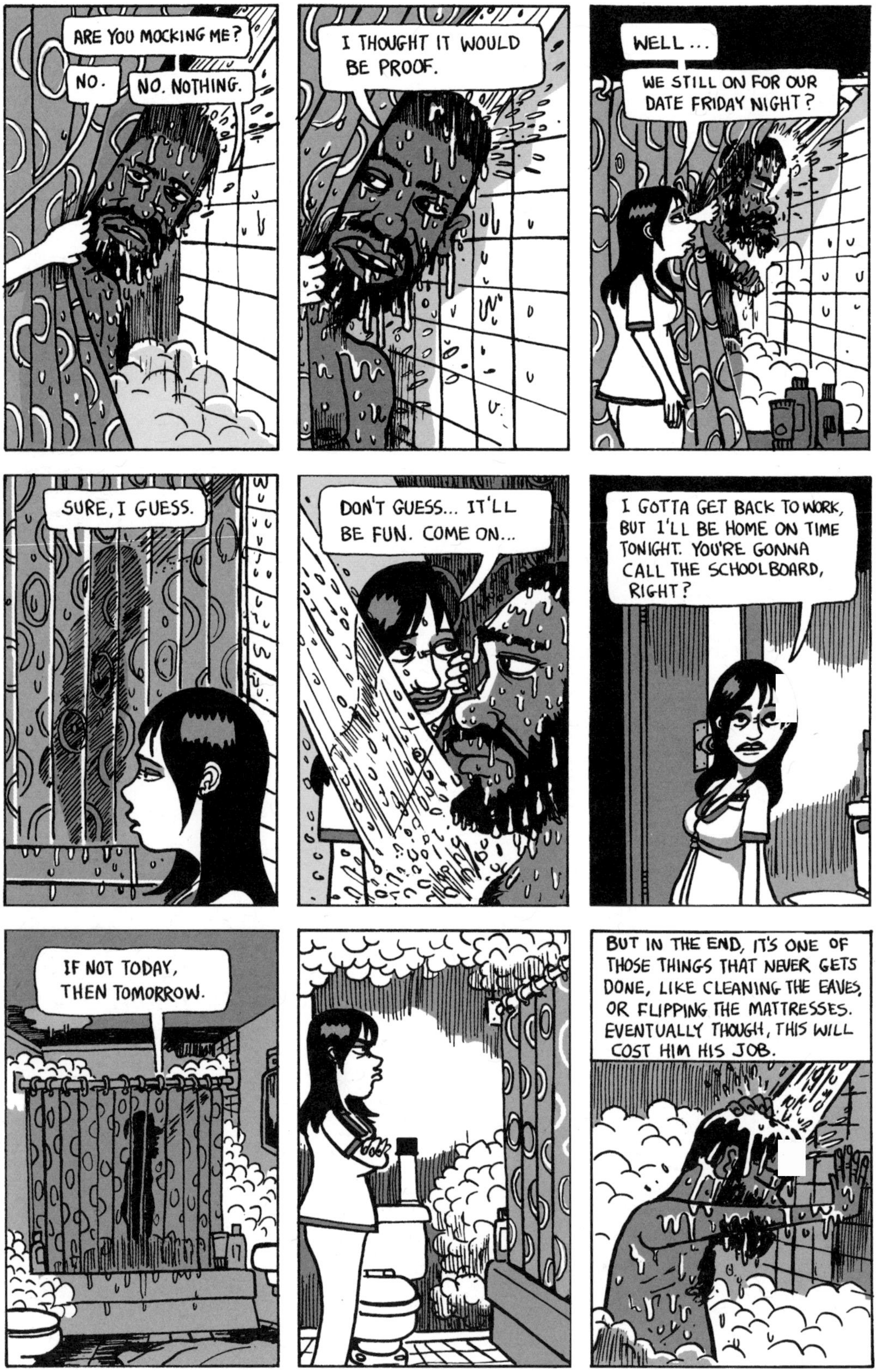
ARE YOU MOCKING ME?
NO.
NO. NOTHING.
I THOUGHT IT WOULD BE PROOF.
WELL...
WE STILL ON FOR OUR DATE FRIDAY NIGHT?
SURE, I GUESS.
DON'T GUESS... IT'LL BE FUN. COME ON...
I GOTTA GET BACK TO WORK, BUT I'LL BE HOME ON TIME TONIGHT. YOU'RE GONNA CALL THE SCHOOLBOARD, RIGHT?
IF NOT TODAY, THEN TOMORROW.
BUT IN THE END, IT'S ONE OF THOSE THINGS THAT NEVER GETS DONE, LIKE CLEANING THE EAVES, OR FLIPPING THE MATTRESSES. EVENTUALLY THOUGH, THIS WILL COST HIM HIS JOB.

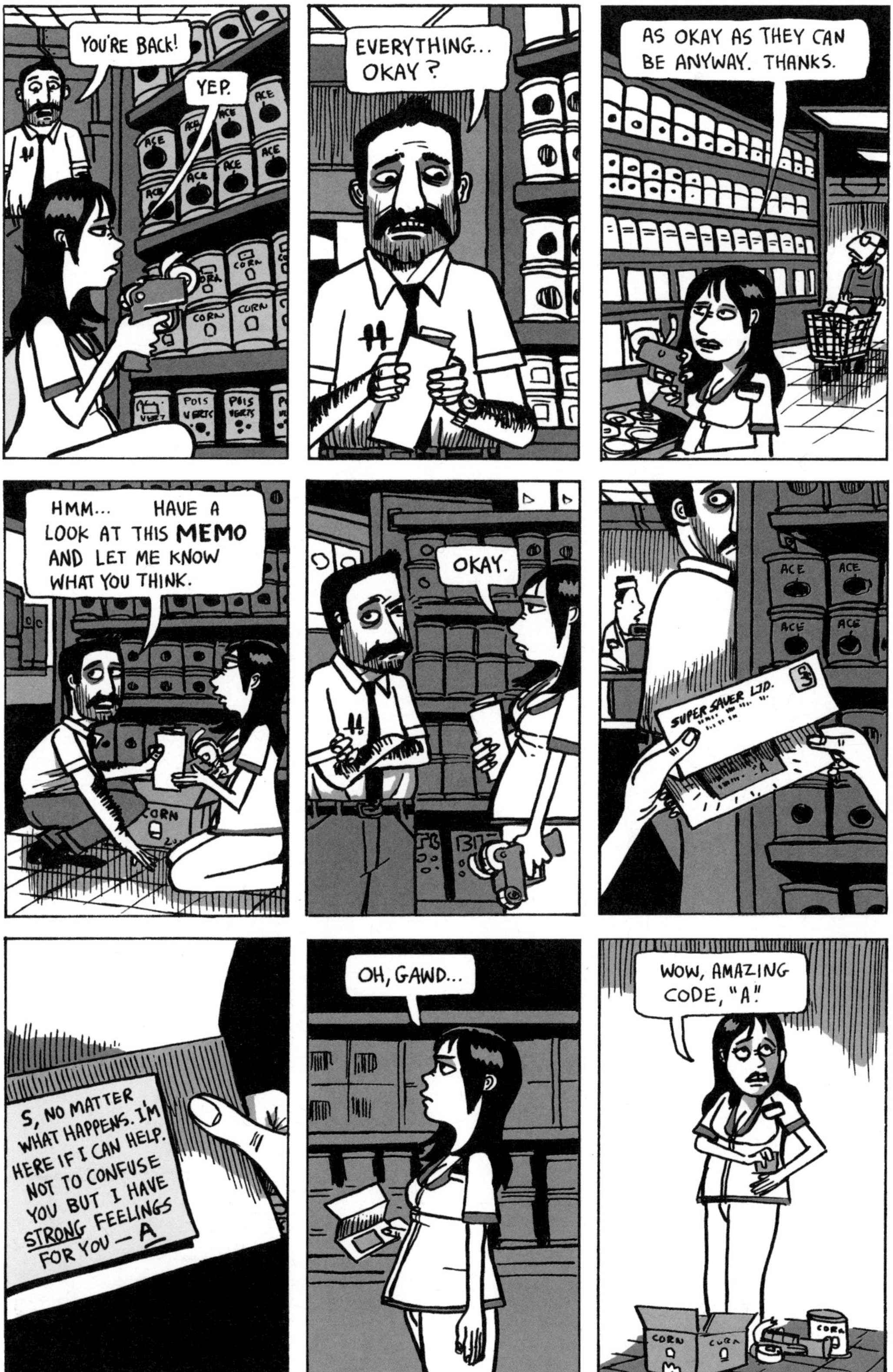
YOU'RE BACK!
YEP.
EVERYTHING... OKAY?
AS OKAY AS THEY CAN BE ANYWAY. THANKS.
HMM... HAVE A LOOK AT THIS MEMO AND LET ME KNOW WHAT YOU THINK.
OKAY.
SUPER SAVER LTD.
S, NO MATTER WHAT HAPPENS. I'M HERE IF I CAN HELP. NOT TO CONFUSE YOU BUT I HAVE STRONG FEELINGS FOR YOU — A
OH, GAWD...
WOW, AMAZING CODE, "A."

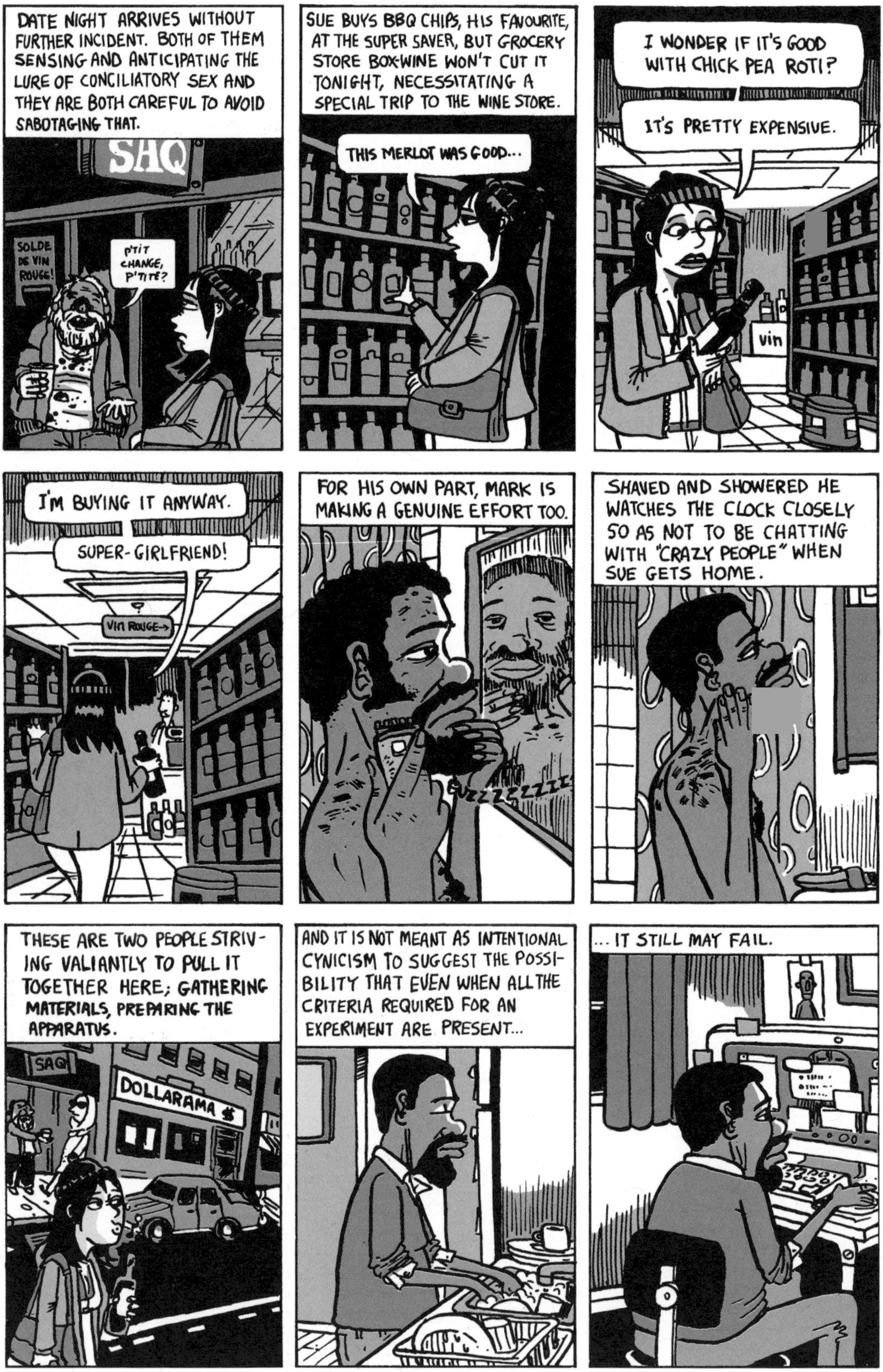
DATE NIGHT ARRIVES WITHOUT FURTHER INCIDENT. BOTH OF THEM SENSING AND ANTICIPATING THE LURE OF CONCILIATORY SEX AND THEY ARE BOTH CAREFUL TO AVOID SABOTAGING THAT.
SAQ
SOLDE DE VIN ROUGE!
P'TIT CHANGE, P'TITE?
SUE BUYS BBQ CHIPS, HIS FAVOURITE, AT THE SUPER SAVER, BUT GROCERY STORE BOX-WINE WON'T CUT IT TONIGHT, NECESSITATING A SPECIAL TRIP TO THE WINE STORE.
THIS MERLOT WAS GOOD...
I WONDER IF IT'S GOOD WITH CHICK PEA ROTI?
IT'S PRETTY EXPENSIVE.
vin
I'M BUYING IT ANYWAY.
SUPER-GIRLFRIEND!
VIN ROUGE→
FOR HIS OWN PART, MARK IS MAKING A GENUINE EFFORT TOO.
BUZZZZZZZ
SHAVED AND SHOWERED HE WATCHES THE CLOCK CLOSELY SO AS NOT TO BE CHATTING WITH "CRAZY PEOPLE" WHEN SUE GETS HOME.
THESE ARE TWO PEOPLE STRIV-ING VALIANTLY TO PULL IT TOGETHER HERE; GATHERING MATERIALS, PREPARING THE APPARATUS.
SAQ
DOLLARAMA $
AND IT IS NOT MEANT AS INTENTIONAL CYNICISM TO SUGGEST THE POSSI-BILITY THAT EVEN WHEN ALL THE CRITERIA REQUIRED FOR AN EXPERIMENT ARE PRESENT...
... IT STILL MAY FAIL.

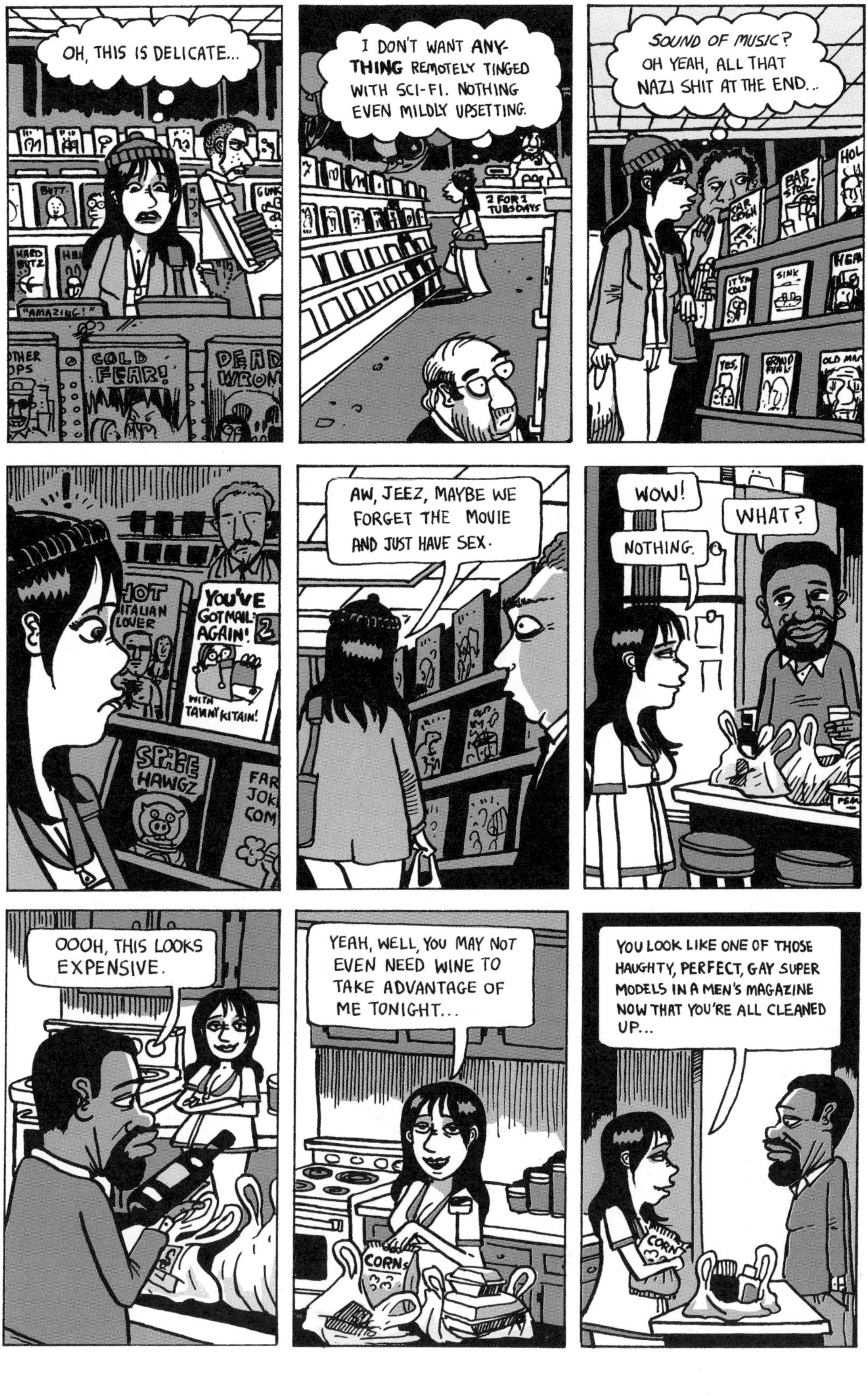
OH, THIS IS DELICATE...
COLD FEAR!
I DON'T WANT ANYTHING REMOTELY TINGED WITH SCI-FI. NOTHING EVEN MILDLY UPSETTING.
2 FOR 1 TUESDAYS
SOUND OF MUSIC? OH YEAH, ALL THAT NAZI SHIT AT THE END...
HOT ITALIAN LOVER
YOU'VE GOT MAIL: AGAIN! 2
WITH TAWNY KITAIN!
SPACE HAWGZ
AW, JEEZ, MAYBE WE FORGET THE MOVIE AND JUST HAVE SEX.
WOW!
NOTHING.
WHAT?
OOOH, THIS LOOKS EXPENSIVE.
YEAH, WELL, YOU MAY NOT EVEN NEED WINE TO TAKE ADVANTAGE OF ME TONIGHT...
YOU LOOK LIKE ONE OF THOSE HAUGHTY, PERFECT, GAY SUPER MODELS IN A MEN'S MAGAZINE NOW THAT YOU'RE ALL CLEANED UP...

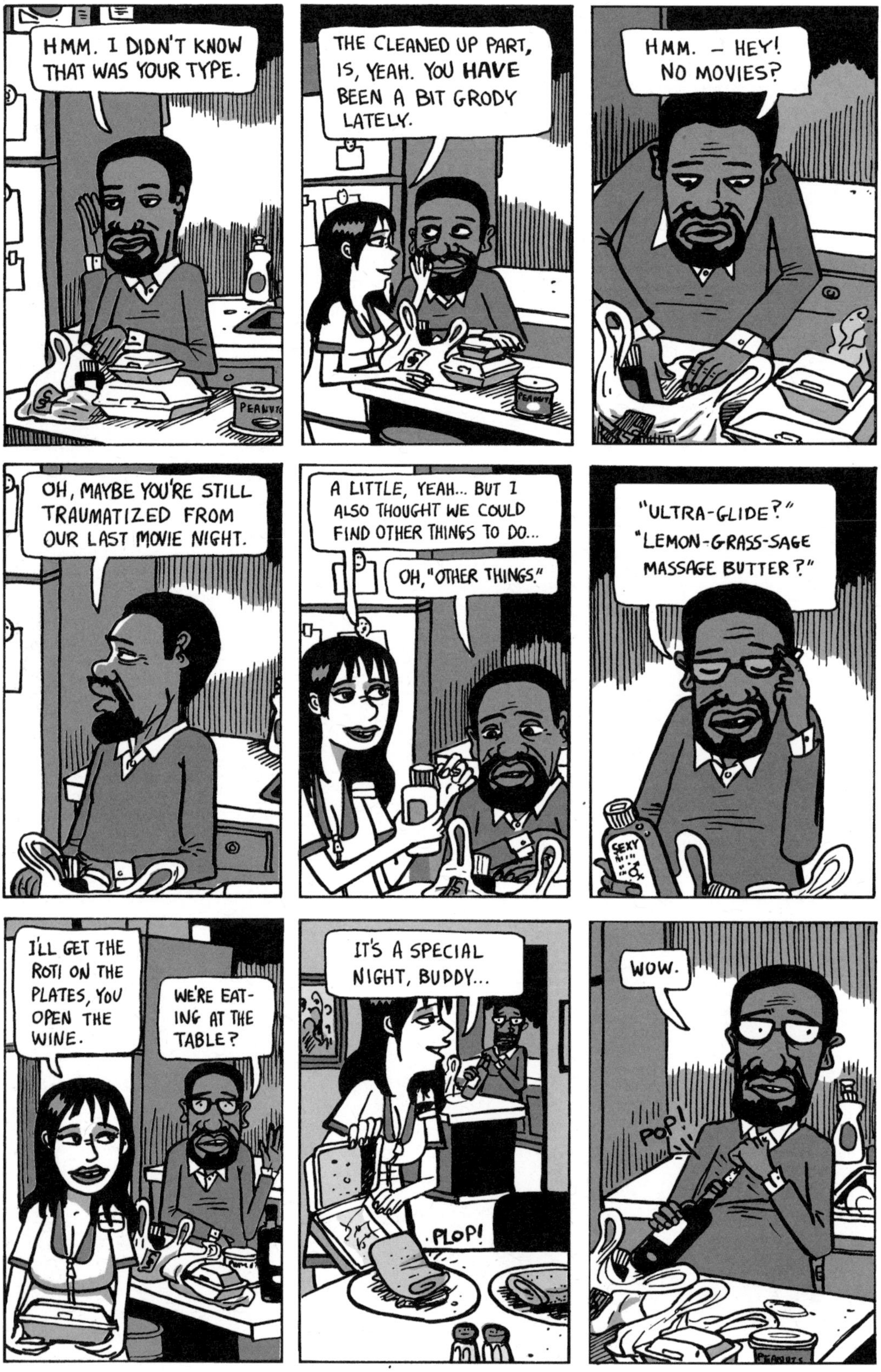

HMM. I DIDN'T KNOW THAT WAS YOUR TYPE.
THE CLEANED UP PART, IS, YEAH. YOU **HAVE** BEEN A BIT GRODY LATELY.
HMM. – HEY! NO MOVIES?
OH, MAYBE YOU'RE STILL TRAUMATIZED FROM OUR LAST MOVIE NIGHT.
A LITTLE, YEAH... BUT I ALSO THOUGHT WE COULD FIND OTHER THINGS TO DO...
OH, "OTHER THINGS."
"ULTRA-GLIDE?" "LEMON-GRASS-SAGE MASSAGE BUTTER?"
SEXY
I'LL GET THE ROTI ON THE PLATES, YOU OPEN THE WINE.
WE'RE EAT-ING AT THE TABLE?
IT'S A SPECIAL NIGHT, BUDDY...
PLOP!
WOW.
POP!

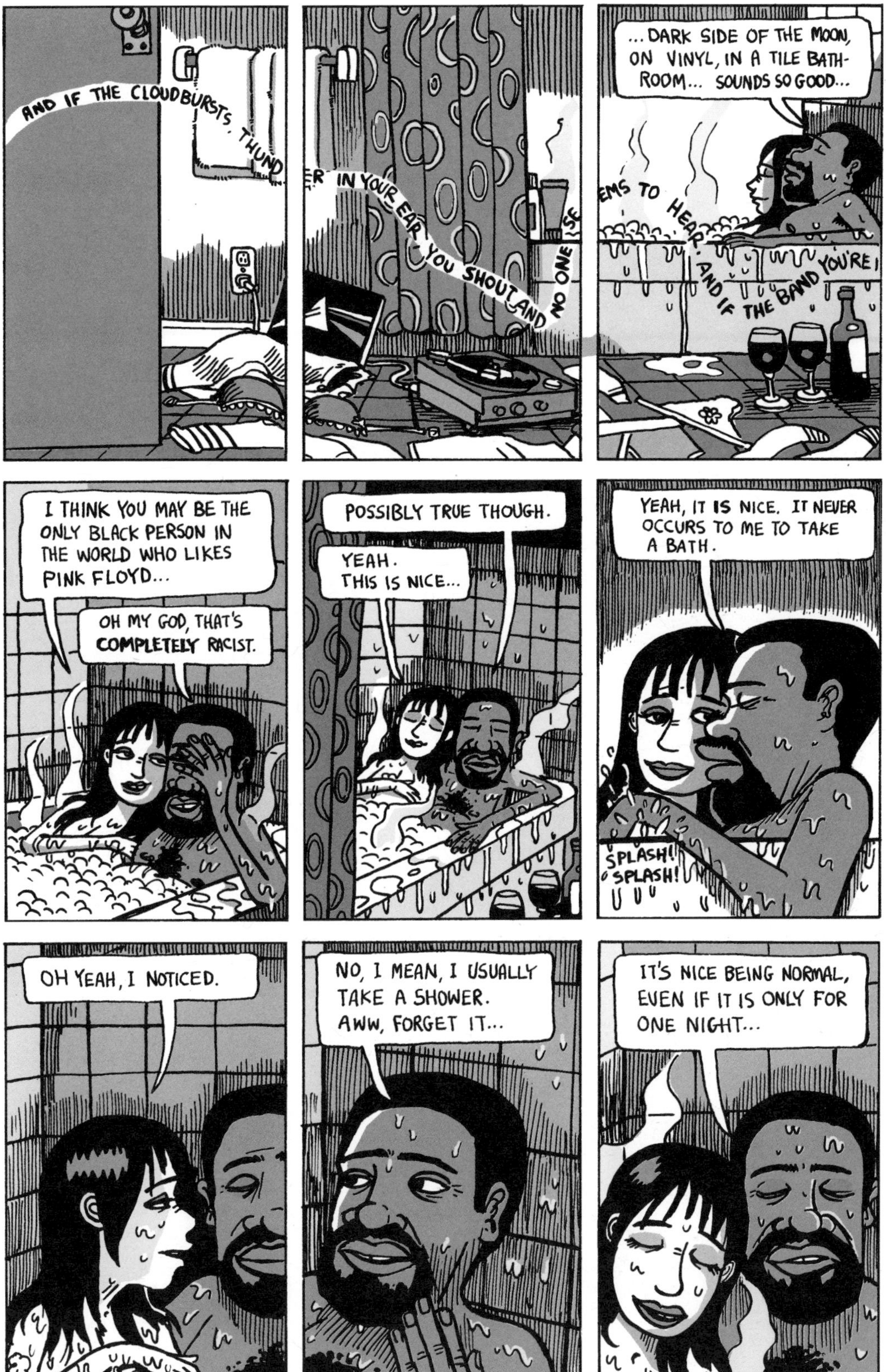

AND IF THE CLOUDBURSTS THUNDER IN YOUR EAR, YOU SHOUT AND NO ONE SEEMS TO HEAR, AND IF THE BAND YOU'RE I
...DARK SIDE OF THE MOON, ON VINYL, IN A TILE BATHROOM... SOUNDS SO GOOD...
I THINK YOU MAY BE THE ONLY BLACK PERSON IN THE WORLD WHO LIKES PINK FLOYD...
OH MY GOD, THAT'S COMPLETELY RACIST.
POSSIBLY TRUE THOUGH.
YEAH. THIS IS NICE...
YEAH, IT IS NICE. IT NEVER OCCURS TO ME TO TAKE A BATH.
SPLASH! SPLASH!
OH YEAH, I NOTICED.
NO, I MEAN, I USUALLY TAKE A SHOWER. AWW, FORGET IT...
IT'S NICE BEING NORMAL, EVEN IF IT IS ONLY FOR ONE NIGHT...

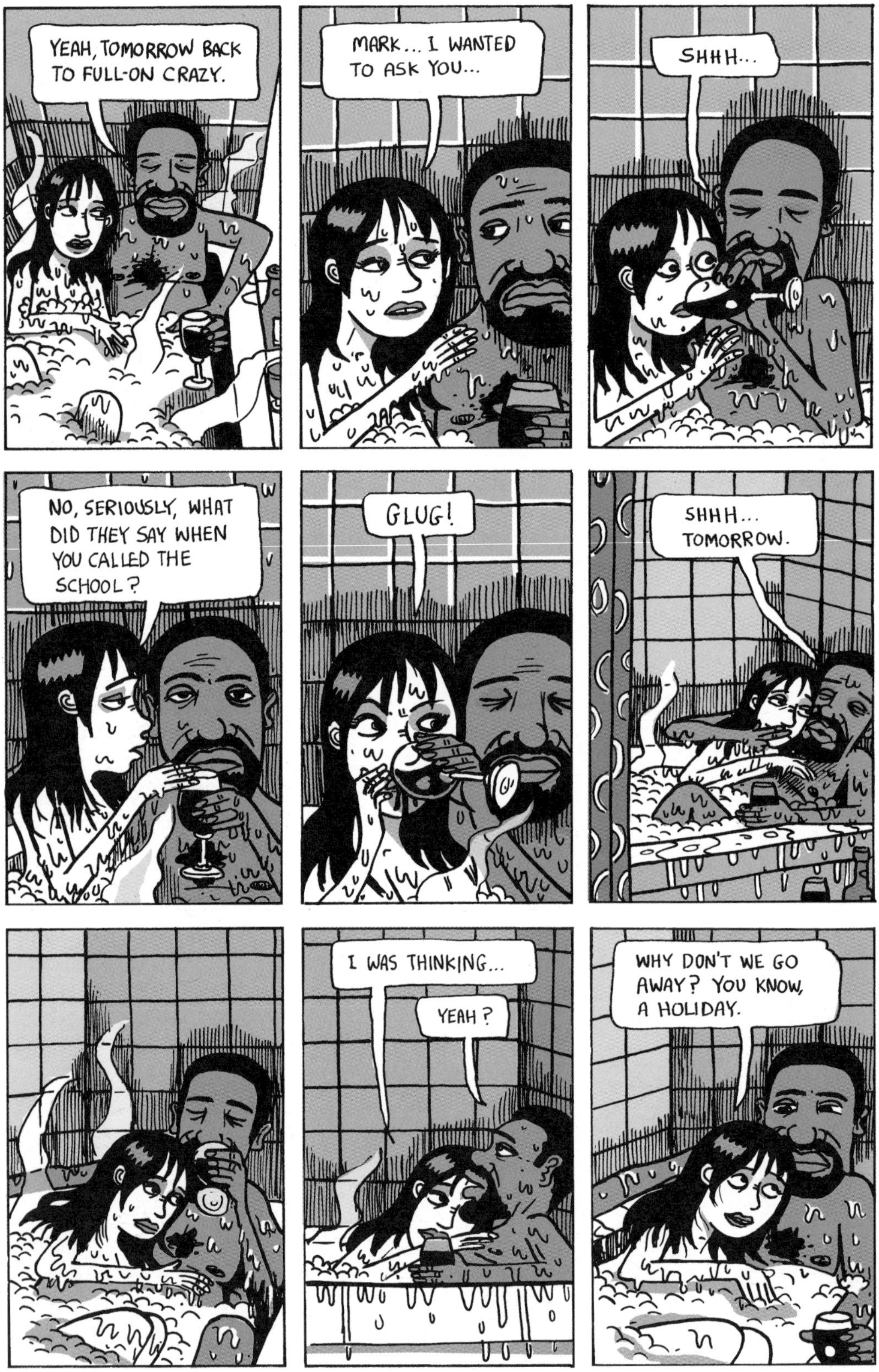
YEAH, TOMORROW BACK TO FULL-ON CRAZY.
MARK... I WANTED TO ASK YOU...
SHHH...
NO, SERIOUSLY, WHAT DID THEY SAY WHEN YOU CALLED THE SCHOOL?
GLUG!
SHHH... TOMORROW.
I WAS THINKING...
YEAH?
WHY DON'T WE GO AWAY? YOU KNOW, A HOLIDAY.

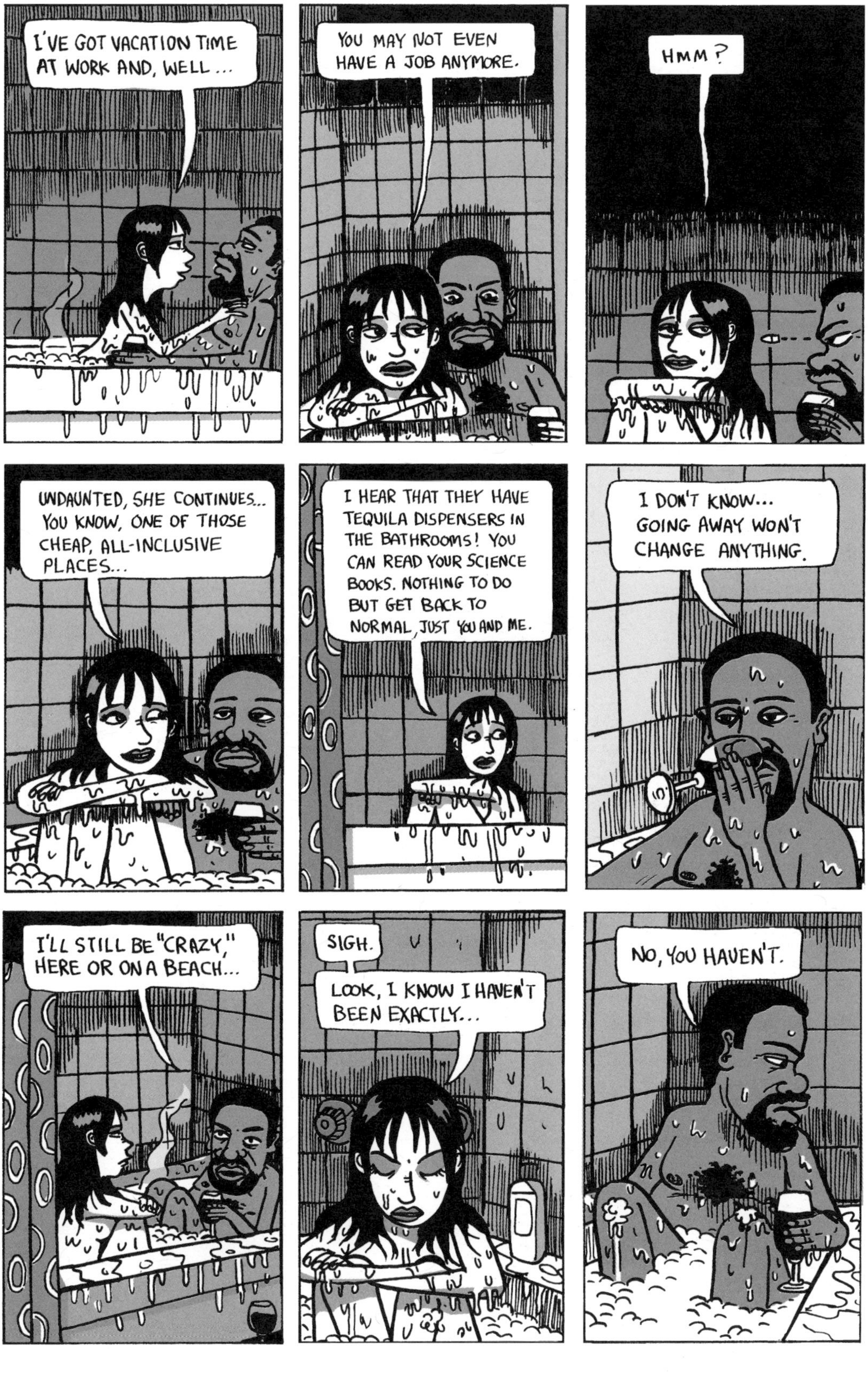
I'VE GOT VACATION TIME AT WORK AND, WELL...
YOU MAY NOT EVEN HAVE A JOB ANYMORE.
HMM?
UNDAUNTED, SHE CONTINUES... YOU KNOW, ONE OF THOSE CHEAP, ALL-INCLUSIVE PLACES...
I HEAR THAT THEY HAVE TEQUILA DISPENSERS IN THE BATHROOMS! YOU CAN READ YOUR SCIENCE BOOKS. NOTHING TO DO BUT GET BACK TO NORMAL, JUST YOU AND ME.
I DON'T KNOW... GOING AWAY WON'T CHANGE ANYTHING.
I'LL STILL BE "CRAZY," HERE OR ON A BEACH...
SIGH.
LOOK, I KNOW I HAVEN'T BEEN EXACTLY...
NO, YOU HAVEN'T.

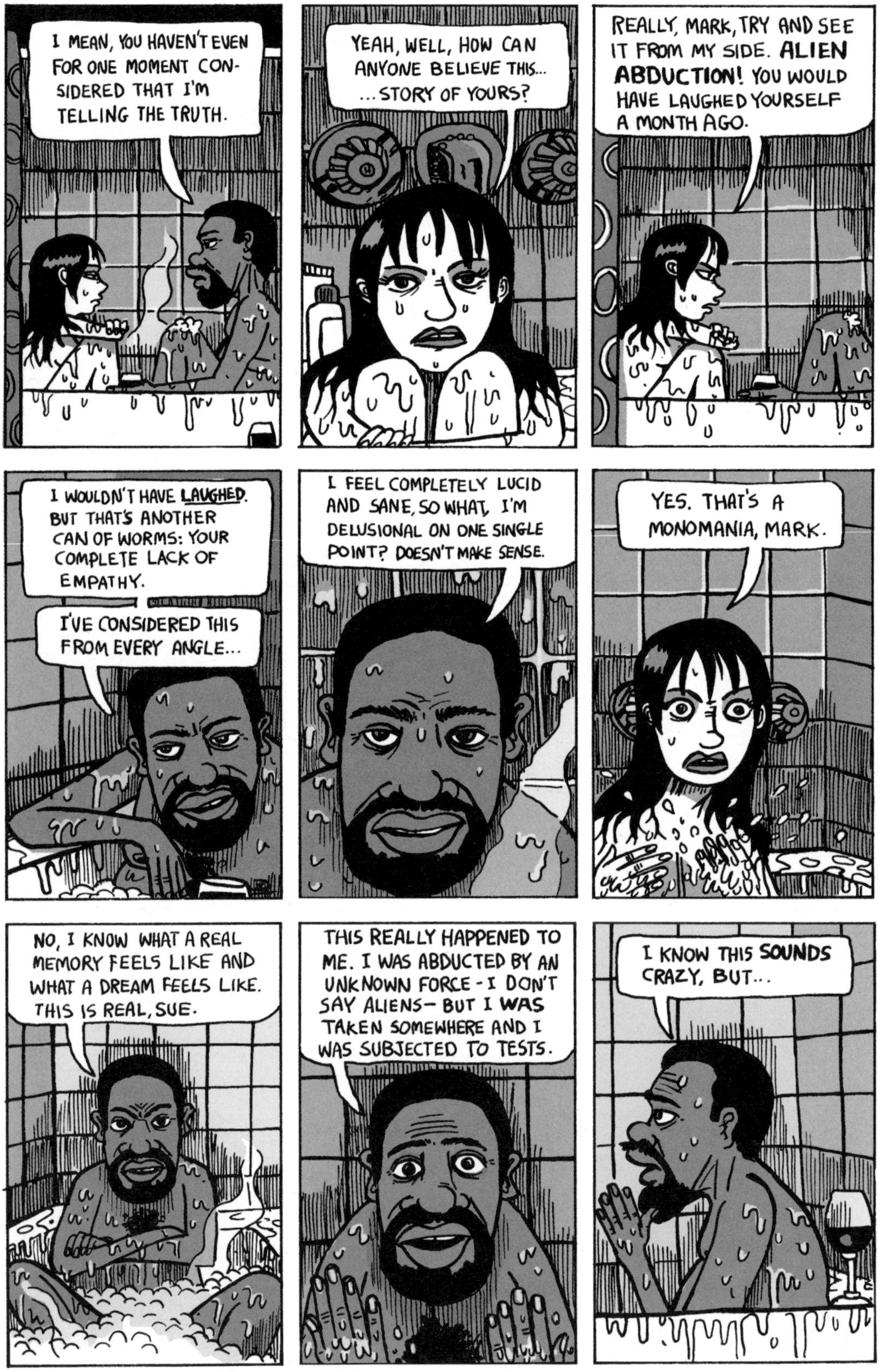
I MEAN, YOU HAVEN'T EVEN FOR ONE MOMENT CONSIDERED THAT I'M TELLING THE TRUTH.
YEAH, WELL, HOW CAN ANYONE BELIEVE THIS... ...STORY OF YOURS?
REALLY, MARK, TRY AND SEE IT FROM MY SIDE. ALIEN ABDUCTION! YOU WOULD HAVE LAUGHED YOURSELF A MONTH AGO.
I WOULDN'T HAVE LAUGHED. BUT THAT'S ANOTHER CAN OF WORMS: YOUR COMPLETE LACK OF EMPATHY.
I'VE CONSIDERED THIS FROM EVERY ANGLE...
I FEEL COMPLETELY LUCID AND SANE, SO WHAT, I'M DELUSIONAL ON ONE SINGLE POINT? DOESN'T MAKE SENSE.
YES. THAT'S A MONOMANIA, MARK.
NO, I KNOW WHAT A REAL MEMORY FEELS LIKE AND WHAT A DREAM FEELS LIKE. THIS IS REAL, SUE.
THIS REALLY HAPPENED TO ME. I WAS ABDUCTED BY AN UNKNOWN FORCE - I DON'T SAY ALIENS- BUT I WAS TAKEN SOMEWHERE AND I WAS SUBJECTED TO TESTS.
I KNOW THIS SOUNDS CRAZY, BUT...

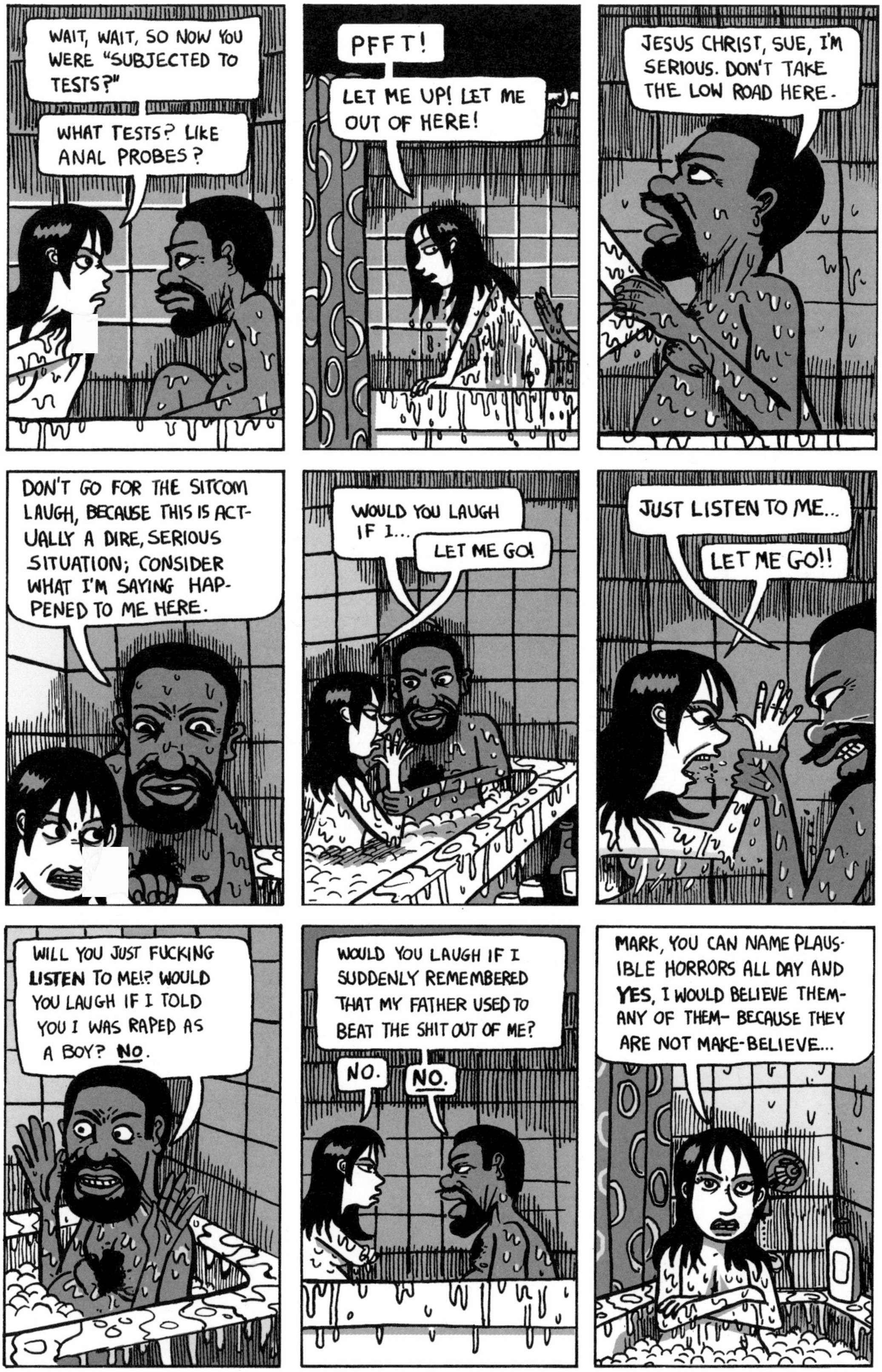
WAIT, WAIT, SO NOW YOU WERE "SUBJECTED TO TESTS?"
WHAT TESTS? LIKE ANAL PROBES?
PFFT!
LET ME UP! LET ME OUT OF HERE!
JESUS CHRIST, SUE, I'M SERIOUS. DON'T TAKE THE LOW ROAD HERE.
DON'T GO FOR THE SITCOM LAUGH, BECAUSE THIS IS ACT-UALLY A DIRE, SERIOUS SITUATION; CONSIDER WHAT I'M SAYING HAP-PENED TO ME HERE.
WOULD YOU LAUGH IF I...
LET ME GO!
JUST LISTEN TO ME...
LET ME GO!!
WILL YOU JUST FUCKING LISTEN TO ME!? WOULD YOU LAUGH IF I TOLD YOU I WAS RAPED AS A BOY? NO.
WOULD YOU LAUGH IF I SUDDENLY REMEMBERED THAT MY FATHER USED TO BEAT THE SHIT OUT OF ME?
NO.
NO.
MARK, YOU CAN NAME PLAUS-IBLE HORRORS ALL DAY AND YES, I WOULD BELIEVE THEM- ANY OF THEM- BECAUSE THEY ARE NOT MAKE-BELIEVE...

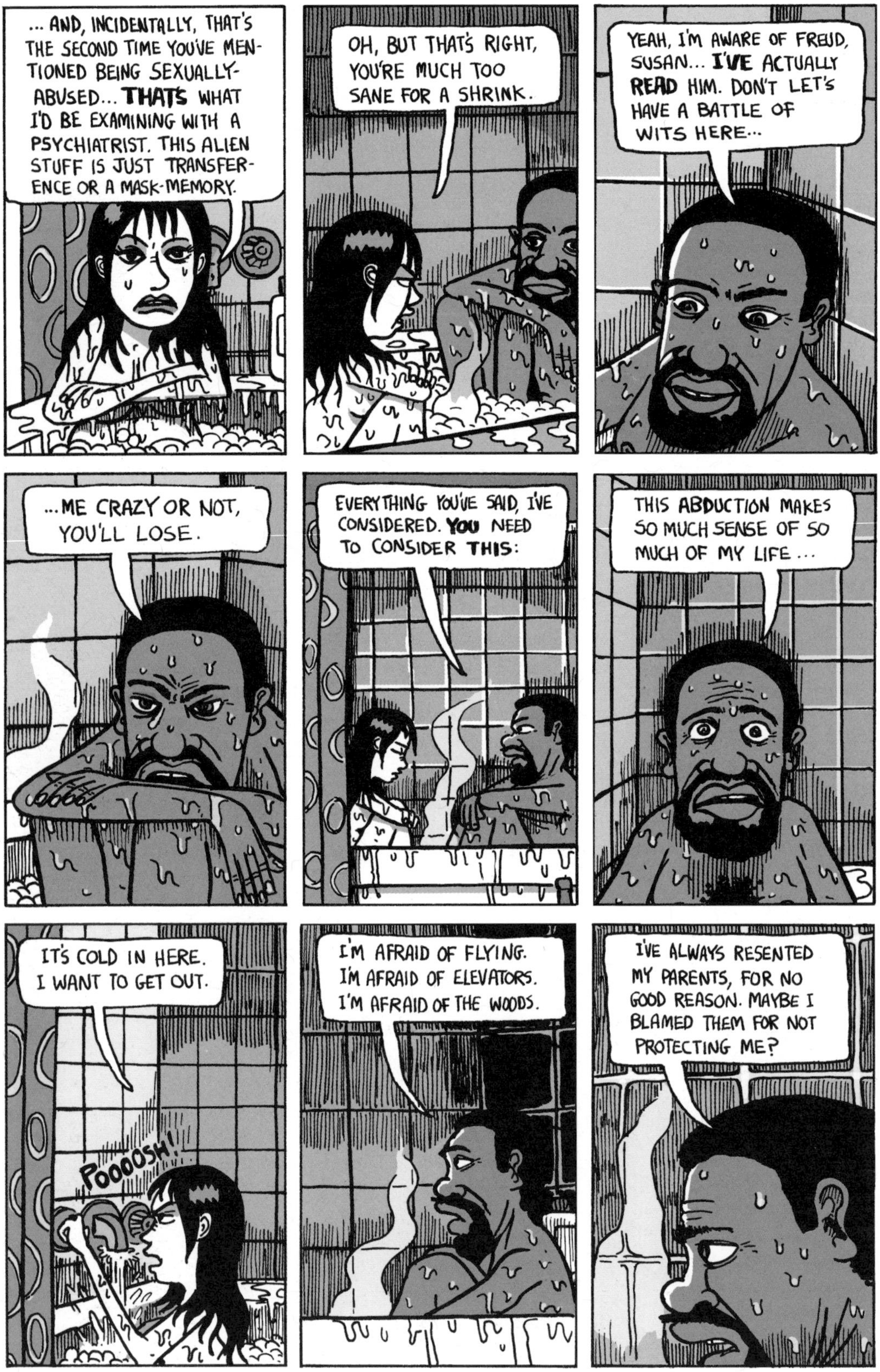
... AND, INCIDENTALLY, THAT'S THE SECOND TIME YOU'VE MENTIONED BEING SEXUALLY-ABUSED... THAT'S WHAT I'D BE EXAMINING WITH A PSYCHIATRIST. THIS ALIEN STUFF IS JUST TRANSFERENCE OR A MASK-MEMORY.
OH, BUT THAT'S RIGHT, YOU'RE MUCH TOO SANE FOR A SHRINK.
YEAH, I'M AWARE OF FREUD, SUSAN... I'VE ACTUALLY READ HIM. DON'T LET'S HAVE A BATTLE OF WITS HERE...
...ME CRAZY OR NOT, YOU'LL LOSE.
EVERYTHING YOU'VE SAID, I'VE CONSIDERED. YOU NEED TO CONSIDER THIS:
THIS ABDUCTION MAKES SO MUCH SENSE OF SO MUCH OF MY LIFE...
IT'S COLD IN HERE. I WANT TO GET OUT.
POOOOSH!
I'M AFRAID OF FLYING. I'M AFRAID OF ELEVATORS. I'M AFRAID OF THE WOODS.
I'VE ALWAYS RESENTED MY PARENTS, FOR NO GOOD REASON. MAYBE I BLAMED THEM FOR NOT PROTECTING ME?

OH MY GOD. YOU'RE **SUPPOSED** TO RESENT YOUR PARENTS...

...AND YOU'VE JUST MADE A LIST OF THE COMMONEST PHOBIAS IN THE WORLD.

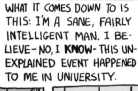

WHAT IT COMES DOWN TO IS THIS: I'M A SANE, FAIRLY INTELLIGENT MAN. I BELIEVE-NO, I **KNOW**- THIS UNEXPLAINED EVENT HAPPENED TO ME IN UNIVERSITY.

IT HAS MADE ME EVERYTHING THAT I AM TODAY-UNHAPPY, DISTANT, DEPRESSED...

YOU WANT US TO GO AWAY TOGETHER AND START OVER AGAIN OR SOMETHING; A NEW START.

WELL, YOU COULD START WITH THE ONE THING THAT I ACTUALLY **NEED** FROM YOU- FOR YOU TO BELIEVE ME.

LOOK, IF THAT'S WHAT YOU NEED, SURE, I CAN **SAY** I BELIEVE YOU WERE ABDUCTED BY ALIENS.

...BUT NO, I DON'T **BELIEVE** YOU WERE ABDUCTED BY ALIENS.

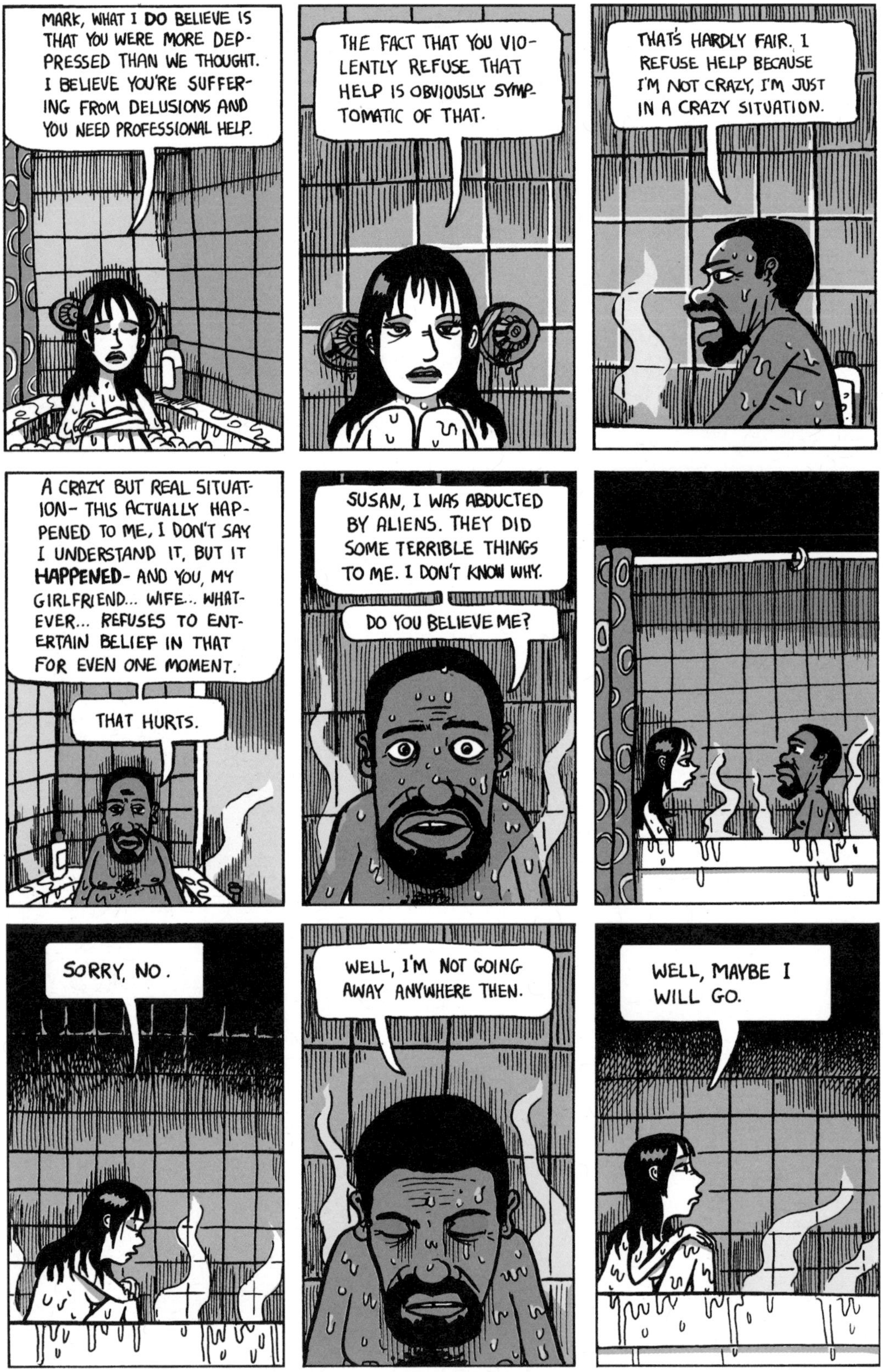
MARK, WHAT I DO BELIEVE IS THAT YOU WERE MORE DEP-PRESSED THAN WE THOUGHT. I BELIEVE YOU'RE SUFFER-ING FROM DELUSIONS AND YOU NEED PROFESSIONAL HELP.
THE FACT THAT YOU VIO-LENTLY REFUSE THAT HELP IS OBVIOUSLY SYMP-TOMATIC OF THAT.
THAT'S HARDLY FAIR. I REFUSE HELP BECAUSE I'M NOT CRAZY, I'M JUST IN A CRAZY SITUATION.
A CRAZY BUT REAL SITUAT-ION- THIS ACTUALLY HAP-PENED TO ME. I DON'T SAY I UNDERSTAND IT, BUT IT HAPPENED- AND YOU, MY GIRLFRIEND... WIFE... WHAT-EVER... REFUSES TO ENT-ERTAIN BELIEF IN THAT FOR EVEN ONE MOMENT.
THAT HURTS.
SUSAN, I WAS ABDUCTED BY ALIENS. THEY DID SOME TERRIBLE THINGS TO ME. I DON'T KNOW WHY.
DO YOU BELIEVE ME?
SORRY, NO.
WELL, I'M NOT GOING AWAY ANYWHERE THEN.
WELL, MAYBE I WILL GO.

HE SITS COMPLETELY STILL, DETERMINED TO IGNORE THE WATER GROWING COLD AROUND HIM.
AN ASCETIC MONK OF TRUTH AND RIGHTEOUSNESS.
BUT THE WATER IS VERY COLD...
POOOSH
...AND HE WONDERS HOW LONG HE SHOULD WAIT BEFORE GETTING BACK TO HIS INTERNET ABDUCTION MESSAGE BOARDS.
SK SKIP SKIP SKIP SKIP
SKIP SKIP SKIP SKIP SKIP

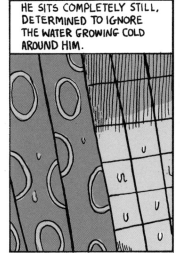

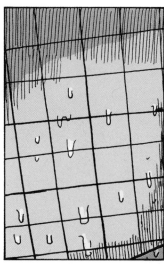

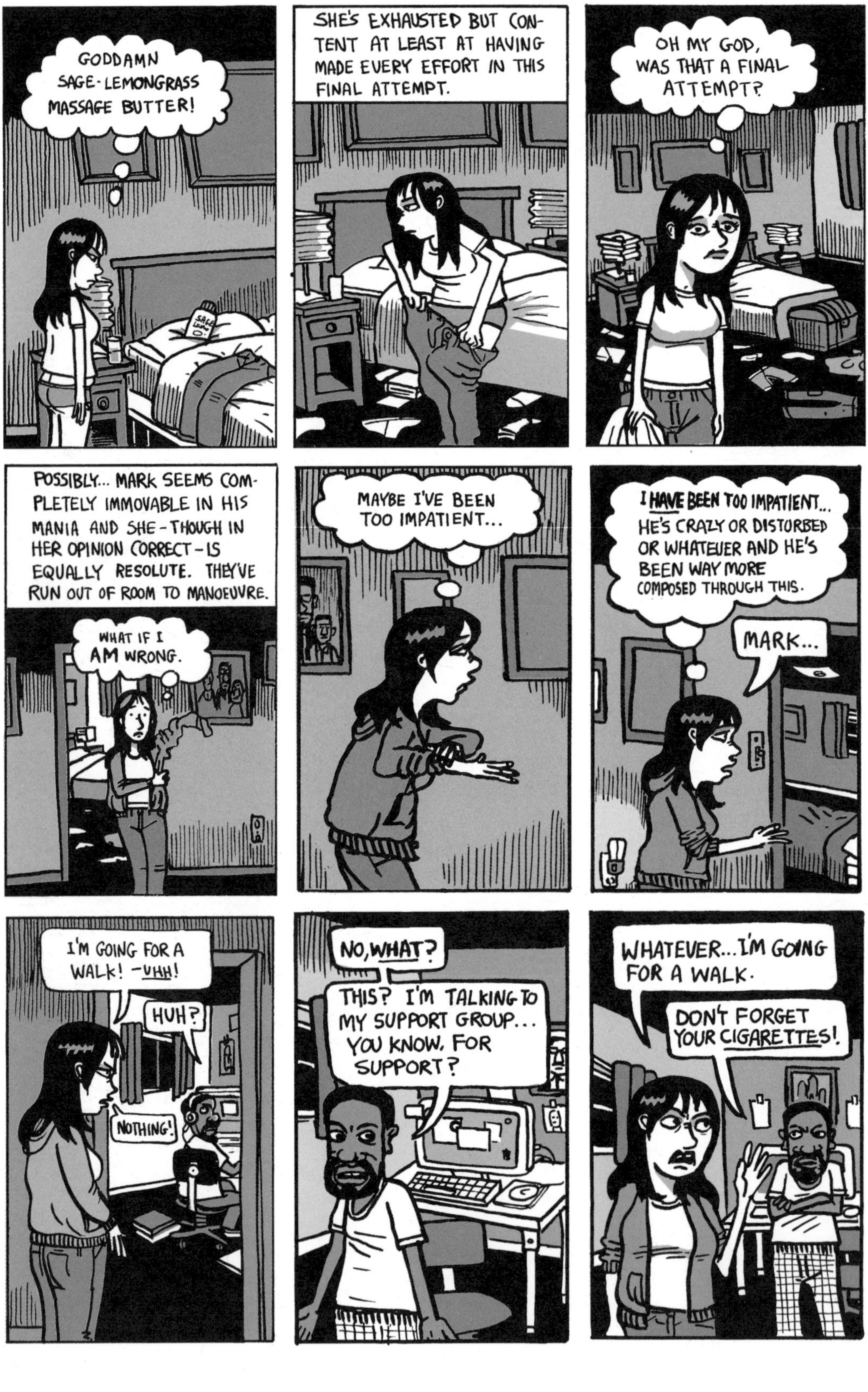
GODDAMN SAGE-LEMONGRASS MASSAGE BUTTER!
SHE'S EXHAUSTED BUT CONTENT AT LEAST AT HAVING MADE EVERY EFFORT IN THIS FINAL ATTEMPT.
OH MY GOD, WAS THAT A FINAL ATTEMPT?
POSSIBLY... MARK SEEMS COMPLETELY IMMOVABLE IN HIS MANIA AND SHE - THOUGH IN HER OPINION CORRECT - IS EQUALLY RESOLUTE. THEY'VE RUN OUT OF ROOM TO MANOEUVRE.
WHAT IF I AM WRONG.
MAYBE I'VE BEEN TOO IMPATIENT...
I HAVE BEEN TOO IMPATIENT... HE'S CRAZY OR DISTURBED OR WHATEVER AND HE'S BEEN WAY MORE COMPOSED THROUGH THIS.
MARK...
I'M GOING FOR A WALK! -UHH!
HUH?
NOTHING!
NO, WHAT?
THIS? I'M TALKING TO MY SUPPORT GROUP... YOU KNOW, FOR SUPPORT?
WHATEVER... I'M GOING FOR A WALK.
DON'T FORGET YOUR CIGARETTES!

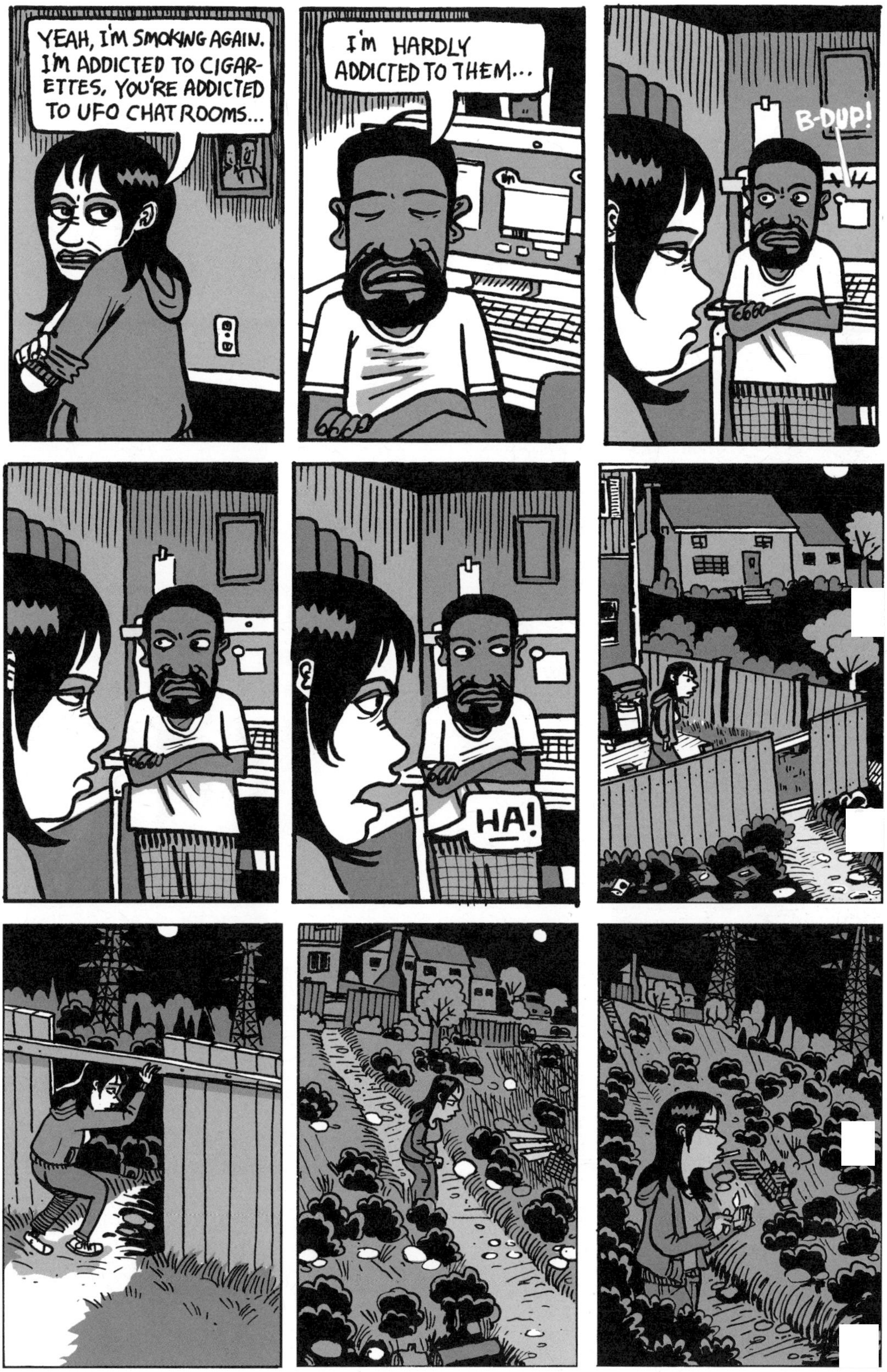
YEAH, I'M SMOKING AGAIN. I'M ADDICTED TO CIGAR-ETTES, YOU'RE ADDICTED TO UFO CHAT ROOMS...
I'M HARDLY ADDICTED TO THEM...
B-DUP!
HA!

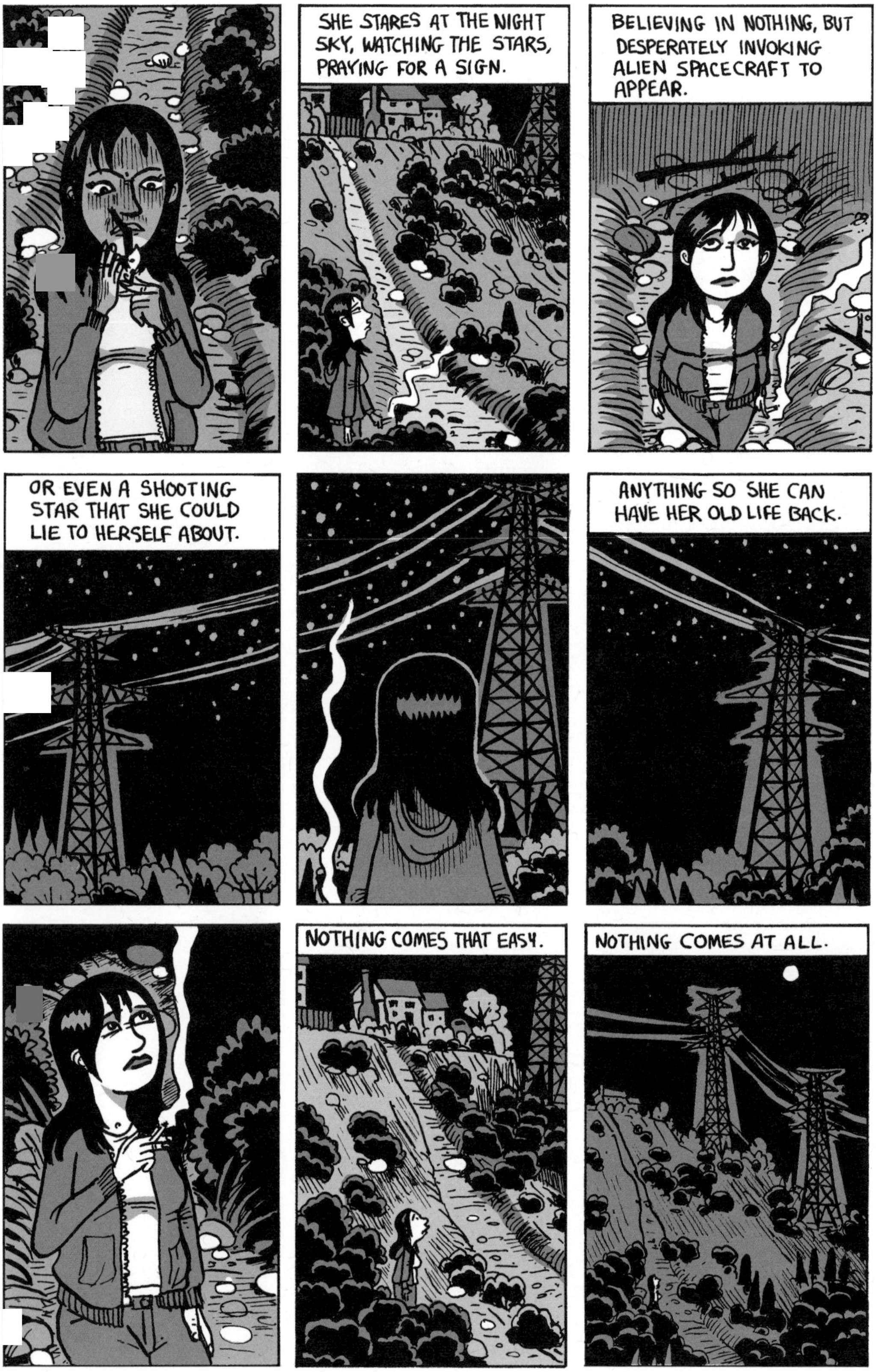

SHE STARES AT THE NIGHT SKY, WATCHING THE STARS, PRAYING FOR A SIGN.
BELIEVING IN NOTHING, BUT DESPERATELY INVOKING ALIEN SPACECRAFT TO APPEAR.
OR EVEN A SHOOTING STAR THAT SHE COULD LIE TO HERSELF ABOUT.
ANYTHING SO SHE CAN HAVE HER OLD LIFE BACK.
NOTHING COMES THAT EASY.
NOTHING COMES AT ALL.

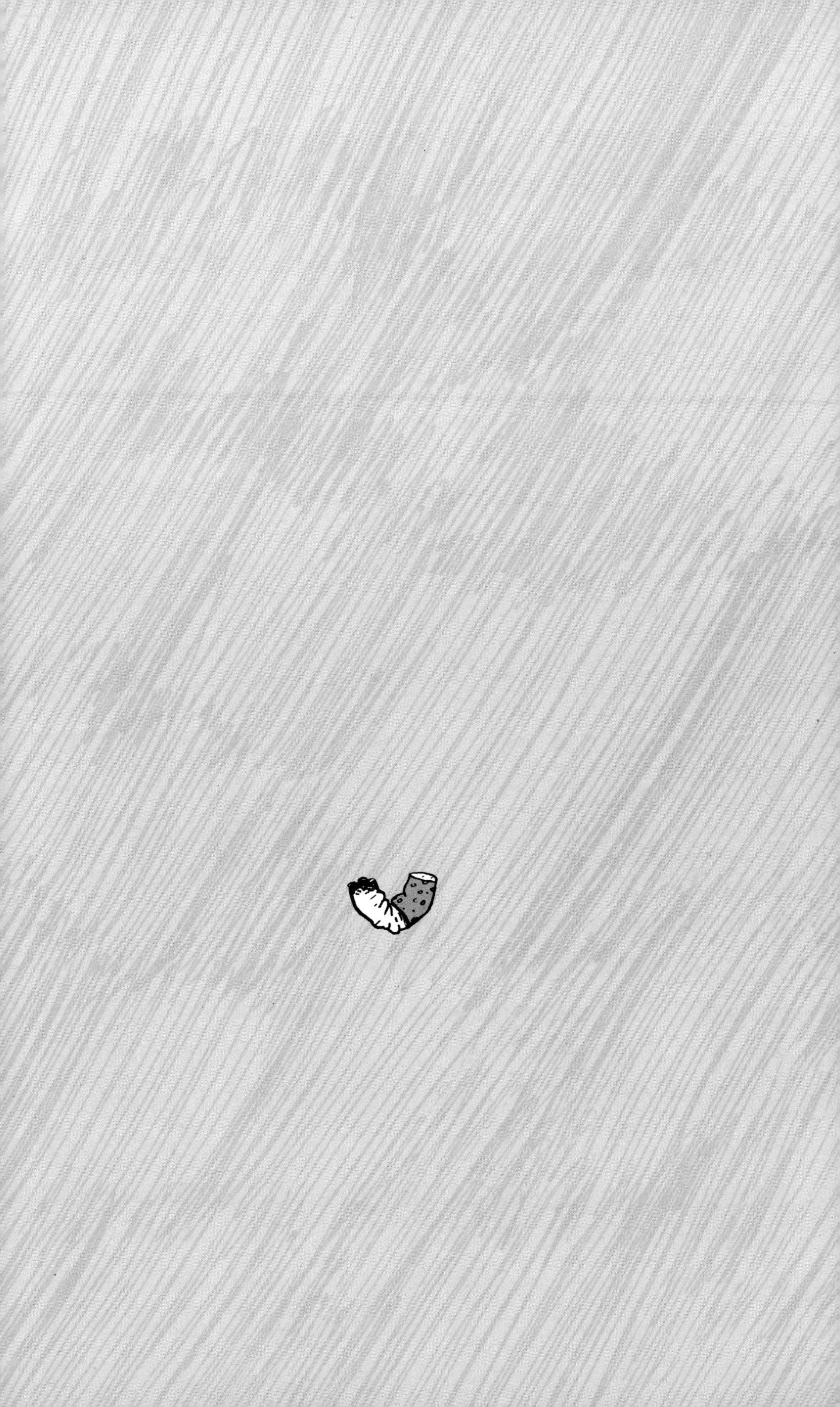

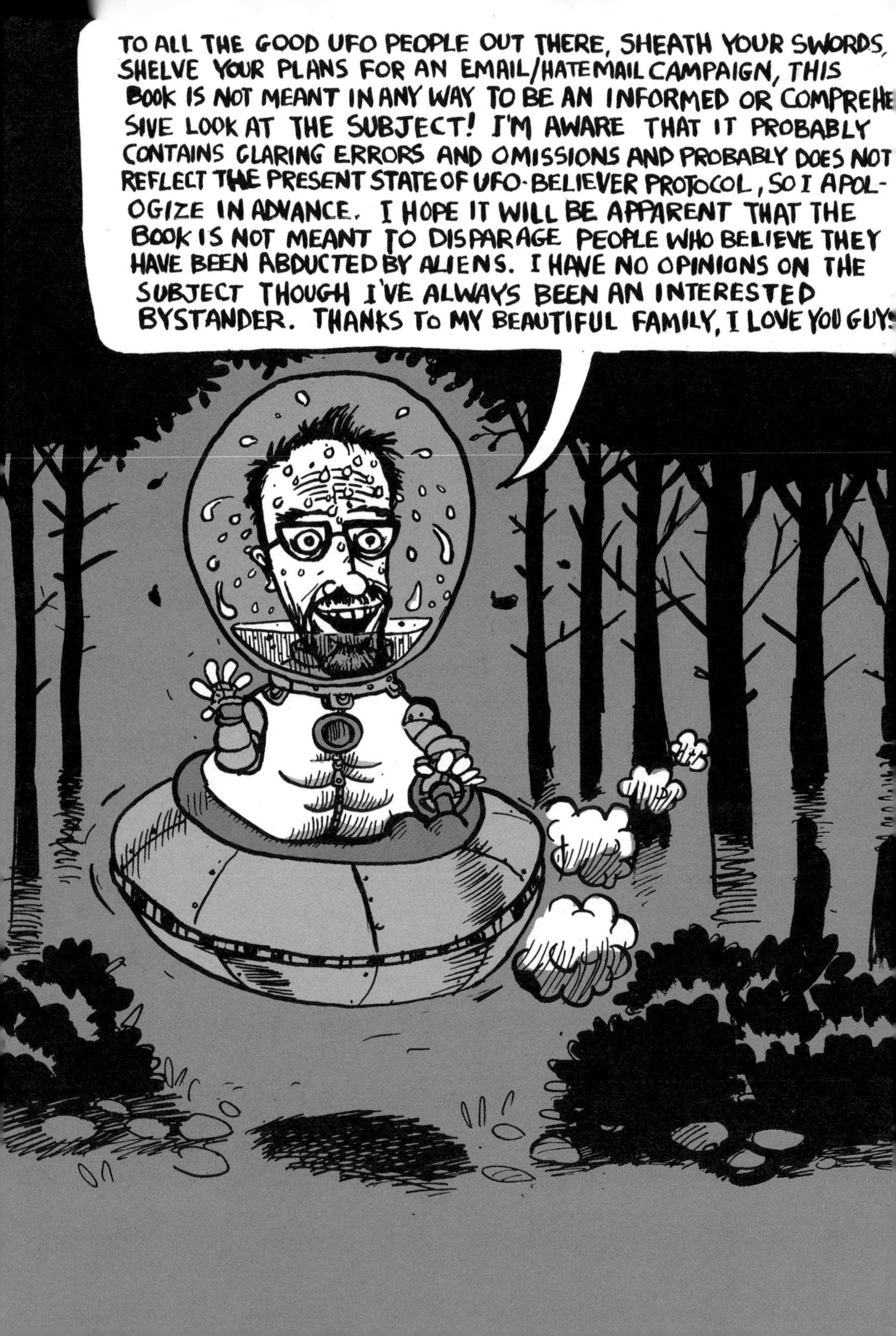
TO ALL THE GOOD UFO PEOPLE OUT THERE, SHEATH YOUR SWORDS, SHELVE YOUR PLANS FOR AN EMAIL/HATEMAIL CAMPAIGN, THIS BOOK IS NOT MEANT IN ANY WAY TO BE AN INFORMED OR COMPREHE SIVE LOOK AT THE SUBJECT! I'M AWARE THAT IT PROBABLY CONTAINS GLARING ERRORS AND OMISSIONS AND PROBABLY DOES NOT REFLECT THE PRESENT STATE OF UFO-BELIEVER PROTOCOL, SO I APOLOGIZE IN ADVANCE. I HOPE IT WILL BE APPARENT THAT THE BOOK IS NOT MEANT TO DISPARAGE PEOPLE WHO BELIEVE THEY HAVE BEEN ABDUCTED BY ALIENS. I HAVE NO OPINIONS ON THE SUBJECT THOUGH I'VE ALWAYS BEEN AN INTERESTED BYSTANDER. THANKS TO MY BEAUTIFUL FAMILY, I LOVE YOU GUY

JOE OLLMANN LIVES IN MONTREAL WHERE HE RARELY LEAVES HIS BASEMENT. IN 2006, HIS SHORT STORY COMICS COLLECTION, THIS WILL ALL END IN TEARS WON THE DOUG WRIGHT AWARD FOR BEST BOOK.

OTHER BOOKS

CHEWING ON TINFOIL
THE BIG BOOK OF WAG!
THIS WILL ALL END IN TEARS
MID-LIFE

CHEWING ON TINFOIL
BY JOE OLLMANN

the big book of WAG!
by joe ollmann

this will all end in tears
comics by joe ollmann
rip!

MID-LIFE
BY JOE OLLMANN

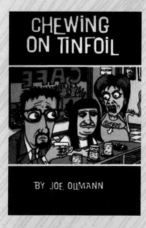

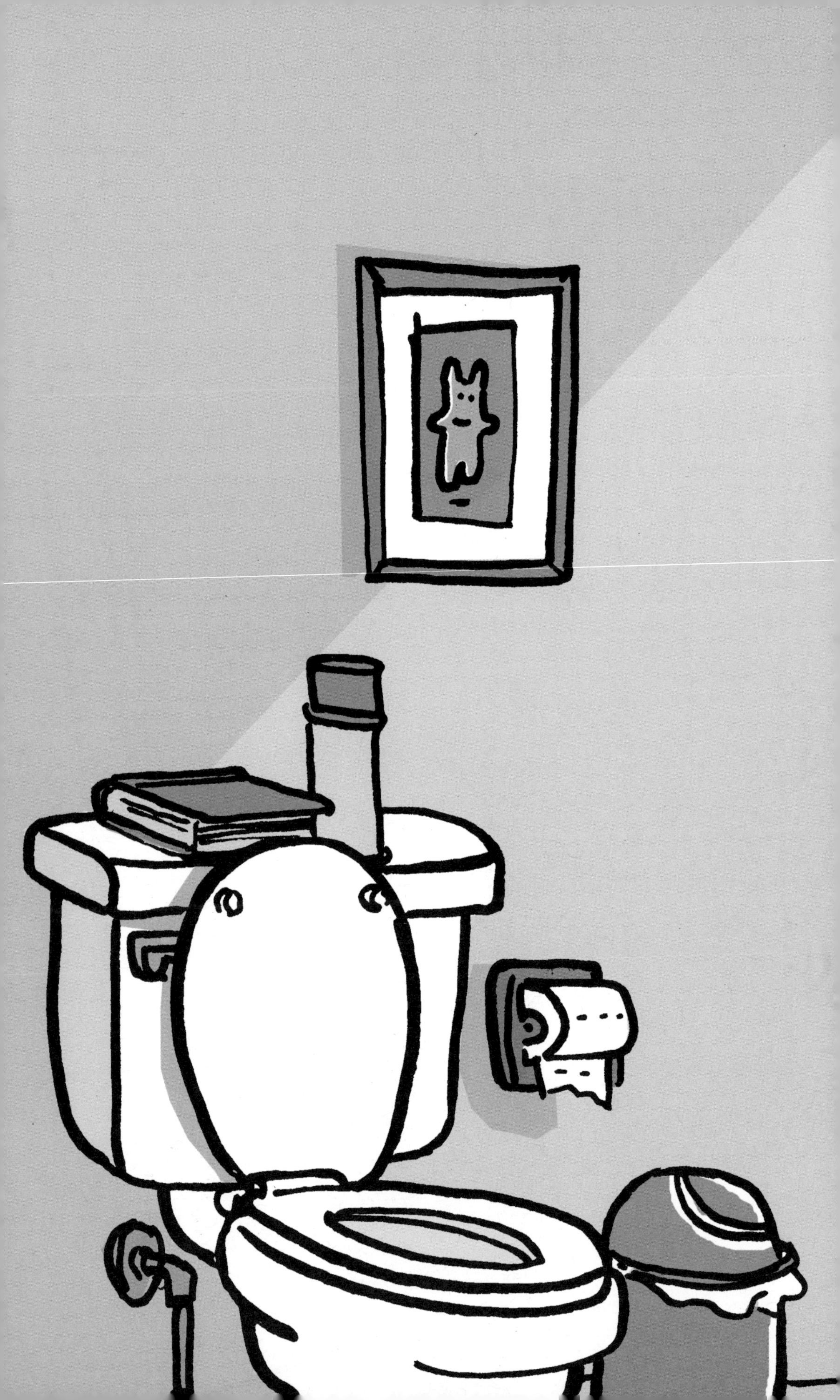

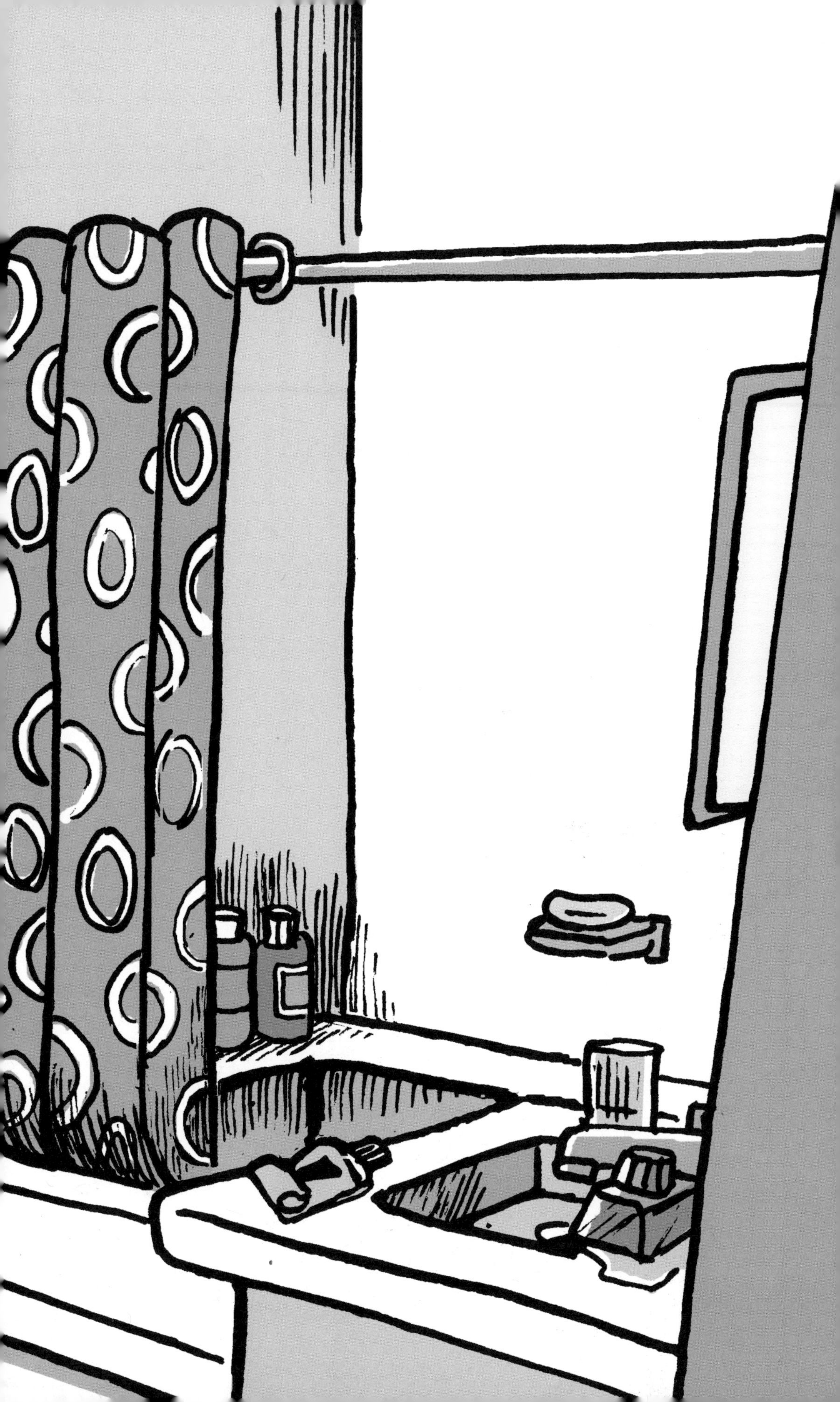

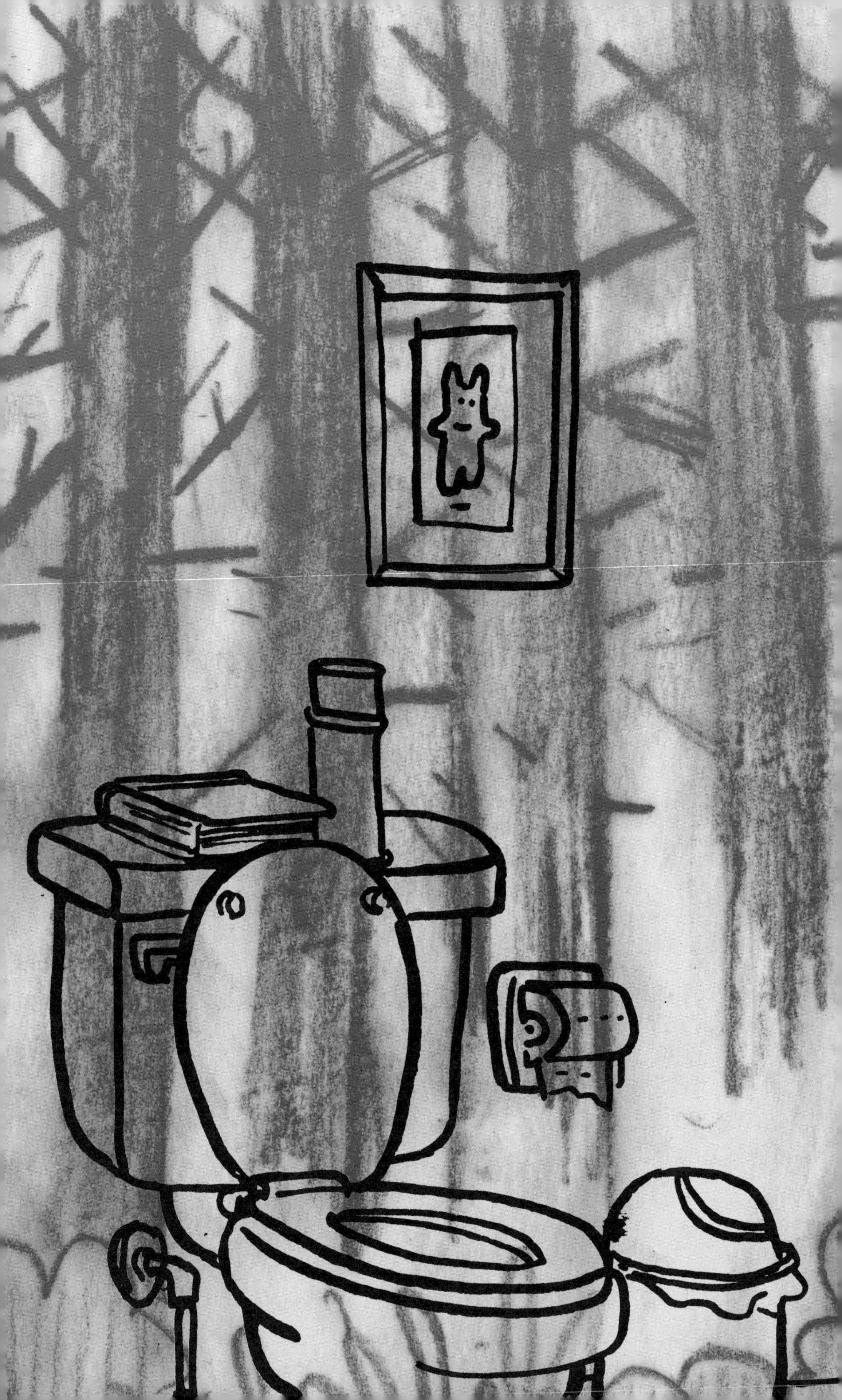

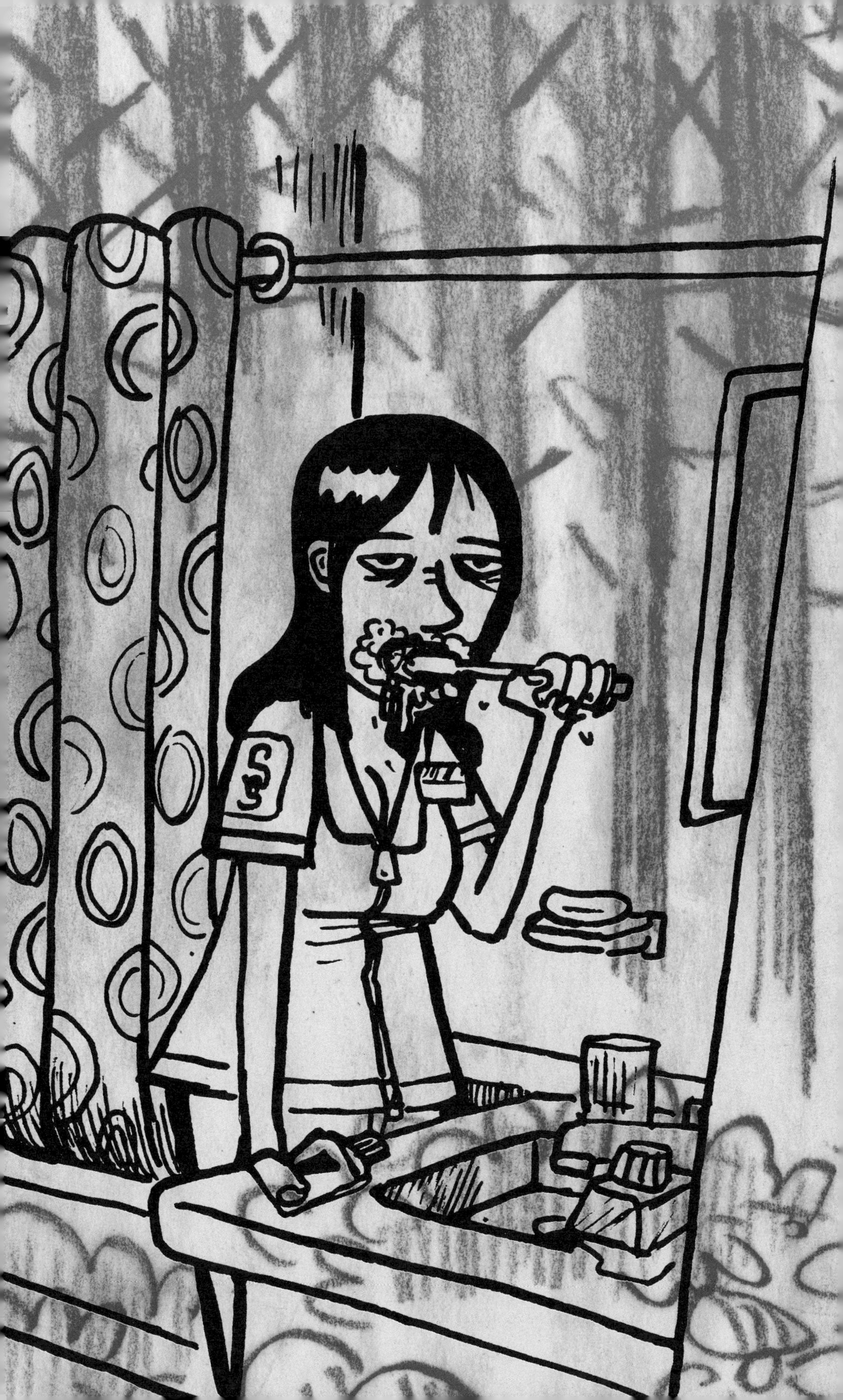

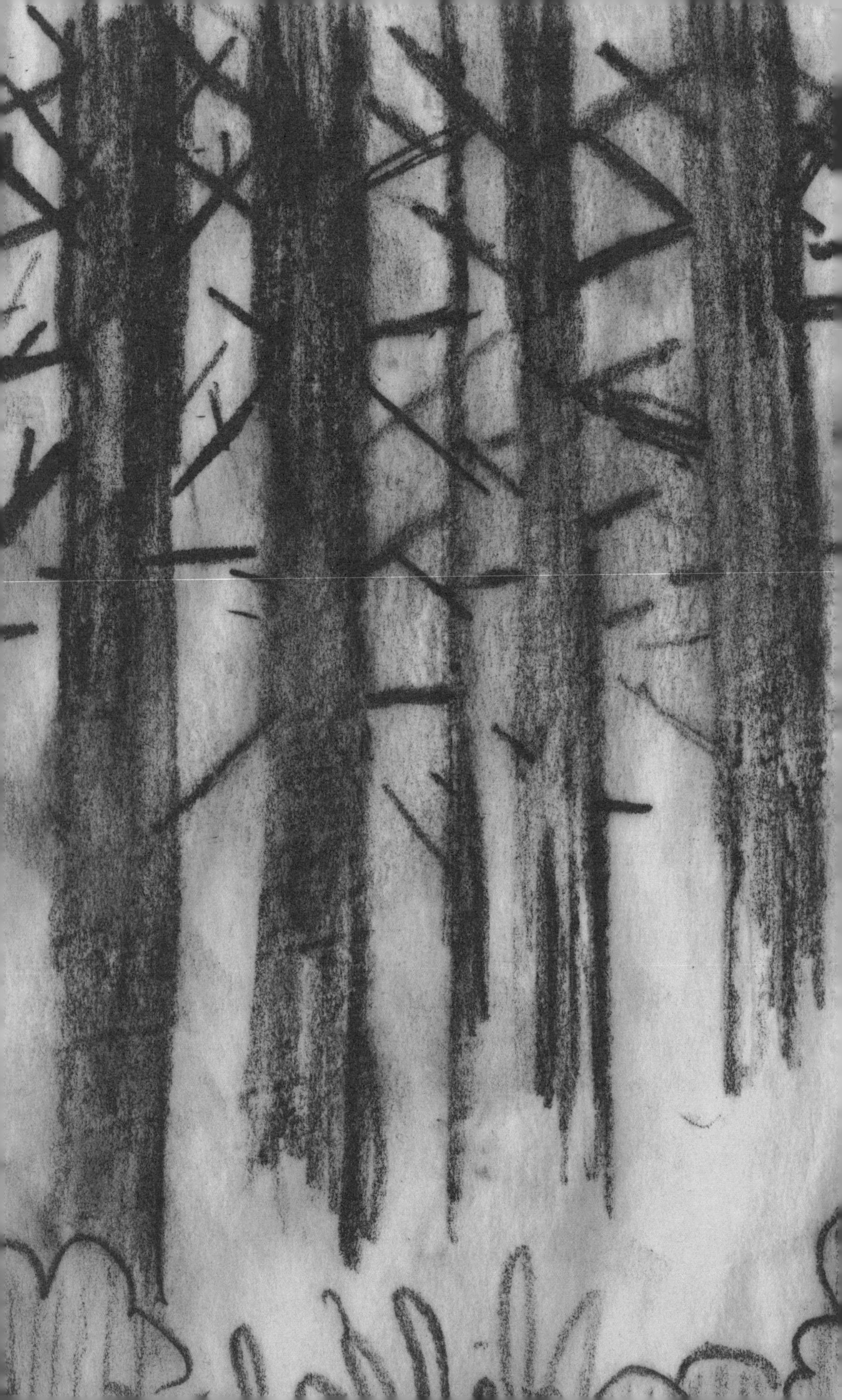

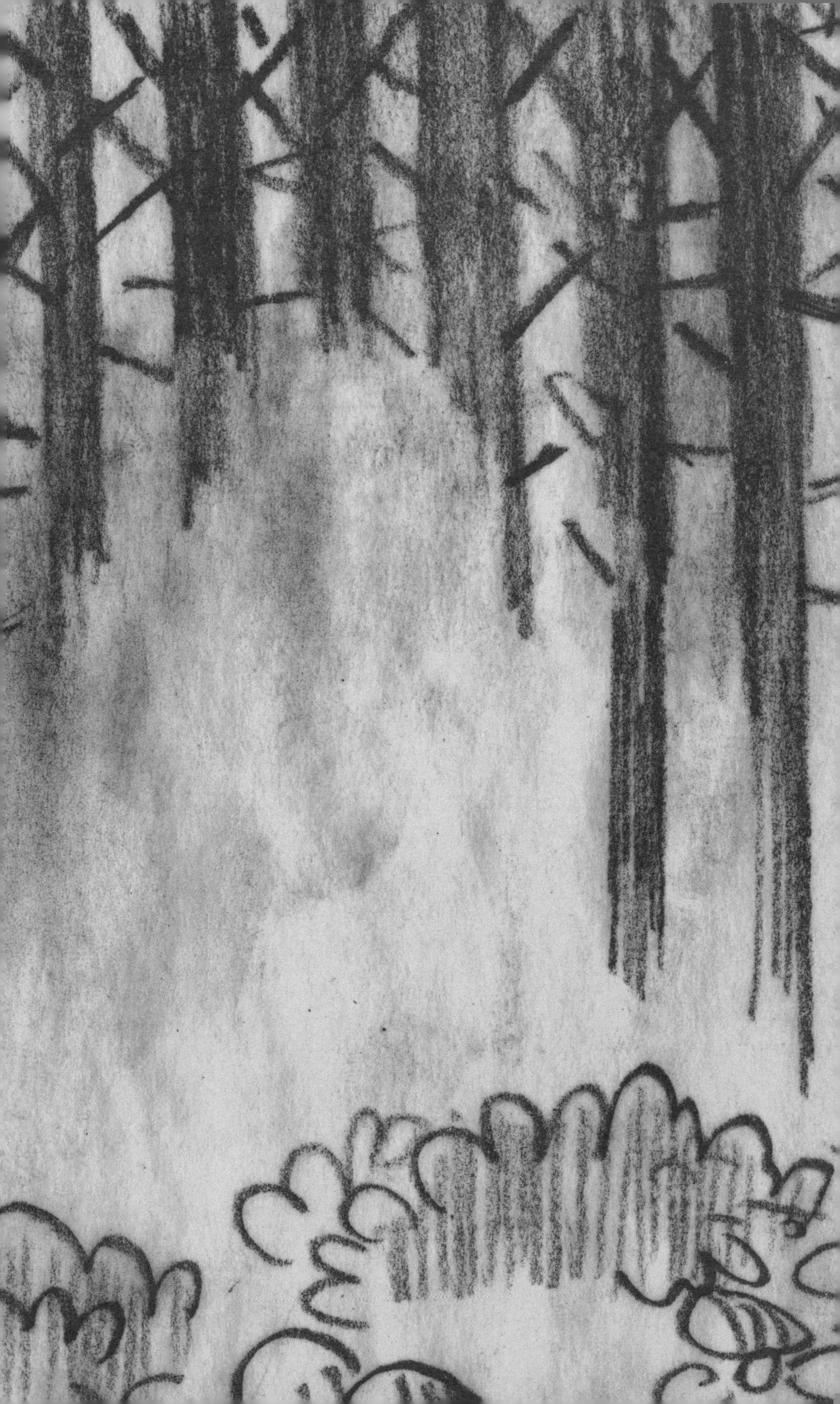

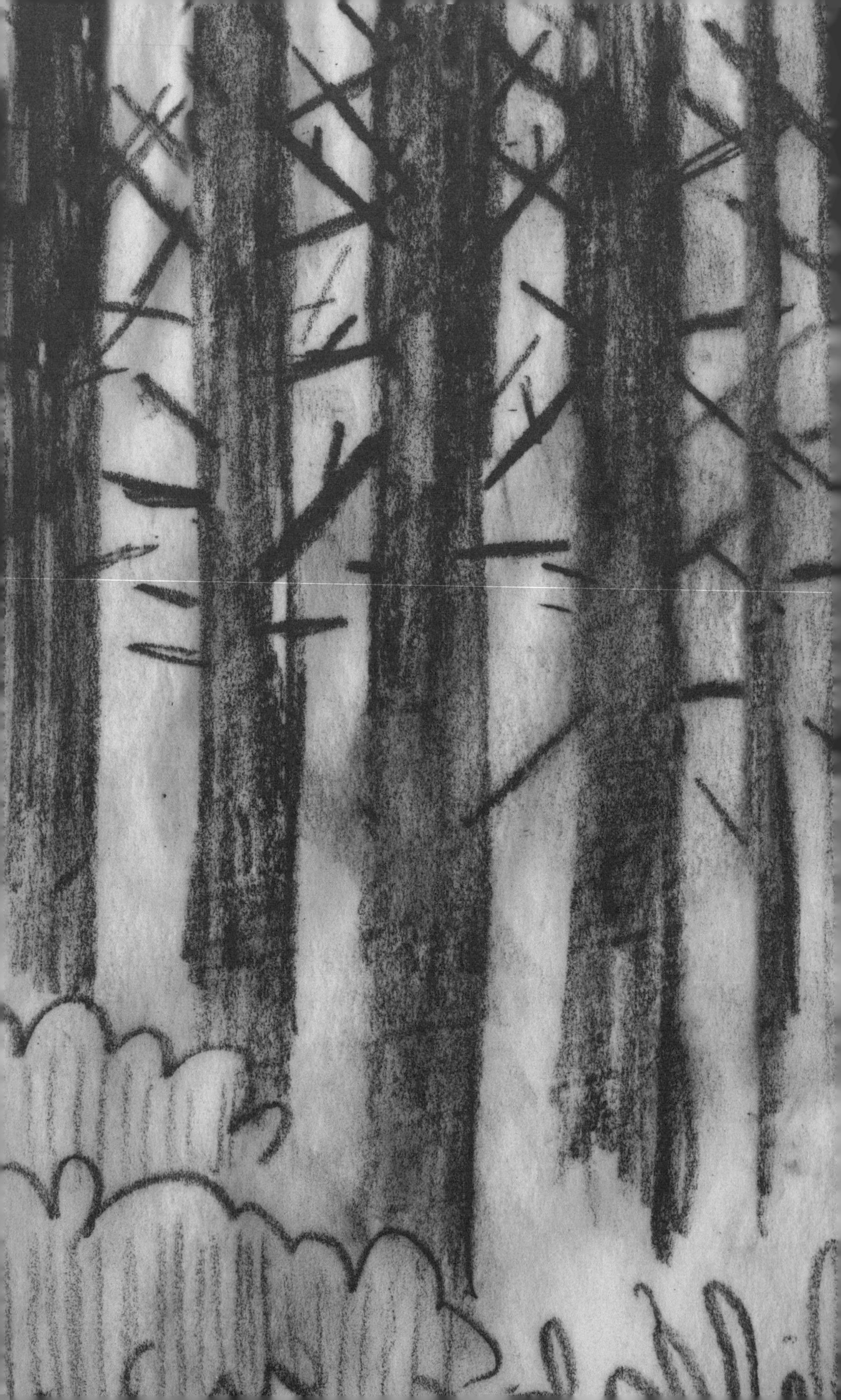